T0291252

# The Red Queen Retail Race

# The Red Queen Retail Race

## An Innovation Pandemic in the Era of Digitization

*Edited by*

RICHARD CUTHBERTSON
OLLI RUSANEN
AND
LAURI PAAVOLA

OXFORD
UNIVERSITY PRESS

# OXFORD
## UNIVERSITY PRESS

Great Clarendon Street, Oxford, OX2 6DP,
United Kingdom

Oxford University Press is a department of the University of Oxford.
It furthers the University's objective of excellence in research, scholarship,
and education by publishing worldwide. Oxford is a registered trade mark of
Oxford University Press in the UK and in certain other countries

Published in the United States of America by Oxford University Press
198 Madison Avenue, New York, NY 10016, United States of America

British Library Cataloguing in Publication Data
Data available

Library of Congress Control Number: 2022948701

ISBN 978–0–19–286261–7

DOI: 10.1093/oso/9780192862617.001.0001

Printed and bound in the UK by
Clays Ltd, Elcograf S.p.A.

# Foreword

The Red Queen Effect is famous from Lewis Carroll's classical novel *Through the Looking-Glass, and What Alice Found There* (1871). In the novel, the Red Queen commented to Alice: 'Now, here, you see, it takes all the running you can do, to keep in the same place. If you want to get somewhere else, you must run at least twice as fast as that.'

This book originated from a research project that was inspired by this metaphor: Red Queen Effect: Strategies for an Innovative Landscape. The research project focused on retailing. Innovations in multi-channel retailing have developed at different rates in different countries. The United Kingdom had been a forerunner and Finland seemed to be lagging behind.

The Red Queen project was well fitted to a funding instrument called the Finland Distinguished Professor of Business. Thus, Business Finland became the main financier of the Red Queen research project. Besides researchers, the project consortium consisted of a number of prominent companies working in the retail sector.

During the Red Queen project, a number of phenomena gained importance. Retailers wanted to better understand customers and their behaviour. They wanted to optimize shopping experiences through multiple channels. They also wanted to deepen customer loyalty, brand experience, and business experience. All these created demand for robust research and information sharing.

We would like to warmly thank Richard Cuthbertson and the other main researchers involved: Lasse Mitronen, Jussi Nyrhinen, Lauri Paavola, Lauri Pulkka, and Olli Rusanen. The project team had a clear-cut orientation and solid research plan, and, at the same time, they seemed to enjoy the study and cooperation.

This topic is even more important now than it was when the project started, as Covid-19 has proven to cause major disruption in the retail sector. That's why it is of the utmost important to get fact-based information. The Red Queen research project and this book represent a major contribution in this field. We hope it will find a large audience in a post-Covid-19 era. It will take all the running you can do to keep up.

*Pekka Pesonen*
Business Finland

# Acknowledgements

This book is one of the results of a research project: Red Queen Effect-Strategies for an Innovative Landscape. While initially planning the research work, our focus was on the immense transformation that the retail sector was experiencing. We saw customer needs changing; we saw new technologies being introduced; and consequently, we saw a new competitive landscape evolving. There was an urgent need to understand these changes better.

However, during the course of the research, we ended up witnessing a much more dramatic transformation than we could have ever anticipated in the project planning phase. Indeed, we witnessed the Covid-19 pandemic taking a sharp economic toll on the retail industry worldwide as many retailers and shopping centres were forced to shut down for months due to mandated stay-at-home orders. As a result of these closures, retailers experienced a huge increase in sales through online channels as customers looked for alternative ways to shop and the effects of the impending retail apocalypse were exacerbated. This rapidly transformed and truly innovative landscape has not only caused retailing to change forever but also changed the way in which we understand innovation.

We would like to thank the project sponsors, not only for funding our work but also for believing in the project and contributing valuable advice along the way. The willingness of the sponsors to give their time so generously is very much appreciated. The main sponsor behind the project was Business Finland, with major contributions also from S-Group, Tieto, Solita, and Citycon. We are also grateful to Oxford University Press, and Adam Swallow in particular, for their advice and support in publishing this book, as well as peer reviewers and a select group of helpful external academics who provided advice along the way, including Arto Lindblom, Lasse Mitronen, and Jonathan Reynolds.

# Contents

# Notes on Contributors

This book is the result of a collaboration between the eight academics listed below. Data was collected, shared, and discussed amongst the group, with authors then allocated to take a lead on developing an individual chapter, while Cuthbertson, Rusanen, and Paavola provided an editorial role to ensure a common approach and style for the resulting text. All chapters were peer reviewed by at least two other academics, as well as by the editors. Following review, the authors made changes until the reviewers and editors were satisfied with the final text. Hence, this should be considered a complete work in itself and not a series of edited papers.

**Richard Cuthbertson** is a senior research fellow at the University of Oxford; Research Director of the Oxford Institute of Retail Management at the Saïd Business School, University of Oxford; a governing body fellow at Green Templeton College, Oxford; and a visiting senior fellow at Aalto University. His research interests focus on innovation within consumer service firms, where the diversity of customer experiences, formats, and channels combine to create a challenging environment for those firms, their supply chains partners, and public policy.

**Mikko Hänninen** is now IT Area Lead, Assortment Planning and Space Management, at SOK (the S-Group), the largest retailer in Finland. He was previously Assistant Professor in Retail Operations Management at Nottingham University Business School. His research has focused on understanding the digital transformation of retailing. His work has been published in journals such as *Journal of Management Studies, Journal of Retailing and Consumer Services,* and *International Review of Retail, Distribution and Consumer Research.*

**Heikki Karjaluoto** is a professor, head of Information Systems Research Division, at the Faculty of Information Technology, University of Jyväskylä, Finland. His research interests include marketing communications, digital marketing, industrial marketing, and customer value. Karjaluoto has published extensively in business and information system journals and is the author of several books. His previous publications have appeared in *European Journal of Marketing, Journal of Business Research, Industrial Marketing Management, Internet Research, Journal of Service Management,* among others.

**Jussi Nyrhinen** is a postdoctoral researcher in sociology at the faculty of humanities and social sciences in University of Jyväskylä, Finland. He also works for the faculty of information technology in University of Jyväskylä. Nyrhinen earned his DSc at Jyväskylä University School of Business and Economics. He has been involved in studies investigating digitalization in the retail business, and the consequent disruptions in consumer behaviour, retail spaces, and local retail firms' strategies and policies. His work has been published in journals such as *Digital Business, Transport Policy, Technology in Society, Journal of Gambling Studies,* and *The International Review of Retail Distribution and Consumer Research.*

**Lauri Paavola** is a postdoctoral researcher and lecturer at University of Eastern Finland (UEF). Before joining UEF, he had worked at Stanford University as a research fellow and at the University of Oxford as a visiting academic. Much of his research and teaching has concentrated on addressing the challenges of digitalization, particularly through technological innovation and data analytics. Lauri earned his PhD at Aalto University School of Business.

**Lauri Pulkka** is now Head of Innovation at Newsec Property Asset Management Finland. During the research documented in this book, he was a postdoctoral researcher at the Department of Built Environment in Aalto University. His research interests include innovation and sustainability in the built environment, interorganizational collaboration, and urban development. Pulkka has been a visiting scholar at the University of California, Berkeley, and a visiting fellow at the Saïd Business School, University of Oxford.

**Olli Rusanen** now works for IBM, with a focus on Sustainability Software, and Order Management for eCommerce. During the research for this book, he was a researcher at Aalto University and a visiting scholar at the University of Oxford, with research interests in retail innovation, retail strategy, and the management of tangible resources, as well as retail adaptation to a digital environment. Rusanen has conducted case analyses of several major retail chains, including Sainsbury's, Tesco, Walmart, Kmart, SOK, and Lidl, in order to understand how resource management practices change as a result of technological change and how the firms pursue competitive advantage in an increasingly digital landscape.

**Outi Uusitalo** is professor of marketing at the Jyväskylä University School of Business and Economics, Finland. Her areas of research interest are digitalizing consumption, retail and service environments, and sustainable marketing and consumption. Uusitalo has published in *Journal of Consumer Culture, Journal of Consumer Behaviour, International Journal of Consumer Studies, European Journal of Marketing, Journal of Business Ethics,* among others. She has acted as chair of the Finnish Association of Consumer Research and editor-in-chief in Kulutustutkimus.Nyt.

# 1

# The Red Queen Retail Race

*Olli Rusanen, Lauri Paavola, and Richard Cuthbertson*

"Now, here, you see, it takes all the running you can do, to keep in the
same place. If you want to get somewhere else, you must run at least
twice as fast as that."

Lewis Carroll (1871, p.33)

## Introduction

Service firms represent more than 70 per cent of gross domestic product (GDP) in
many advanced economies and are typically bimodal in distribution; either large
capital-intensive corporations serving a mass market or small family-run enterprises serving a local geographically small market. Digital innovation enables new
entrants, both mass and niche, to bypass heavy investments in fixed assets, such
as real estate, within a market and to potentially circumvent regulatory issues, for
example, by operating from another country. Technology-oriented global competition combines scale-driven cost advantage with novel service design for a
fresh customer experience (Smedlund, Lindblom, & Mitronen, 2018; Treadgold &
Reynolds, 2020). Such new forms of digital competition have created substantial
challenges for established retailers and service providers in every market across the
globe. The title of this chapter, the Red Queen Race, is inspired by Alice's encounters with the Red Queen in the classical novel *Through the Looking-Glass, and
What Alice Found There* by Lewis Carroll (1871). Following the recent Covid-19
pandemic, services have now moved through the looking-glass. When observing
the Red Queen's race, the Queen comments: 'Now, here, you see, it takes all the
running you can do, to keep in the same place. If you want to get somewhere
else, you must run at least twice as fast as that' (Lewis Carroll, 1871, p.33). This
metaphor is illustrative of the service sector, which is in rapid transition from a
slow world towards a Red Queen's race, where companies need to learn novel
ways of competing in the emerging digital competitive landscape. Moreover, the
impact of this change is not restricted to the service sector nor the digital space but
transforms the whole retail value chain, including product suppliers, real estate
owners, transport specialists, and public policymakers. It is creating a revolution

Olli Rusanen, Lauri Paavola, and Richard Cuthbertson, *The Red Queen Retail Race*. In: *The Red Queen Retail Race*.
Edited by Richard Cuthbertson, Olli Rusanen, and Lauri Paavola, Oxford University Press. © Olli Rusanen, Lauri Paavola,
and Richard Cuthbertson (2023). DOI: 10.1093/oso/9780192862617.003.0001

in how a consumer society operates, replacing investment in the physical confines of products, stores, and geographical areas with investment in the digital universe of information, relationships, and social networks.

Red Queen rivalry is not only beneficial for the consumer and society through lower prices, but it is beneficial for the rivals themselves (Barnett & Hansen, 1996). It forces companies to take competitive action, which in turn forces them to develop new competencies and then helps them to become more competitive in the long term. In all this, public policy plays a key role in establishing a viable contractual space and encouraging change with substantial differences in political, legal, and institutional settings across different countries.

This book considers different aspects of the Red Queen Rivalry in the post-pandemic world: how innovation through technological change is transforming the service sector in different markets, how changing consumer needs and behaviours are forcing firms to alter their operations, how firms need different competitive strategies to respond to this changing landscape in different markets, how those strategic plans need new modes of implementation, and how public policy will need to adapt.

## Digitalization is the new norm for the Red Queen Retail Race

Digitalization is a force that drives new forms of consumption and competition across all service sectors. Retail, the focal sector of this book, is in the process of substantial change. Historically, retailer power has been created by physical assets—large supermarkets, hypermarkets, and shopping centres, coupled with global logistics solutions. During the twenty-first century, the competitive repertoire of retailers has increasingly been altered towards digital actions (Grewal, Roggeveen, & Nordfält, 2017). There are new forms of competition changing the retail landscape: global digital marketplaces (platforms) and omni-channel retailers that mix digital and physical assets to create a seamless customer experience across different channels.

First, the platform economy has introduced a new competitive category of global platforms with distinct networks, competitive repertoire, and resource base. Supply chain platforms leverage technological capabilities and open interfaces to build competitive advantage for certain product lines (manufacturing examples include Boeing and Renault-Nissan), while industry platforms utilize open ecosystems with common governance methods to build open market spaces either locally or globally (Gawer, 2014). Examples include Facebook, Google, and Apple, and in retail Amazon, Alibaba, and eBay are examples of global industry marketspaces. The competitive advantage of platforms is derived from their ability to steer platform access and manage platform routines (Boudreau, 2010; Paavola, 2018), leveraging network effects in two-sided platforms (Cennamo & Santalo, 2013; Rochet & Tirole, 2003), and the ability to bundle resources and capabilities across the entire ecosystem of platform participants (Armstrong, 2006; Hänninen, Rusanen, & Paavola, 2018; Lavie, 2006).

Second, retailers are becoming increasingly omni-channel in order to adapt to the Red Queen Race. Omni-channel consumption refers to disruptive challenges to the service sector created by new technologies: barriers of buying are eroding while consumers can access information anywhere and anytime through mobile channels (Rigby, 2011). Omni-channel retailers integrate different channels to create a seamless consumption experience across the physical and digital spectrum (Piotrowicz & Cuthbertson, 2014). Digital channels are utilized in a complementary fashion; for omni-channel retailers, the co-existence of new digital channels increases the value of physical channels (Gong, Smith, & Telang, 2015; Rusanen, 2018; Schramm-Klein et al., 2011; Zhang et al., 2010).

Omni-channel retailers use new technologies to promote the value of their existing physical resources. Through analytics, by combining customer data with various data sources, retailers can make more informed decisions across the business, both in the digital and physical channels (Piotrowicz & Cuthbertson, 2014). Retail is altered by big data (George, Haas, & Pentland, 2014), analytics, and artificial intelligence (AI) (Bradlow et al., 2017) and the utilization of mobile channel interactions (Grewal, Roggeveen, & Nordfält, 2017). Data is systematically collected, and individual silos are organized into holistic big data and analysed using modern technologies. Internal data is collected from operational processes and logistics and combined with customer point-of-sales and loyalty data (Bradlow et al., 2017). These internal sources of data are combined with external sources (social media, analyst agencies, etc.) to create an overall picture of customer expectations, the buying journey, and individual needs. In addition to analysing purely numerical data, it is also possible to leverage unstructured data (picture, audio, video) to analyse consumer behaviour in social media and changing fashion trends.

This book contributes to the empirical knowledge across organization studies, marketing, operations, and strategic management. By integrating theories of innovation management, competitive strategy, resource management, and organizational structure into a framework of organizational adaptation, we seek to analyse how organizations in retail are adapting to the disruption caused by retail digitalization. The goal of this book is to advance our understanding of new strategy implementation during technological disruption by analysing and comparing experiences in the retail sector across different markets.

We address the following main question: How can retail organizations adapt to the transformation brought about by the Red Queen Race?

This book considers the following themes:

- How is innovation through technological change transforming the retail sector?
- How are consumer needs and behaviours changing?
- How are firms adapting to the evolving context?

## Three themes of this book

The main phenomenon of this book is the 'Red Queen Retail Race', which implies that the competitive landscape sets the requirements for a faster pace of change and requires new ways of competing. We explore technological changes, omni-channel consumption patterns, changing competitive landscapes and strategies, and their implementation in several retail markets. While digital innovation is affecting every market, the implementation of innovation is distinct in every market. Thus, we consider the competition between different retailers in different markets. Each market has its own Red Queen Race at its own speed, rules, and culture. This book considers the Red Queen Race through three main lenses: the changing competitive landscape, customer behaviour in an omni-channel landscape, and organization structure and strategy implementation.

## Theme I. Changing competitive landscape

Disruptive technologies have been studied extensively from many different angles ever since Christensen published his highly cited book in 1997. Disruptive technologies are considered to alter the competitive landscape in any given industry by enabling the creation of new innovations. These disruptive innovations can create new markets and value networks, eventually disrupting the existing market and competitive situation. The pace of change varies across markets and customers, from innovators to laggards (Rogers, 2003). As a result, the retail sector is altered by several disruptive technologies (online retailing, big data, analytics, AI) and disruptive business models (omni-channel retailing, global platforms), while different retailers in different markets adapt to these disruptions in widely different ways.

Technological change and business model innovation dramatically alter the competitive landscape of the retail sector. Technological change enables new forms of competition and often reduces entry barriers so that new competitors can enter the market. We take an industry view and argue that while technological change undoubtedly is a threat to existing firms it also enables existing firms to grow and offer services in new ways that did not exist before (Porter, 1981, 1996). Established firms face the constant pressure as to whether they can seize the opportunity of new innovations or will fall victim to technological change. We study innovation activities from the industry viewpoint and analyse how companies manage their activities vis-à-vis current competitors and new entrants. We argue that firms need to find new ways to compete through differentiation. The concept of the Red Queen Race implies a contextual change in the retail space, with implications in several areas: retail technology, the competitive landscape, consumption patterns, business models, and organizational structures, as well as in the broader society.

## Theme II. Customer behaviour in an omni-channel landscape

Changing customer behaviour is a crucial element of the retail competitive land-scape. Under this theme, we combine firm-level strategic analysis with consumer studies. This combination enables us to provide a comprehensive view regarding the challenge of technological change in the retail sector. We argue that it is impor-tant to analyse the interaction between firm strategies and consumer behaviour, that is how they affect each other. Moreover, it is essential to study how tech-nological changes influence consumer behaviour. According to Dholakia et al. (2010) channel acceptance is affected by customers' adaptation of technologies as well as various lifestyle factors such as the appreciation of traditions or the seeking of experiences. Various studies (e.g. Kumar & Venkatesan, 2005; Wal-lace, Giese, & Johnson, 2004) show that well-developed omni-channel customer experiences increase purchases and customer loyalty. However, several compa-nies, especially at times of transformation, have come across challenges trying to expand their customer experience online. Neslin and Shankar (2009) emphasize the understanding of consumers' lifestyles and demographics to provide con-sistent service and interaction across channels. Further research and practice regarding consumers' attitudes and behaviours are still required in order to meet customers' expectations in both online and offline channels to develop a seamless omni-channel experience.

## Theme III. Organization structure and strategy implementation

The two previous themes deal with the nature of change and future success fac-tors but do not address how to manage the transformation process. Under this third theme, we join the contemporary criticism of strategy research that it is not enough to understand the nature of change and associated critical success fac-tors. We need more knowledge on how the change process should be managed in practice (Langley et al., 2013; Whittington, 2006). The organizational structure consists of processes and routines that play a key role in a firm's ability to adapt to technological change. We study the role of the organization as an important aspect of strategic change. Innovation research often ignores the practical aspects of how change should be achieved. Large firms have complex structures that have a huge impact on the way firms can achieve change. For example, Burgelman (1994, 1996, 2002) studied strategic change in Intel Corporation where the change pro-cess was autonomous. In the 1960s and 1970s, Intel was officially a memory chip firm; processors fell outside of Intel's official strategy but were nevertheless devel-oped through an autonomous bottom-up process. Indeed, innovation literature, especially open innovation, has argued for the benefits of including organizational members from various levels of the organization in the innovation process. Simi-larly, open strategy literature has argued that strategy work should actively include lower organizational levels in both strategy and innovation work. In addition to studying strategy processes, we study the role of organization routines. By recognizing its operating routines at different levels, an organization can identify its effective and ineffective operating patterns (Eisenhardt & Martin, 2000). Routines are considered to act as an organizational memory, which forms the basis for learning and storing knowledge (Becker, 2004). This brings the role of the organization structure and its practices to the forefront of both strategy and innovation research.

Finally, we conclude this theme by considering the timing of innovation in different markets. Competition, technology infrastructure, consumer awareness, and public policy all play a role in affecting the successful introduction of new innovations to a market. For managers, the most difficult question is not whether digitization will impact a market but when. Introduce a new service too early and it may die before becoming established, draining investment and staff. Introduce it too late and the organization may be swept away by pre-emptive competition.

## Intended benefits

The intended benefits from reading this book fall into two categories: academic and practical. This book provides novel insight into innovation, strategy, and organization structure in a global, digital, consumer society. This provides valuable frameworks for future research. The practical benefits include the possibility to influence corporate and public policy actions in order to seize opportunities and alleviate the negative effects of disruptive technologies on the largest sector in developed economies in terms of GDP.

For practitioners, there is much focus on utilization and implementation. We use the retail industry as an example of the broad ecosystem, meaning it encompasses both the production and the user side of the service sector. It is not limited to firms and organizations working in retail but also those working with retailers, for example in construction and real estate, logistics, media, and the public sector.

For policymakers, this book explores many timely industry-specific topics. How will digitalization affect physical retail structure and urban planning? What kind of support do firms require for internationalization as e-commerce opens the door to global markets even for small players? What kind of pressure for regulatory change will emerge in the next five to ten years as e-commerce develops?

## Outline of book chapters

### Introduction

This book contains 10 chapters in total that cover the three themes. Below are outlines for each chapter.

Chapter 1 (The Red Queen Retail Race) provides the overall context of the global, digital, consumer society. It explains the concept of the Red Queen Race in retailing—running faster to stand still—as well as the lasting impact of the Covid-19 pandemic. The Red Queen Race captures the notion that competition is beneficial for society: firms compete to develop new competencies, increase quality, and drive down prices, with consumers being the winner. Over the course of time, with new technology and new consumer demands, companies learn to compete in these new situations or they perish. Organization learning is not only a key force that drives innovation and thus competitive action, it is also triggered and driven by the competition itself. Companies compete in the short term through pricing and promotional rivalry, in the medium term through product and service development, and in the long term through resource portfolio restructuring and competence development. Competitive pressure is a driving force that intensifies each of these forms of competition. In their notion of Red Queen competition, Barnett and Hansen (1996) argue that rivalry is not only beneficial for the consumer and society through lower prices but that rivalry is beneficial for the rivals themselves. Rivalry forces companies to take competitive action, but it also forces them to develop new competencies, which then ensures that they are competitive in the long term. In all of this, public policy plays a key role in encouraging change while protecting the weak.

## Changing competitive landscape

Chapter 2 (The New Rules of the Red Queen Retail Race) explains how retailing has changed over the last few decades and accelerated during the recent pandemic. There are six cases presented here that explain the impact of the new rules of the Red Queen Retail Race—a move away from mass volume-driving resources. During the twentieth century, major retail chains competed through investments in volume-driving resources that leveraged supply innovation, product assortment, and physical space that in turn delivered competitive advantage through economies of scale. Lately, the value of volume-driving resources has declined, thus creating a challenge for retail resource management. Retailers aspire to find new sources of growth and identify emerging value drivers. A model is presented that examines a gap between large retailers' current competencies and emerging value drivers. The model was developed through comparative longitudinal case analysis of six major retailers in Finland, the United Kingdom, and the United States. In the late twentieth century some of the largest businesses in the world were from the retail sector. These firms leveraged innovations on the supply side and through standardization and economies of scale empowered their customers with larger assortments and low prices. During the last ten years, many of these businesses have been struggling to cope with a declining unit value of volume-driving physical resources. Our model summarizes four key competencies and four emerging value drivers. Major established retailers' core competencies are built around supply technologies, product orientation, the physical environment, and standardization—all driving economies of scale. Emerging drivers of resource value are increasingly less tangible: demand-driven innovations through big data, service orientation, digital solutions, and personalized relationships.

Chapter 3 (Digital Impacts) looks at how innovations are diffused from first movers to more traditional industry players in retailing and consumer services, focusing especially on how incumbent retailers can continue to challenge their new digitally native rivals and adapt to the new rules of the Red Queen Race in retailing. Overall, the past decade has seen new business models emerge to meet the changing expectations of customers. In this chapter, we focus on one important business model innovation that has emerged—digital platforms. Digital platforms aim to change the way customers interact and transact with retailers. The primary focus of this chapter is thus on introducing platform-based business models and their implications for industry structure and competitive dynamics. Digital platforms are transforming the retail exchange logic, and as a result this business model innovation will need to be understood by incumbent retailers to stay relevant amidst the new digitally native competition. An illustrative case of Amazon.com and its business model development is provided, Amazon.com being a global pioneer of e-commerce via digital platforms and a good example of how digitalization infuses new business that then changes the competitive landscape.

Chapter 4 (Physical Impacts) explores the impact of digitalization and e-commerce on retail property and the urban structure, particularly in the context of shopping centres. This chapter explains the impact of the Red Queen Race in retailing on real estate. There are indications as to where such business is heading, what key competences of the future are, who will emerge victorious, and who may fail. First, we present different perspectives of the impact on the ongoing digital revolution on retail property. How do organizations perceive the future of the shopping centre business? In addition to teasing out various perceptions, we attempt to discern what they mean for the organization, consumers, and the business ecosystem today and in the future. Second, we describe in detail an application of the scenarios methodology as an approach to prepare for an uncertain future with multiple possible outcomes, depending upon the firm's strategic choices and the overall market context, at least partially defined by public policy.

## Customer behaviour in an omni-channel landscape

Chapter 5 (Customer Experiences) examines the digital disruption of the traditional physical-based retail trade on the servicescape as the retail service experience is dispersed across online and offline stores in the context of a Red Queen Race in retailing. However, there is limited evidence as to how a service experience in an omni-channel environment is constructed. This chapter shows how the interplay of digital servicescape and physical servicescape forms the overall service experience in an omni-channel retail environment. We illustrate this phenomenon using focus group interview data. The findings elucidate how social interaction and retail space in online and offline stores can affect both cognitive and socio-emotional aspects of the service experience. We further examine how the interplay of digital and physical servicescapes can enhance the experience if the service is designed consistently. The implications of this chapter provide guidelines for ser-vice designers to develop service concepts that form their servicescape through both digital and physical channels.

Chapter 6 (Customer Loyalty) considers the impact of the Red Queen Race in retailing on customer loyalty. Although over 90 per cent of commerce in the retail sector is still carried out in brick-and-mortar stores, the rapid growth of online shopping, especially before visiting a physical outlet, is transforming the rules of retailing. Both practitioners and scholars are increasingly trying to understand the interaction between the online and offline channels. This chapter seeks to exam-ine this interplay from the perspective of cognitive and emotional aspects of the service experience and how this builds loyalty in an omni-channel retail environ-ment. It reports results on a large-scale consumer survey ($N=880$). The results of the study show that among omni-channel customers, brick-and-mortar stores still play a crucial role in forming the service experience. Additionally, the findings elucidate how positive experiences enhance a customer's willingness to share data about themselves with a retailer. Finally, this chapter examines the relationships between customer loyalty, measured as share of wallet and positive word of mouth, in offline and online environments.

## Organization structure and strategy implementation

Chapter 7 (Implementing Strategy) presents a case study on the turnaround of a large cooperative grocery retailing organization (SOK) as it adapts to the new rules of the Red Queen Race in retailing. This firm was characterized by highly rou-tinized and stable practices suitable for the old rules of the retail race. Though the organization went through a major turnaround, it did not primarily result from the implementation of new work practices but rather from the ability of the manage-ment to steer the existing practices into a more sustainable direction and to enable them to be recreated internally. Our case illustrates that sustainable development is not so much about having the most advanced and well-designed processes or technologies in place, but instead, it is more about the correct institutional pres-sures, namely in our case the economic and social tensions. We highlight these issues when we conclude the chapter by considering organizational sustainability from a managerial perspective.

Chapter 8 (Organizational Routines) presents a case study analysis of organi-zational routines in the field of grocery retailing and how they change under the new rules of a data-rich Red Queen Race. The chapter focuses on specific processes that enable retailers to understand and respond to the behaviour of a mass of individual customers. We observe and analyse how different variables behind these specific adaptation processes have resulted in varied performance outcomes and varying paths of development within the field. Unlike what is typically considered, we show that the implementation of new technologies or processes is not in itself any solution for organizations. Our research highlights that the successful management of such processes requires an understanding of the factors that support their intended outcome. We argue that only by understanding these contextual factors can an organization meet the challenges of the Red Queen Race and gain the full benefits of digitalization.

Chapter 9 (The Timing of Innovation) examines innovation as a process and discusses three themes that emerge when a process view of the Red Queen Race is adopted. Innovation is often discussed in terms of new products and services—in terms of the outcomes of a Red Queen Race. The outcome, however, is neither the start nor the end of innovation. First, adopting the process view gives more attention to the activities taking place from the conception of the idea to its manifestation in practice. Second, the process view broadens the concept of innovation by expanding the focus from the innovator to the network of actors that impact the innovation process. Third, the process view is equally interested in the diffusion of innovation—in what happens after realizing the idea. The process view of innovation is extremely relevant for the ongoing disruption of the retail sector because it helps us understand why some of the ideas we have been anticipating for years may only break through at moments of crisis, such as the Covid-19 pandemic. Organizations are not logs in a river but active agents in steering the change. We use two models to explain the interorganizational dynamics of innovation: the gravitational slingshot model for the early phase and the smart timing of innovation for the adoption phase. The chapter is concluded with a synthesis connecting the two models.

## Conclusions

Chapter 10 (Implications for Managers, Firms, and Markets) brings together the conclusions of our previous chapters to show how firms can capture and leverage the new rules of the Red Queen Race in retailing, especially given the impetus created through the Covid-19 pandemic. Furthermore, we consider the public policy implications of the new ways of working in a global, digital, consumer society. What is the role of public decision-makers in a world of ecosystems, networked routines, and consumer engagement? Where are the boundaries of competition when commercial firm strategies are collaborative? What are the implications for employment in a networked platform of global and local providers? What is the balance between transport infrastructure and real estate planning to support consumer convenience and customer experiences? What are the tax implications of a global firm offering a local service or a local firm offering a global service? How can public policy best ensure a sustainable, innovative, and competitive service sector? Current research has focused almost extensively on the formulation of retail strategy to meet the challenges of digitalization. However, much less attention has been given to how digitalization should be managed in practice. In this chapter, we join the contemporary criticism of strategy research that we need more practical knowledge on how the change process required to adapt to the Red Queen Retail Race should be managed in practice.

# References

Armstrong, M., 2006. 'Competition in two-sided markets'. *The RAND Journal of Economics*, 37(3), 668–691.

Barnett, W. P. & Hansen, M. T., 1996. 'The red queen in organizational evolution'. *Strategic Management Journal*, 17(S1), 139–157.

Becker, M. C., 2004. 'Organizational routines: a review of the literature'. *Industrial and Corporate Change*, 13(4), 643–678.

Boudreau, K., 2010. 'Open platform strategies and innovation: granting access vs. devolving control'. *Management Science*, 56(10), 1849–1872.

Bradlow, E. T., Gangwar, M., Kopalle, P., & Voleti, S., 2017. 'The role of big data and predictive analytics in retailing'. *Journal of Retailing*, 93(1), 79–95.

Burgelman, R. A., 1994. 'Fading memories: a process theory of strategic business exit in dynamic environments'. *Administrative Science Quarterly*, 39(1), 24.

Burgelman, R. A., 1996. 'A process model of strategic business exit: implications for an evolutionary perspective on strategy'. *Strategic Management Journal*, 17(S1), 193–214.

Burgelman, R. A., 2002. 'Strategy as vector and the inertia of coevolutionary lock-in'. *Administrative Science Quarterly*, 47(2), 325.

Cennamo, C., & Santalo, J., 2013. 'Platform competition: strategic trade-offs in platform markets'. *Strategic Management Journal*, 34(11), 1331–1350.

Christensen, C. M., 1997. *The innovator's dilemma: when new technologies cause great firms to fail*. Harvard Business School Press.

Dholakia, U. M., Kahn, B. E., Reeves, R., Rindfleisch, A., Stewart, D., et al., 2010. 'Consumer behavior in a multichannel, multimedia retailing environment'. *Journal of Interactive Marketing*, 24(2), 86–95.

Eisenhardt, K. M. & Martin, J. A., 2000. 'Dynamic capabilities: what are they?' *Strategic Management Journal*, 2000(21), 1105–1121.

Gawer, A. 2014. 'Bridging differing perspectives on technological platforms: toward an integrative framework'. Research Policy, 43, 1239–1249.

George, G., Haas, M. R., & Pentland, A., 2014. 'Big data and management'. *Academy of Management Journal*, 57(2), 321–326.

Gong, J., Smith, M. D., & Telang, R., 2015. 'Substitution or promotion? The impact of price discounts on cross-channel sales of digital movies'. *Journal of Retailing*, 91(2), 343–357.

Grewal, D., Roggeveen, A. L., & Nordfält, J., 2017. 'The future of retailing'. *Journal of Retailing*, 93(1), 1–6.

Hänninen, M., Rusanen, O., & Paavola, L., 2018. 'Creating the foundation for a functioning internal platform'. In A. Smedlund, A. Lindblom, & L. Mitronen (eds), *Collaborative value co-creation in the platform economy*: 147–165. Springer.

Kumar, V. & Venkatesan, R., 2005. 'Who are the multichannel shoppers and how do they perform? Correlates of multichannel shopping behavior'. *Journal of Interactive Marketing*, 19(2), 44–62.

Langley, A., Smallman, C., Tsoukas, H., & Van de Ven, A. H., 2013. 'Process studies of change in organization and management: unveiling temporality, activity, and flow'. *Academy of Management Journal*, 56(1), 1–13.

Lavie, D., 2006. 'The competitive advantage of interconnected firms: an extension of the resource-based view'. *Academy of Management Review*, 31(3), 638–658.

Neslin, S. A. & Shankar, V., 2009. 'Key issues in multichannel customer management: current knowledge and future directions'. *Journal of Interactive Marketing*, 23(1), 70–81.

Paavola, L., 2018. 'Understanding platform transformations through routine interactions'. In A. Smedlund, A. Lindblom, & L. Mitronen (eds), *Collaborative value co-creation in the platform economy*: 147–165. Springer.

Piotrowicz, W. & Cuthbertson, R., 2014. 'Introduction to the special issue information technology in retail: toward omnichannel retailing'. *International Journal of Electronic Commerce*, 18(4), 5–16.

Porter, M. E., 1981. 'The contributions of industrial organization to strategic management'. *The Academy of Management Review*, 6(4), 609–620.

Porter, M. E., 1996. 'What is strategy?' *Harvard Business Review*, 74 (November–December), 61–78.

Rigby, D., 2011. 'The future of shopping'. *Harvard Business Review*, 89(12), 64–75.

Rochet, J.-C., & Tirole, J. 2003. 'Platform competition in two-sided markets'. Journal of the European Economic Association, 1(4), 990–1029.

Rogers, E. M., 2003. *Diffusion of innovations* (5th ed.). Free Press.

Rusanen, O., 2018. 'Crafting omnichannel strategy: identifying sources of competitive advantage and implementation barriers'. In W. Piotrowicz & R. Cuthbertson (eds), *Exploring omnichannel retailing: common expectations and diverse realities*: 35. Springer.

Schramm-Klein, H., Wagner, G., Steinmann, S., & Morschett, D., 2011. 'Cross-channel integration—is it valued by customers?' *The International Review of Retail, Distribution and Consumer Research*, 21(5), 501–511.

Smedlund, A., Lindblom, A., & Mitronen, L. (eds), 2018. *Collaborative value co-creation in the platform economy*. Springer.

Treadgold, A. D. & Reynolds, J., 2020. *Navigating the new retail landscape: a guide for business leaders* (2nd ed.). Oxford University Press.

Wallace, D. W., Giese, J. L., & Johnson, J. L., 2004. 'Customer retailer loyalty in the context of multiple channel strategies'. *Journal of Retailing*, 80(4), 249–263.

Whittington, R., 2006. 'Completing the practice turn in strategy research'. *Organization Studies*, 27(5), 613–634.

Zhang, J., Farris, P. W., Irvin, J. W., Kushwaha, T., Steenburgh, T. J., et al., 2010. 'Crafting integrated multichannel retailing strategies'. *Journal of Interactive Marketing*, 24(2), 168–180.

# 2

# The New Rules of the Red Queen Retail Race

*Olli Rusanen*

## The importance of resources

This chapter examines resource management processes during a Red Queen Race. A Red Queen Race implies a changing competitive context that forces companies to develop new capabilities (Barnett & Hansen, 1996). The resource portfolio of a firm is the combination of resources acquired in the past, with typically only a small fraction of resources acquired in the recent past. Thus, even if resource management processes (Sirmon, Hitt, & Ireland., 2007) are adapted to reflect a new competitive context, firms compete through their entire resource portfolio, which to a large extent is a result of decisions made long before.

Economies of scale and scope occupy a central position in the strategic management literature. Foundational works viewed strategy as the design of a structure that can exploit economies of scale and scope (Chandler, 1990). In a resource-based view, economies of scale and scope are viewed as resources that lead to superior quality-cost position for the firm (Wernerfelt, 1984). Within a given market, only a few firms can possess the necessary resources for generating volume and eventually reap the cost advantage associated with economies of scale. Thus, for major firms, volume-driving resources form the foundation of cost advantage and are thus particularly important resources for strategic management.

The resource management process consists of structuring the resource base, bundling resources to form capabilities, and leveraging capabilities in the external environment (Sirmon, Hitt, & Ireland, 2007). Structuring involves acquiring new resource types that have the potential for generating volume. These resources are then accumulated to create economies of scale. Firms can possess higher order capabilities that enable them to systematically develop and identify new types of resources with volume-driving potential and then accumulate them rapidly over rivals (Teece, Pisano, & Shuen, 1997; Winter, 2003). The acquisition and accumulation of volume driving resources are embedded in competitive rivalry and catalysed by technological development. The ability to perform these two structuring processes is particularly important for determining cost leadership of the sector. Over time, all participants of scale-based rivalry develop

Olli Rusanen, *The New Rules of the Red Queen Retail Race*. In: *The Red Queen Retail Race*.
Edited by Richard Cuthbertson, Olli Rusanen, and Lauri Paavola, Oxford University Press.
© Olli Rusanen (2023). DOI: 10.1093/oso/9780192862617.003.0002

improved capabilities for acquiring new volume-driving resources and accumulating existing volume-driving resources, which drive down prices for the benefit of customers but also rivals due to improved resource management capabilities. This competence creation process is also known as the Red Queen Race (Barnett & Hansen, 1996).

Structuring a resource portfolio also includes the option to divest some resources. Divestment is the recommended option for low-value or value-destroying resources as it creates slack and flexibility. Organizations have inertia, sunk costs, and imperfect information that may prevent them from divesting (Sirmon, Hitt, & Ireland, 2007). There is also an alternative rationale to refrain divestment because it is possible that divestment of a volume-driving resource is not economically feasible even when the unit value is declining. In retail, Treadgold and Reynolds (2020) have discussed about potential deaths of hypermarkets but their core position generating sales volume is crucial cost-efficient operations, creating inertia for major established retailers.

Volume-driving resources occupy a strategic position in the resource portfolio, and they form a foundation for bundling processes. Over time, firms acquire adjacent resources that form profitable bundles with volume-driving resources. In this sense, volume-driving resources occupy a special position for firms that pursue a cost leadership strategy based on economies of scale. These firms can face a paradoxical situation: volume-driving resources cannot be divested while the declining unit value renders processes of acquisition and accumulation ineffective, and they have a spill-over effect to entire resource bundles of complementary resources. This creates a barrier for the whole resource management process and can potentially lead to a situation where a firm is unable to invest or divest while performance is declining. There is a gap in the resource management process literature about the management of resources in a situation of declining unit value of volume-driving resources. The objective of this chapter is to examine the resource management process of retailers that face the problem of declining unit value of volume-driving resources. There is one research question: how does resource management process change as a result of the declining unit value of volume-driving resources?

This question is pursued through a longitudinal comparative case study in three competitive retail markets: Finland, the United Kingdom, and the United States. The retailers examined are Walmart, Kmart, J Sainsbury, Tesco, S Group, and Lidl Finland. This sampling enables identifying generalizable results about changes in the resource management process due to a declining unit value of volume-driving resources.

This chapter is structured as follows: (1) an overview of the central terminology; (2) a literature review covering the resource management process in the retail sector; (3) a methodology section explaining the choices of the longitudinal comparative case studies; (4) an analysis section examining the investment pattern in the three competitive paired case studies in each market; (4) a discussion synthesizing the results into a model of strategic assets, emerging value drivers, and the resource management process in the retail sector; (5) a conclusion revisiting the problem of declining unit value of volume driving resources and summarizes the learnings from this chapter; (6) and finally, an examination of the implications for academia and practice.

## Terminology and definitions

The following constructs are central for this book chapter.

## Economies of scale and scope

In the 1960s, strategic management was understood as a designing firm structure to utilize economies of scale and scope. Economies of scale describe a situation where fixed investments are divided across a large sales volume to realize a small average unit cost. Economies of scope describe a situation where a single investment can be utilized across several different product types (Chandler, 1990). Economies of scale and scope identify resources that are potential sources of sustainable competitive advantage (Wernerfelt, 1984). In the retail sector, large stores enable economies of scope and deliver in-store efficiency, as the same store sells thousands of different products. On the other hand, managing a portfolio of stores that are bundled with supply chain management and sourcing provides a potential source of economies of scale.

## Ex ante and ex post value

Researchers distinguish between ex ante and ex post value (Schmidt & Keil, 2013). Ex ante value is the value that management perceives before the resource is deployed. It is the expected value and is driven by perceived value drivers. Ex post value is the delivered value that a resource performs. Ex ante value materializes in investment decisions while ex post value materializes in income statements. Schmidt and Keil (2013) propose that resource-based view scholars examine ex ante value, that is. investment decisions, when examining the resource management of firms.

## Retail chains and multi-/omni-channel retailing

Due to the development of new store concepts during the twentieth century, many retailers organized as retail chains. Many organizations acquired and accumulated several different store types to match different customer needs and market segments (Neslin & Shankar, 2009) and to meet the regulatory requirements of local communities (Wood et al., 2010). This multi-channel strategy enabled a retailer to create economies of scale as different stores had overlapping assortments with high product volumes. Digital channels created major challenges for established retailers (Grewal, Roggeveen, & Nordfält, 2017) and scholars began to emphasize the role of channel integration (Herhausen et al., 2015; Zhang et al., 2010). Omni-channel retailing examines the integration problem where retailers acquire digital channels and bundle them with physical stores and operational resources (Verhoef, Kannan, & Inman, 2015). It consists of three choices about the channel stage, type, and agent (Saghiri et al., 2017) to adapt and build competitive advantage (Rusanen, 2019).

## Resource management process

Resource management process consists of structuring, bundling, and leveraging. Structuring consists of acquiring new resource types, accumulating the existing resource base, and divesting unfit, non-valuable, or value-destroying resources. Bundling is the process of connecting different resources to form capabilities. Leveraging is the process of mobilizing, coordinating, and deploying capabilities to exploit external opportunities (Sirmon, Hitt, & Ireland, 2007). In the retail sector, structuring involves the development of new store concepts and the accumulation of volume-driving resources. The resources are bundled to form capabilities that utilize economies of scale in the pursuit of sustainable competitive advantage. Finally, the case studies will show that loyalty programmes, customer data, and analytics are examples of emerging leveraging activities.

## Self-service stores

A major innovation of the twentieth century was the invention of the self-service store. This led to the development of the supermarket format (primarily food) and discount store (initially non-food) and the experimentation with larger store types. A hypermarket is a supermarket that also has a full non-food range and was initially developed in Europe. A supercentre is a non-food discount store that also has a full food range and was initially developed in the United States. Hypermarkets and supercentres are often located out of town and are generally accessed by car. Hard discounter formats (Aldi/Lidl) offer a limited product range with large economies of scale. These stores mostly sell food items, but they also have a weekly changing non-food range that can sell, for example, clothes, tools, and kitchen accessories.

## Volume-driving resources and the declining unit value problem

Volume-driving resources are resources that generate the necessary sales volume for economies of scale. These resources occupy a strategic position because they are crucial for cost positioning but also because firms bundle adjacent resources with volume-driving resources. For example, one activity of omni-channel retailing is bundling of volume-driving physical resources with emerging digital resources (Rusanen, 2019). The declining unit value problem can disrupt the resource management process because volume-driving resources are inert and hard to divest due to these resource bundles, while the declining unit value disrupts the acquisition and accumulation processes.

## Resource management process in the retail sector

This section reviews the literature about the resource management process in the retail sector. Four topics are discussed: (1) the resource-based view and the resource management process, (2) the problem of a declining unit value of volume-driving resources, (3) resource properties: scalability and fungibility, and (4) digitalization of the retail sector as a catalyst of change.

First, the resource-based view provides a theory of sustainable competitive advantage. The resource-based view is founded on the idea that a firm's resources are crucial determinants of its ability to produce products and services. Economies of scale and scope can be considered as a resource (Wernerfelt, 1984). Resources are assumed to be imperfectly mobile and heterogeneous. If a resource is valuable, rare, inimitable, and non-substitutable, then it is a source of sustainable competitive advantage (Barney, 1991). In the retail sector, the cost advantage of major retailers is built on mass sourcing, a substantial store portfolio, and efficient logistics. Imitation of this kind of resource portfolio is time-consuming and costly so any cost advantage is likely to be enjoyed over smaller rivals for an extended time period. Further, the existing resource endowment both enables and limits the available option set because resource heterogeneity is a source of asymmetrical decisions (Wernerfelt, 2011). Major retailers have a different set of options than smaller retailers. A profitable action for one firm might not be profitable for another firm due to differences in volume-driven cost efficiency. Further, there may be specific resources that are particularly valuable for major retail chains but not for specialized retailers, and this can create a path of reinforcing decisions that create heterogeneity in a market's competitive landscape. During the twentieth Century, major retailers have created competitive advantage based on the acquisition of volume-driving resources to utilize economies of scale and scope.

Second, the problem of the declining unit value of volume drivers is a theoretically unexplored issue. A volume-driving resource is defined as a resource that generates the necessary sales volume for economies of scale. The combination of resources and capabilities that utilize strategic industry factors is called strategic assets (Amit & Schoemaker, 1993). Firms that have accumulated a substantial base of volume-driving resources that are bundled with other adjacent resources to form capabilities can encounter problems in these strategic assets. An exogenous fall in unit prices of volume-driving resources can create major problems for such firms. Resources with a declining unit value can still form valuable bundles but the falling unit prices are signals of potential problems on the horizon. Resources with low value are candidates for divestment (Sirmon, Hitt, & Ireland, 2007), while a strategic status as a volume-driving resource can prevent divestment. This leaves the firm in an unclear situation where it is both difficult to divest and also not feasible to invest.

But how is unit value defined? It is tautological to state that valuable resources are a source of sustainable competitive advantage (Kraaijenbrink, Spender, & Groen, 2010). A solution for this tautology problem is to distinguish between ex ante and ex post value (Schmidt & Keil, 2013). The contemporary resource-based view examines investment decisions as they reveal managerial ex ante valuations. Realized performance in the income statement is also important because it might affect upcoming ex ante valuations. In particular, the declining ex post unit value of volume-driving resources influences the ex ante valuation of potential new resources. Established firms have acquired volume-driving resources over a long period of time, and they have processes in place to routinely build a larger portfolio of such resources, creating a virtuous cycle where positive ex post performance leads to high ex ante valuations and investment decisions. Over time, such a firm generates more volume, which results in improved cost competitiveness. However, when the competitive context changes in the Red Queen Race, such virtuous circles can be halted, rendering carefully established resource management processes non-feasible in the new context. If the ex post performance of the volume-driving resources declines, there will be changes in ex ante valuations of future resource decisions. The virtuous circle becomes a vicious circle.

Third, resources can be scalable and fungible. Scalable resources enjoy only minor expansion-related costs: after acquiring a scalable resource, it can be used in different scales without a need to acquire new resources. Fungible resources have multiple uses that can be applied in several different contexts (Levinthal & Wu, 2010). A firm brand is a typical example of a resource that is both scalable and fungible, as the same brand can be leveraged by different products or services at various growth rates.

A volume-driving resource is not automatically scalable or fungible. In retail, a large store has physical limits in sales volume that it can realistically produce, and in order to scale the system, the retailer must accumulate more stores or extend the existing footprint. Further, a store concept has limited fungibility. It is possible to use a space in various ways, but a physical space nevertheless has a fixed location and size that make changes costly and will limit its fungibility. Thus, physical retail space has both limited scalability and limited fungibility. Fixed assets can have several uses but there are clear constraints and inertia in achieving change. Large stores have limited maximum capacity. Limits in scalability emphasize the role of the resource acquisition process. Limited scalability has led many retailers to take an active expansion strategy that identifies a volume-driving resource and accumulates that resource rapidly in order to generate enough volume for economies of scale, for example by opening more stores. The emergence of omni-channel retailing (Neslin & Shankar, 2009) can be viewed as a response to limited fungibility. Since a store format has limited uses, retailers have developed new ways to use existing formats and have also created entirely new store formats for different competitive contexts.

Fourth, digitalization is a catalyst of change in the retail sector, which was accelerated by the Covid-19 pandemic. The retail sector is experiencing a drastic change due to digitalized assets (Grewal, Roggeveen, & Nordfält, 2017) and business challenges such as omni-channel retailing (Saghiri et al., 2017), which has implications for resource management (Rusanen, 2019). Physical resources in the retail sector have limited scalability and limited fungibility but digitalization has created new resource types that have a very different operating logic. Intangible knowledge-based resources are valuable in quickly changing and complex environments (Miller & Shamsie, 1996). Digitalization has created a surge of new knowledge-based intangible resource types. Digital resources can be highly scalable and fungible. For example, data analytics can be used by firms with low or high market share and it can be applied to different business segments (Bradlow et al., 2017). A retailer can utilize the data for developing products and services and there is no obvious limit to the fungibility of customer data analytics. The invention of the self-service format enabled retailers to lower prices by eliminating costly non-scalable services. In the digital environment, many services have become automated, scalable, and fungible. In an increasingly digital context, new digital services can be crafted with only a small increase in variable costs.

Retailers that face the problem of the declining unit value of their volume-driving resources need to change the resource management process. Channel management requires the adaptation of existing volume-driving resources or expanding into new areas. This implies finding a balance between new digital resources and existing physical channels. Such omni-channel resource management has the potential to create new growth for retailers by providing a seamless customer experience across the digital and physical channels (Brynjolfsson, Hu, & Rahman, 2013) but this requires the integration of physical channels with supply chain and digital solutions, such as mobile and social media (Piotrowicz & Cuthbertson, 2014). These developments emphasize a holistic approach to retail resource management and the importance of a new approach towards the strategic management of resources.

## Comparative longitudinal multiple case analysis

This book chapter examines how retailers respond to the declining unit value of volume-driving resources. As discussed, such phenomenon can be studied by observing retail investment patterns, as they are driven by changes in resource ex post value and lead to changes in resource ex ante valuations. In order to accomplish this objective, this chapter considers a longitudinal analysis of multiple comparative case studies. It examines two retailers each in three markets: S Group and Lidl in Finland, Sainsbury's and Tesco in the United Kingdom, and Walmart and Kmart in the United States. These cases are selected because each of these retailers has built a portfolio of volume-driving resources in order to utilize economies of scale as a base for cost-efficient operations and market leadership within their respective countries. Further, several retailers have experienced problems with volume-driving resources: this sampling enables to make generalizable observations about changes in the investment pattern when the unit value of a volume-driving resource declines.

The time periods chosen to be examined cover the structuring of volume-driving resources, bundling them with adjacent resources in order to create scale-based capabilities, observing the declining unit value problem and the changes in the resource management pattern as a result of this problem. In the United States, the discount format was developed in 1962; in the United Kingdom, Sainsbury's experimented with hypermarket formats in the late 1970s and Tesco invested aggressively in this format in late 1990s; in Finland, major store structuring decisions happened in the mid-1980s and Lidl entered the Finnish market in 2002. All cases are examined until 2017, except for Kmart due to a Chapter 11 filing in 2002.

Data collection is focused on identifying strategic events by analysing major investment decisions. Theoretically, this corresponds to ex ante valuations made by managers: resources are valuable if managers expect them to be valuable and this is realized in an investment decision (Schmidt & Keil, 2013). Annual reports are selected as the primary data source as they provide both quantitative and qualitative data about the ex ante resource valuations. Annual reports also enable comparability within markets due to the consistent regulatory standards for reporting. Reporting for public companies is regulated and must provide accurate and truthful information about core resources and financial performance. The annual report data is complemented with official corporate announcements about strategic events, books, or news articles about specific events, as well as interview data (N = 56). Annual reports, especially in the case of Lidl, contain mostly quantitative data, so utilizing additional data sources such as interviews and news sources was necessary to build a valid and reliable description about Lidl's resource management process that can be utilized for comparing it with S Group. For each case, the volume-driving resources were identified and examined through the relevant financial data. Quantitative data about complementary resources bundles was then examined. This enabled an understanding of the growth, peak(s), and decline of the resources. This was followed by a study of strategic events to explain the pattern of resource management process. The objective is to identify strategic events that top management themselves highlight as particularly important sources of growth or profitability and then to analyse changes in those resources over time and in comparison to a rival company. The primary data was supplemented with secondary publicly available data: news, industry reports, and academic research about the companies.

## Strategic assets, store investments, and emerging value

In this section, I will examine the resource management process in the three competitive pairs. (1) For each competitive pair, I will examine the acquisition of strategic assets that formed the foundation of competitive advantage for the retailers. (2) Next I will examine the large store investment pattern and performance—volume-driving resources—which have created a need to redefine the resource management process of the major retail chains. (3) Finally, I will examine key characteristics in the investment pattern of the major retail chains in order to understand emerging value drivers (ex ante valuation). These three areas are examined all the cases. I have organized the cases as competitive rivalries: Kmart–Walmart (United States), Sainsbury's–Tesco (United Kingdom), and S Group–Lidl (Finland).

### Kmart and Walmart (United States)

S.S. Kresge opened its first K Mart discount store in 1962, when it was operating Kresge and Jupiter variety stores. The discount concept quickly became the spearhead operation of the company, which eventually led the company and the store type to be branded as K Mart discount store (later Kmart) and Kmart Corporation. The discount format was a major success and the company's total sales grew from 1 billion in 1966 to 14.2 billion in 1980. The stores carried a wide assortment of non-food products in a 3,700–7,800 square metre store. The products were priced aggressively and supported by a Kmart's 'Blue Lights' advertisement campaign. The discount concept utilized the sourcing of affordable products and scope-based in-store efficiency. The large assortment of non-food products and increased package sizes in a self-service environment enabled the lowering of costs due to economies of scope within an individual store. For Kmart, cost leadership of the 1960s was established by the size of individual stores.

Wal-Mart (later Walmart Corporation) opened its first Discount City in 1969 in Arkansas. The store concept had substantial similarity with Kmart's discount operation, and it carried a wide product assortment in an out-of-town location, accessible by car.

Walmart and Kmart had different approaches both in store location strategy and supply chain management. Kmart defined a potential market as large Standard Metropolitan Statistical Areas (SMSAs) areas and targeted only major cities in all 50 states. By 1979, Kmart had expanded to 261 out of 275 SMSAs in 48 states; Walmart was still operating in 11 mid-West states. Walmart expanded to towns and states adjacent to existing operations utilizing a distribution-oriented strategy. This economics of density enabled Walmart higher volume and efficiency in its distribution centre (Basker, 2007). In fact, in the 1970s, the Walmart expansion strategy was mainly determined based on access to a central distribution centre. This different investment pattern resulted in an asymmetry in the rivals' abilities to utilize new logistics technologies efficiently. In the 1980s, both companies invested in logistics technologies and information technology (IT) systems. However, Walmart, operating with a higher volume, was able to improve its inventory turnover from 95 (1975) to 68 (1990) while Kmart's inventory turnover in fact worsened from 90 (1976) to 106 (1990), due to a strategic shift towards diversified operations.

In the 1980s and early 1990s, Kmart attempted to replicate the scope-based format design in specialty retailing. It initiated a diversification programme where it acquired several unrelated businesses and expanded the store size and the assortment range. Kmart acquired Border bookstores, Payless drug stores, Office Square and OfficeMax, The Sports Authority, Designer Depot & Garment Rack clothes stores, Builders' Square do it yourself (DIY) chain, and Furr's Cafeterias.

Both companies invested in membership warehouse businesses. Walmart opened its first Sam's Club membership warehouse in 1983, and the clubs were often located in adjacent cities with an existing discount store, attracting traffic from households and small businesses. Kmart entered this business in 1988 with Makro and PACE stores. Kmart's scale development in the core discount store business and in membership warehouse operations was limited by the acquisitions of unrelated store concepts—during the 1980s, Walmart bypassed Kmart both in sales and profits.

In the late 1980s, both companies started to find new sources of growth. Walmart trialled with four Hypermart* USA stores that eventually led to the development of the Supercenter concept. Walmart Supercenters carried a discount store with non-food range and also a food range. Kmart trialled its American Fare operation and developed a similar Supercenter format. However, the performance of Kmart's trials and its early Supercenters was lower than that of the Walmart Supercenters because Walmart had integrated its non-food volume with logistics investments in the 1980s to develop greater sourcing and logistics-based capabilities.

In the 1990s, Kmart attempted to revitalize its operations. It divested specialty retail operations and focused on discount-driven concepts. Its discount stores were rebranded as Kmart Traditional, Big Kmart, and Supercenter. At its peak, the number of Big and Traditional Kmart stores was 2,323 while there were 124 Supercenters. This can be compared with Walmart's peak of 1,995 Discount Cities and 2,612 Supercenters. The main reason why Kmart could not meet the challenge of Walmart was that it did not have comparable scale and could not take advantage of global sourcing and logistics technology as efficiently as Walmart did. The transition into the Supercenter format was comparably low scale. Both companies invested heavily in warehouses, automation, logistics technology, and in-store technology, but Walmart was able to bundle store and logistics resources and integrate the operations at a corporate level. For example, Walmart developed a crossdocking system in the late 1980s but Kmart did not adopt the system as it was not efficient for a non-dense store network. Kmart filed for Chapter 11 in 2001 and was acquired by Sears in 2002.

Walmart opened its first Neighborhood market in 1998, a smaller store concept. The Neighborhood market carries mostly groceries and pharmacies, with a goal to enhance accessibility and convenience. In 2011, local services were further expanded through the Walmart Express convenience format.

Walmart pioneered digital channels through the launch of Walmart Online (later Wal-Mart.com) in 1996–1997, 'a shop without shop', but already in 1999 it faced difficulties in making profits in the online channel as it was treated as a substitute of physical channels. In 2007, its site-to-store service was launched, which allowed customers to purchase products online and pick them during store visit. This service enabled Walmart to offer customers an extended range of products with added convenience during their weekly shopping visit. Since 2009, Walmart has systematically argued that channel integration and creation of seamless shopping experience are crucial factors to improve convenience anywhere and anytime. Customers were increasingly using mobile in-store, and stores were considered also as showrooms for the online channel. Since 2009, Walmart has launched several initiatives to strengthen the interplay between the physical and digital: in-store wireless networks, mobile self-checkout, Sam's Club eValues personalized discount campaign, Pick Up Today service, Scan and Go App, and Walmart Pay for smart phones. In 2016, Walmart acquired Jet.com and its smart-cart technology. These initiatives were also supported by two-day shipping in 2018.

Data mining initiatives were pioneered in early 1991, based on point-of-sale data, with the original goal to optimize store fulfilment and sharing data with suppliers through Retail Link. In this way, suppliers were able to utilize sales information in product development, especially for private brands. Data analytics was further utilized through Sam's Club membership data and the data from online and mobile channels in the twenty-first century. This is further enhanced through the analysis of social media data. The goal of data analytics has expanded from logistics and product development to create personalization and convenience for online shopping. In annual report 2016 (p.7), Walmart stated that the 'use of data, algorithms, advanced forecasting capabilities – and more – is of extreme strategic significance'.

## Sainsbury's and Tesco (United Kingdom)

J Sainsbury Plc and Tesco Plc have their roots in UK grocery retailing dating from the late nineteenth and early twentieth centuries. 'The best butter in the world' was an original slogan used by Sainsbury's in the nineteenth century and targeted workers and the middle class with a premise of quality food at a reasonable price. This food-oriented mission has driven the business design of Sainsbury's for well over 100 years. In the 1970s, Sainsbury's was growing quickly, and it was supported by a strong brand. Tesco made a strategic acquisition in the 1960s and it refurbished and modernized the acquired stores until the mid-1980s.

Both Sainsbury's and Tesco utilized and developed the self-service supermarket concept. This led to experimentation with larger store sizes and the utilization of out-of-town locations accessible by car. In 1975, 11 per cent of Tesco's stores were over 25,000 square feet compared with 64 per cent in 1987. In the early 2000s, stores under 20,000 square feet were considered small, while the largest stores were over 60,000 square feet. The average sales area of Sainsbury's supermarkets grew from 9,600 square feet (1975) to 16,000 square feet (1985) and to 26,300 square feet (1995). Sainsbury's had early experiments with the hypermarket format as it launched the Savacentre chain in 1978. This 73,000 square feet hypermarket carried a full Sainsbury's supermarket food range that was coupled with a non-food offering provided by British Home Stores (BHS). Sainsbury's acquired the Savacentre joint venture in the 1980s but opened only 13 Savacentres in the United Kingdom. Hence, Savacentre never became a major volume driver and as a result did not create economies of scale in non-food operations. In the late 1990s, the Savacentre format was merged with the large supermarket format of Sainsbury's.

In the 1980s, both companies invested heavily in supply chain management, sourcing, and IT systems to cater for their growing supermarket networks. Both firms adopted barcode scanning, point of sale (POS) systems, and enterprise resource planning (ERP) systems, which led to sharp improvement in the inventory turnover.

Tesco renewed its store branding in 1994–1995. The new store concepts were Express, Metro, Compact Superstore, and Superstore and were designed based on town-specific requirements. Express carried a limited grocery range in a small outlet, designed for the town centre, while Superstore had a full food assortment in non-central urban areas. In 1996, a new regulatory rule, PPG6, was launched that was designed to limit the building of large stores and hypermarkets in out-of-town locations. Sainsbury's stated that this fitted well with its strategy of moving towards medium-sized hypermarkets. In contrast, Tesco launched a hypermarket chain, Extra, in 1998. In the early twenty-first century, Tesco had a store concept portfolio that could be customized for the requirements of individual towns: small Express stores for expensive city centre locations, Metro and high street stores for daily pedestrian grocery shopping, Superstores in non-central areas, and Extra hypermarkets for food and non-food in out-of-town locations. Sainsbury's did not have a comparable standardized store concept range, with its supermarket being a varying concept from small self-service stores to large hypermarkets. Tesco grew as the market leader, especially due to the volume generated by the growth of the Extra format. In 2009, Tesco had 177 Extra stores and 448 Superstores while Sainsbury's had 35 hypermarkets with over 60,000 square feet sales area and 165 supermarkets with a sales area of 40,000 to 60,000 square feet. This difference in large supermarkets and hypermarkets enabled Tesco to gain a volume-driven cost advantage in the late 1990s and early twenty-first century.

Tesco's cost advantage was further improved by its internationalization programme that had begun in 1993. It entered into several markets in Europe, Asia, and the United States typically by acquiring a local retail chain to establish a minimum scale and then by building store concepts such as Express and Extra. Exporting these physical store concepts proved to be a successful strategy as Tesco was able to generate global volume especially for its non-food lines. It opened a global sourcing office in China to improve this sourcing of non-food lines to global hypermarket operations.

In the early twenty-first century, Sainsbury's was in difficulty because of volume disadvantage, an unclear brand strategy, and an unrelated diversification programme. In the 1980s, Sainsbury's was successful in its experimentation with larger supermarkets and started to look for new sources of growth with largely unrelated diversification. It opened two Homebase DIY stores in 1982 and entered the US grocery retail business through the acquisition of Shaw's. In the 1990s, these formats accounted for approximately 25 per cent of its annual investments but delivered only limited synergies or scale as there was only minor overlapping between business areas. In the early 2000s, the lack of focus on investing in the core operations of grocery retailing and the inability to match Tesco's systematic volume-driven scale cost competitiveness had driven Sainsbury's into crisis. It initiated a major change programme to improve its supply chain management, IT systems, infrastructure, stores, and organization. It divested Homebase in 2001 and Shaw's in 2003 and re-focused on its core supermarket business. Sainsbury's had problems with the new logistics investments in its automated distribution centre and with IT outsourcing and subsequent insourcing during 2000–2006, and cost efficiency targets were not reached by its early recovery programmes.

Tesco was active in developing own-label products and invested in long-term relationships with key producers. Sainsbury's had experimented in own-label products throughout the twentieth century, but its own-label strategy was renewed in the twenty-first century as a result of the Making Sainsbury's Great Again (MSGA) recovery programme. It initiated a 'good, better, best' hierarchy of own-label products. The programme also involved a 'Tell Justin' scheme (Justin King, the CEO at the time) to improve relations for their employees and to identify areas for improvement.

In the twenty-first century, both Sainsbury's and Tesco noticed that small grocery outlets with high margins can utilize effectively their existing logistics competencies. Since 2003, Tesco has acquired T&S and One Stop local store chains and merged some into the Express format. Sainsbury's had experimented with two convenience stores in 1999, and in 2004 it had 146 convenience stores. In 2009, Sainsbury's had 290 convenience stores while Tesco had 1,473 local stores. The volume contribution is small, but these outlets can be built in high-traffic city centre locations and are accessible to pedestrians. As a result, they form a high-margin bundle that utilizes existing scale-based competencies. The re-focus on smaller store formats was driven by the identified need to add local services and convenience for customers. In 2018–2019, Sainsbury's attempted to merge with Asda, which could have had a substantial impact on market positions, but it was blocked by the Competition and Markets Authority.

During the recession of 2008, Tesco's performance declined. In particular, the large outlets, Superstore and especially Extra, did not perform as expected. The non-food range of the hypermarkets had suffered from changing consumer behaviour, macro-economic cycles, and new rivals, both physical and digital. Tesco announced the end of its space race programme, which marked a strategic move away from opening hypermarket stores towards local convenience stores and online. In 2017–2018, Tesco merged with Booker Group, which is a food wholesale retailer. The logic of this merger is to strengthen Tesco's position in out-of-home and on-the-go food services and to realize operational synergies.

The UK retailers have been frontrunners in loyalty programmes and data analytics. In the 1990s, both companies introduced loyalty cards. Sainsbury's Homebase was a first mover, but Tesco was able to be the first mover in grocery retailing with the Clubcard. This created incentives for consumers to concentrate purchases in Tesco stores, while the consumer data was used for investment decisions. Tesco outsourced its analytics to a partially owned subsidiary, Dunnhumby, which quickly improved the ability of demand-driven decision-making. Early analytics initiatives had shown that buying frequency increased while average basket size was decreasing. Tesco utilized early experimentation in analytics for moving towards smaller store segment and for determining the appropriate store type in location decisions. In comparison, similar analytics initiatives of Sainsbury's developed only a decade later. During strategical renewal programmes, Sainsbury's Reward Card was replaced by Nectar and it was coupled with analytics with Aimia. Especially through the MSGA programme, Sainsbury's has highlighted its intention to use the analytics of customer data in designing business operations and strategic decision-making.

Both companies have experimented with digital consumer technology throughout the twenty-first century. The firms are pioneers in self-service checkouts and experimented with quick checkout technology. Nowadays both firms utilize digital channels, such as mobile, to provide accurate information for customers. The firms attempt to create a seamless consumer experience in both digital and physical channels, and the point of collection is determined by the customer (physical shopping, click & collect, or home delivery).

Both companies have over two decades of experience in Internet retailing. In the late 1990s, Sainsbury's viewed Internet retailing as a substitute for brick-and-mortar stores, relied on centralized delivery, and cut back on investments in physical outlets. Tesco viewed Internet retailing as a complement and utilized its existing stores as a picking station for home deliveries. The profitability of Internet retailing remained marginal, if not negative, and the complementary approach was more successful than the centralized substitute strategy of Sainsbury's while volumes were small. As volumes grew, efficiency of centralized distribution increased.

As a result of problems in the sales of non-food items and large store sales, both firms continue to seek ways to increase the performance of large outlets and innovative ways of selling non-food. The acquisition of Argos by Sainsbury's is particularly interesting. Argos utilizes digital channels as a complement for its physical channels: Argos's digital channel carries a wide assortment of non-food products (long tail) but sell only a limited range in small physical outlets. Customers can order the product and collect it from the store or have it delivered to home. The Argos acquisition has widened Sainsbury's non-food offering in both online and physical outlets. The acquisition enables Sainsbury's to build a service that offers a wide assortment of non-food products in a limited supermarket space. In 2019, Sainsbury's made a strategic decision to invest in a digital future. As a result, Sainsbury's have invested in several digital areas such as opening new Argos stores within Sainsbury's location, investments to in-store digital technologies, investments to the digital channel, and the acquisition of Nectar from Aimia to improve data analytics competencies.

Covid-19 has further enhanced the role of digital channels. Both retailers made it a priority to keep customers safe. Early in the pandemic, grocery sales saw a sharp increase. Both companies have made efforts to increase their online capacity. Sainsbury's also prioritized online services for elderly and vulnerable customers during the pandemic. Tesco announced a 30 million GBP support package for local communities. The investments in omni-channel capabilities have created necessary flexibility to both Sainsbury's and Tesco as the pandemic has had an asymmetric impact on different channels.

## S Group and Lidl (Finland)

S Group is a Finnish consumer cooperative with business areas ranging from grocery retailing, non-food retailing, and automotive to hotel and restaurants. It is the market leader with over 45 per cent market share in grocery retailing. This has not always been the case. In the 1980s, S Group was in a deep crisis, and the new CEO launched a strategic recovery programme called S83. The programme launched the S Group brand name and it is led by central organization SOK (Suomen Osuuskauppojen Keskuskunta). In the early 1980s, S Group was highly diversified, and its operations included industrial operations and its own factories. In 1983, it consisted mainly of small local cooperatives that had a limited ability to acquire large stores and utilize economies of scale. As a result of the S83 implementation, the industrial operations were divested and the group focused on retailing, especially grocery retailing. It underwent major layoffs and restructuring, wherein the cooperative network adopted a regional structure with substantially larger average cooperative size. Local cooperatives merged into regional cooperatives: in 1983, S Group had 178 cooperatives, which reduced by 48 per cent due to mergers in a single year. By 1992, it had 23 regional cooperatives. The main driver of corporate restructuring towards fewer regional cooperatives was the changing retail context due to urbanization as consumers moved to the larger cities, enabling larger stores. Small cooperatives were not able to undertake the large investments necessary to develop a hypermarket format, and the coordination between different cooperatives was not efficient.

In the early 1980s, S Group was not competitive in the large cities and most of its cooperatives were in small towns. The outdated local cooperative structure had been unable to meet the changing technological and business model development needs of an urbanized society. The structural changes driven by S83 were supported by the birth of national retail chains in 1985. A supermarket format, S Market, was created as a spearhead format. In 1987, Prisma stores were rebranded as car-accessible hypermarkets. Prisma was designed as a one-stop shop, with the full S Market grocery range alongside a large non-food range. The renewed regional cooperative structure enabled the cooperatives to undertake large hypermarket investments and locate the hypermarkets in large cities.

In the late 1980s, S Group invested in warehouses, supply chain technologies, and IT systems. It adopted barcode scanning and POS systems and utilized ERP systems for inventory management in the 1990s. In 1991, S Group formed Inex Partners for centralized sourcing and logistics. Inex Partners was founded as a joint venture with a rival cooperative, Eka. Through the combined sales of S Group and Eka, the joint venture had a higher volume than the market leader at that time, K Group, and created a foundation for cost leadership in the Finnish grocery retail industry. SOK eventually acquired Inex Partners from Eka as a fully owned subsidiary. In the 1990s, S Group had made a substantial shift in cost positioning due to the focus on large store units (Prisma and S Market) that was supported by centralized logistics and renewed IT systems. S Group based its strategy on cost leadership driven by bundling logistics with those large formats.

Another major event was the customer ownership strategy that was initiated in late 1980s and supported by a bonus card. S Group is a customer cooperative, which means that cooperatives are owned by the customers. The profits are distributed to customer-owners based on annual purchases. Before the bonus card, bonuses were calculated annually from receipts and it often took a full working day for the customers. Therefore, S Group adopted a loyalty card, as a technological solution to manual calculation by customers, with a progressive bonus system from 1–5 per cent of sales, and during campaigns the bonus can be doubled. The card initially received resistance from many cooperatives as the renewed bonuses were considered as an additional expense. The central organization SOK lobbied heavily for the adoption of the card and bonus system, and after the positive sales development experienced by the cooperatives that had adopted it earlier, the system grew as a national solution in the mid-1990s. The bonus card rewarded customers for concentrating purchases in S Group stores. This led to rapid sales growth that created volume for the newly founded Inex Partners throughout the 1990s and the early twenty-first century. In the early twenty-first century, S Group developed actively its own-label product range for offering affordable and branded food ranges for its customer-owners.

S Group was active in the store format development throughout the 1990s. The ABC service station concept bundled the supermarket with the gas stations and their restaurants. In a tightening regulatory environment, S Group was able to justify building large out-of-town units in high-traffic locations since they are primarily gas stations. In a highly concentrated market, both market leaders S Group and Kesko expanded large hypermarket stores, opened often inside large shopping centres, and S Group built new large out-of-town service stations. This sector development led to legislation changes to tighten the planning regulation for large units in 2011.

During the recession of 2008, S Group's volume-driving outlets encountered problems. Sales per store had declined since 2006 (Prisma) and 2008 (S Market). Figure 2.1 displays the sales development of S Group stores. Real sales of Prisma hypermarkets declined by 41 per cent during 2006–2015. This reflects the development of increasing competition from hard discounters, specialized stores, and the emergence of Internet retailing. This was emphasized by the increasing price transparency of the online channel. The recession also played an important part in explaining the changing consumption behaviour as consumers postponed purchasing certain non-food products. S Group underwent restructuring and launched a 'cheapening' scheme where prices of selected products were lowered. This everyday low price (EDLP) campaign was designed to address the decline of the unit value of large outlets.

In the twenty-first century, S Group has been active in bundling services with the volume-driven businesses. It launched the S Bank, offering customer-owners a low-cost service utilizing space in their hypermarkets. It also launched a mobile application designed to enable customer-owners to manage their personal purchases through S Bank and their shopping behaviour in S Group stores and hotels.

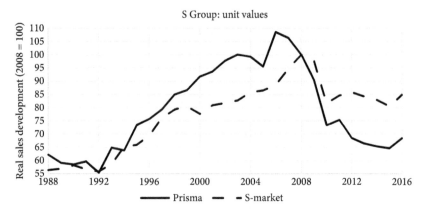

**Figure 2.1** Unit values of volume-driving resources (S Group) based on average sales per store

All values are adjusted for inflation using consumer price index and time-series are normalized (year 2008 = 100).

In 2017, digital services were considered as one of the main investment areas to enhance competitiveness. This was coupled with the statement that S Group's focus is moving from 'mammoth-sized department stores towards human-sized stores' (annual report 2017, p.12), which are convenient and easy to access, supported by multi-channel development and Internet retailing. In 2018, S Group launched Food Market Herkku as a premium service-oriented food convenience store chain.

Lidl entered the Finnish market in 2002. It has a hard discounter business model. Upon entering the market, Lidl opened 800–1,300 square meter stores with 15 employees and 1,000 products. It has several own-label products but decided to include several externally branded products after its market entry. Lidl utilizes European-wide scale in sourcing and logistics in its own-label products. For nationally sourced products, it is crucial to build sufficient volume for sourcing power and economies of scale. By limiting the assortment breadth, Lidl reaches a high volume of sales for nationally sourced products, despite a low market share.

Upon entry, Lidl made a rough plan of 140 store openings in Finland. Based on this plan, Lidl determined the locations of two first distribution centres to optimize distribution routes in the long run. This approach summarizes well the hard discount expansion strategy of logistics-driven growth. The first actual decision is the location of the distribution centre, which is followed by rapid store openings to ensure making use of economies of scale. This approach is very similar to that of Walmart in 1970s, which produced maps with the distribution centre in the middle and store openings surrounding this central point. Lidl opened 20–30 stores annually and in 2007 it had 109 stores serviced from two distribution centres. Lidl hit breakeven in 2008 with cumulative nominal deficits of 92 million euros.

Lidl stores were located at non-central, lower cost areas, often near hypermarkets. The stores were subjected to less regulation than hypermarkets since they were smaller than the large store limit determined by the Finnish construction and planning legislation. The locations of these stores were accessible by car and there was already high customer traffic, as they were often located near the two large hypermarket chains Prisma (operated by S Group) and Citymarket (operated by K Group). The CEO of SOK named this approach publicly as a 'parasite strategy', which became a popular description of Lidl in the Finnish press for the first few years in the market.

In 2009 Lidl initiated a campaign to improve its brand value and reputation towards stakeholders. This included a strategy of rebranding Lidl from a lowest price retailer towards a company that offers products and services for price-conscious customers, and it proved successful. The renewed brand image received positive attention: in 2015–2016, Lidl won the buzz brand index that measures positive brand messages in Finnish social media among customers. Lidl's product focus shifted from lowest price as it coupled selected premium offering as part of product portfolio.

Lidl has found creative ways of using digital advertising and social media to gain visibility for its brand and specially to create interest for non-food products. It has added service elements to non-food offering. Lidl stores have a weekly changing non-food offering. In order to lower purchase barriers, the products have a two-week return policy and many products have a three-year guarantee. Lidl has utilized digital solutions for creating excitement and to incentivize the following of their weekly advertisements about non-food offering. Its website and mobile application were renewed. Both digital channels were designed for advertising, especially the changing non-food offering in-store. In this way, Lidl has utilized digital channels to improve the performance of store sales. In 2020, the Lidl Plus application was introduced, which is a counter to S Group's loyalty card, but also utilizes the advertising features of the earlier mobile application, coupled with digital receipts.

In social media, Lidl has been able to achieve a status of reference price in certain product categories. Especially in DIY segment, customers review Lidl products regularly in social media. For example, in the 'home workshop' website, where DIY hobbyists review new tools and evaluate whether they are worth buying, there were 720 entries totalling 49 pages of reviews and 229,000 reads (accessed on 8 December 2017). The point is that Lidl is the only retail chain that has its own thread for product reviews and that is why it forms a reference price for cheap products with reasonable quality—a feature that competitors have been unable to match. This is an example of a consumer-driven electronic word of mouth. Lidl has also been active in driving social media programmes and event marketing, such as a Master of Barbeque—tour (Fin. Grillimaisteri). Another, smaller, example is the online broadcast of celebrity chef Hans Välimäki working as a cashier in checkout.

Lidl has been very active in redesigning integrated solutions that utilize technology mobile, and social media to create visibility and positive messages about the company and its latest offering.

In-store technologies and services have been updated as part of an investment programme. In 2011, Lidl began to invest heavily in store refurbishments and expansions. The updated stores are larger (approximately 1,600 square meters), have a modern look and feel, and carry an extended product range. Lidl created an in-store bakery that offers fresh bread. Service quality was improved due to hiring practices: employees per store were 14–20 until 2011, but the number had increased to 31 in 2017.

The strategy of a renewed brand, premium (but relatively low-cost) offerings, increased service levels, and the utilization of digital channels for marketing have had a major impact on the performance of Lidl. Further, in a period of recession, customers have emphasized price as a buying criterion. Both Lidl and S Group have emphasized price leadership as a primary objective of their strategies. However, the impact on performance has differed. While S Group's post-recession unit value of large stores has declined, the unit value of Lidl stores has increased rapidly in a period of recession. Figure 2.2 shows that average real sales per store have increased 83 per cent since 2008.

In 2011–2017, Lidl was increasing sales quickly, but its new store openings had been minimal. Net profit per store increased from €232,000 (2011) to €425,000 (2017). Recession can explain part of this growth as customers have emphasized more price in their consumption decisions. Lidl has been able to drive growth by investing in services, in-store technologies, quality products, digital applications,

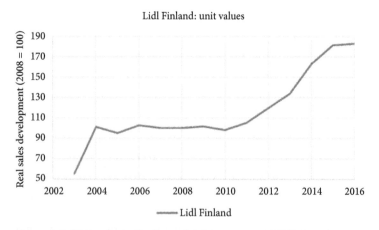

**Figure 2.2** Unit values of volume-driving resources (Lidl) based on average sales per store

All values are adjusted for inflation using consumer price index and time-series is normalized (year 2008 = 100).

and relationship management with customers and suppliers. Interestingly, even in an era of price consciousness, Lidl has not implemented any major cost efficiency programmes. It is utilizing existing cost efficiency but has updated its hard discount business model from being a low-price retailer to offer solutions for cost-conscious customers (e.g. families with children). Lidl has emphasized its public image and branding, added quality product lines, renewed its digital strategy, and improved its in-store services.

Covid-19 has had a major impact on both Lidl Finland and S Group. The food segment has experienced an expansion as customers shift consumption from inside-restaurants to home-made or ordered food items. S Group's all other business areas have experienced decrease in sales—especially travel and hotel segments have had a major decline in revenues, and so has the department and specialty store segment. The demand of S Group's grocery Internet retailing has 'multiplied in a short period of time'. The Finnish market shows similar evidence as experienced globally: omni-channel retailing has enabled companies to transfer part of their sales losses in physical environment to increase of sales in digital channels.

## The declining value of volume-driving resources

This analysis of six major retailers in three markets shows commonalities. They all base their operations on cost advantage created through economies of scale over different time periods as they acquire, accumulate, and bundle resources. They have faced problems associated with volume-driving resources, especially Kmart. They have explored new ideas and solutions that have sometimes enabled them to continue growth and sometimes failed. Lidl Finland has been particularly interesting because its investment programme over the past decade in a depressed economic environment yet managed to achieve impressive developments in sales per store.

Kmart is an example of a firm that could not successfully manage the transition into the Supercenter business that requires the utilization of existing competencies in non-food retailing while also expanding into food retailing. Kmart could not respond to the Red Queen Race and failed to take advantage of potential economies of scale. Kmart's period of growth utilized economies of scope and developing in-store efficiency, but their utilization of supply-based technologies was incomplete.

The examined firms' strategic assets have been acquired during decades of competition to establish cost leadership by utilizing economies of scale and scope. This has been established by standardizing the volume-driving resources that enable to take advantage of the self-service concept in an efficient manner. The 1980s was critical in all three markets (the United States, the United Kingdom, and Finland), where firms experimented with larger and larger stores and invested heavily in logistics technologies and IT systems. The retailers were able to offer a wide assortment of food and non-food products in large stores that were in out-of-town locations and accessible by car. Thus, there are four commonalities in strategic assets in the examined cases: supply chain innovations, new product developments, large physical stores, and standardized volume-driven operations. By utilizing the standardization of large physical units and leveraging supply technologies, the examined companies have competed to establish cost leadership at delivering low prices for large product assortments.

The cases, except Lidl (which has a much smaller product assortment), also emphasize the problem of the declining unit value of volume-driving resources. All examined cases have taken actions to deal with this change in the strategic landscape. Strategic assets form a core part of strategy by driving down costs and enabling firms to offer a wide assortment of products in a large physical space, but in the new Red Queen Race focused on digital rather than physical mass, these firms are unable to take the theoretically identified option of divesting (Sirmon, Hitt, & Ireland, 2007; Sirmon et al., 2011). These cases highlight the utilization of a variety of actions to leverage volume-driving resources or increase their unit value. This has impacted the ex ante valuation of new resource acquisitions and materialized as a change in investment patterns. These cases illustrate four areas where ex ante valuations have shifted: from supply- to demand-driven innovation, from products to services, from physical to digital, and from the sheer customer volume to increasingly emphasize the quality of those relationships.

Major retail chains have competed through volume asymmetries by developing logistics capabilities, controlling large physical spaces to offer a broad product assortment at a low price. These cases show that these dimensions are still very important for retailers, but they don't produce the same competitive advantage as the rules of the Red Queen Race change in this age of digitization. The cases show that retailers have increasingly started utilizing innovation in the demand environment by utilizing customer data to analyse consumption patterns and create new solutions. Retailers have increasingly utilized digital solutions and channels to complement existing offerings in the physical space. These changes match with research findings on omni-channel retailing where retailers build a seamlessly integrated capabilities between the physical and digital retail spaces (Piotrowicz & Cuthbertson, 2014; Rigby, 2011). Digital services are bundled with physical products, with the objective of achieving complementary benefits between these two types of offering. Further, as retailers have utilized a more fine-grained approach to develop the customer offering, especially in digital channels, retailers are increasingly customizing their solutions for specific customer needs or locations. Retailers have invested in relationships towards different stakeholders. Lidl's brand campaign, Tesco's loyalty programme, Sainsbury's Argos acquisition, and S Group's 'cheapening' campaign show the benefits of a customer focus in modern retail.

## The gap between strategic assets and emerging value drivers

Firms accumulate strategic assets and competencies to establish sustainable competitive advantage (Prahalad & Hamel, 1990). This chapter illustrates how firms have attempted to restart or maintain growth in a situation where strategic assets have ceased to be a continuing source of competitive advantage. The option to divest is recommended for resources with declining value (Sirmon, Hitt, & Ireland, 2007; Sirmon et al., 2011), but this option is not always feasible for strategic assets. Thus, the objective of this chapter is to understand how the declining value of volume-driving resources affects ex ante valuations of investments and the resource management process.

The traditional retail sector has now encountered a problem of the declining value of volume drivers: unit sales of hypermarkets, supermarkets, and department stores have declined in the twenty-first century (Treadgold & Reynolds, 2020). Established resource management theory suggests that low-value resources should be divested, but because of sunk cost bias and structural inertia, divestments may not occur. In the examined cases, divestment decisions are not made due to complementarities with other resources. This creates a situation for retailers where they resist divestment of resources, not because of sunk cost biases or inertia as theory suggests but because of scale-based complementarities with adjacent resource bundles. As a result, such firms need to find ways to improve the value of their established resource base and capitalize emerging value drivers. They also need to deal with slack and flexibility problems that this strategy creates. In short, retailers must bridge a gap between existing strategic assets and emerging value drivers.

The findings are summarized in a model (Figure 2.3) that highlights the gap between strategic assets and the emerging value drivers of resources. The model contains four characteristics of core competencies that historically have been the sources of sustained competitive advantage and growth in the examined cases. These characteristics correspond with emerging value drivers based on ex ante value of recent investment pattern in the examined cases. Increasingly, resources with high ex ante value share one or several of these value drivers. Finally, the model contains four main activities that characterize resource management process in the examined cases.

The left side of the triangle contains the firm's strategic assets—the key attributes that retailers have used to build cost leadership. The growth of major retailers was based on their ability to acquire and bundle resources that were characterized by four aspects: supply innovation, product orientation, physical space, and volume-driven economies of scale. These retailers capitalized heavily on logistical developments in the 1980s and investment in IT systems for efficiently delivering products to stores within their supply chain. The retailers moved to larger store sizes, which became the source of sales volume and market share. These

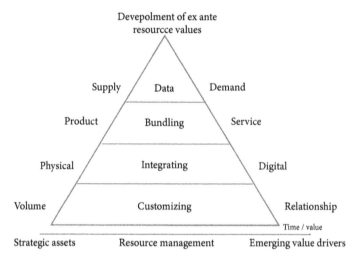

**Figure 2.3** Impact of digitalization on consumer services in the retail sector

changes enabled firms to expand their assortment range and invest in own-label products—and occupy a dominant position within the value chain. The firms gained economies of scale on product, store, and logistics levels, which led to a major period of growth. The left-hand side of the triangle is still important, but recent performance data has shown that what was previously a source of unique competitive advantage has become a common best practice for major retail chains in the twenty-first century.

The right side of the triangle contains the emerging value drivers. These are areas where retailers have paid increasing attention as the unit value of volume-driving resources has declined. The four emerging attributes of resource values are demand, service, digital, and relationships. Resource management consists of the utilization of data as a leveraging resource, bundling core competencies with emerging value drivers, the seamless integration of the digital and physical, and finding ways to efficiently customize offering to personalize relationships while exploiting both economies of scale and scope.

This chapter examines resource management when there is a gap between established strategic assets and emerging value drivers. The twentieth century retail race was built on controlling a portfolio of large physical spaces in key locations and integrating them with logistics systems. The Red Queen Race of the retail sector has changed: the emerging value drivers are increasingly intangible and knowledge based. In the retail sector this involved activities in demand innovation, intangible services, digital knowledge-based resources, and relationship management. The resource management process emphasizes leveraging customer data in business development, unique bundling of product offerings with value-adding services, integrating physical and digital channels for an omni-channel strategy, and identifying high-margin customization opportunities. The firms still utilize their existing strategic assets: supply innovation, broad product assortment, physical space, and a standardized volume-based strategy to create economies of scale. The emerging value drivers are based on an expectation of identifying solutions with high margins, identifying highly specialized needs, and creating an attractive offering for customers that has the potential to support growth in volume-driving resources.

The gap between strategic assets and emerging value drivers is driven by exogenous changes in technology, changing consumer behaviour, omni-channel business models, and the macro-economic environment. The existing strategic assets of retailers have limited fungibility and scalability. As a result, major retailers have historically become masters of accumulating highly standardized resources that have performed in a superior way for several decades. In an increasingly digital environment where customers can compare offerings efficiently, omni-channel retailing attempts to bundle physical spaces with digital resources to increase both scalability and fungibility. The emerging value drivers reflect this reality, as retailers have not significantly divested volume-driving resources but rather invested for new services as bundles to product offering and created digital solutions to promote performance of physical environment. Retailers have utilized customer data for new offering development and increasingly customized their offering to match needs of specific locations, or specific customer segments. Covid-19 has functioned as a catalyst of change, as customers have shifted towards digital channels while reducing shopping in the physical context when possible. This corresponds to retail theory, as retailers are becoming increasingly omni-channel to reflect changes in a competitive context—the Red Queen Retail Race.

## The search for growth in the Red Queen Retail Race

The service economy has not rendered established ways of doing business obsolete. Consumers still demand novel products at scale-driven low prices. However, the value-added is shifting towards digitalized services in a relationship-driven ecosystem. Firms need to further develop capabilities that utilize these aspects of a 'consumer society' (Furseth & Cuthbertson, 2016). In the model, retailers are facing a situation where the capabilities of many firms are located on the left-hand side of the triangle. However, future value is increasingly located on the right-hand side of the triangle. Firms can either take advantage of this shift or fall victim to it.

For practitioners, many retailers face the problem of the declining unit value of volume-driving resources. Supply innovation, product orientation, large physical space, and standardization and volume-based strategies are still important, but their competitive performance has declined. In the twenty-first century, these resources have become easier to imitate and now can be considered as best practices in the retail sector, not a source of sustained competitive advantage.

Retailers had begun to identify new sources of growth in the 2000s and then were forced to act in the face of the Covid-19 pandemic. The emerging value drivers that characterize contemporary retailers' investment pattern are increasingly based on innovation on the demand side, incorporate service elements, utilize intangible digital resources, and are sources of relationship management. The next chapter considers proponents of these new value drivers.

# References

Amit, R., & Schoemaker, P. J. 1993. 'Strategic assets and organizational rent'. *Strategic Management Journal*, 14(1), 33–46.

Barnett, W. P. & Hansen, M. T., 1996. 'The red queen in organizational evolution'. *Strategic Management Journal*, 17(S1), 139–157.

Barney, J. 1991. 'Firm resources and sustained competitive advantage'. *Journal of Management*, 17(1), 99–120.

Basker, E. 2007. 'The causes and consequences of WalMart's growth'. *Journal of Economic Perspectives*, 21(3): 177–198.

Bradlow, E. T., Gangwar, M., Kopalle, P., & Voleti, S., 2017. 'The role of big data and predictive analytics in retailing'. *Journal of Retailing*, 93(1), 79–95.

Brynjolfsson, E., Hu Y. E., & Rahman, M. S. 2013. 'Competing in the age of omnichannel retailing'. *MIT Sloan Management Review*, 54(4): 23–29.

Chandler, A. 1990. *Scale and scope: the dynamics of industrial capitalism (5th printing ed.)*. Harvard University Press.

Furseth, P. I., & Cuthbertson, R. 2016. *Innovation in an advanced consumer society: value-driven service innovation*. United Kingdom: Oxford University Press.

Grewal, D., Roggeveen, A. L., & Nordfält, J., 2017. 'The future of retailing'. *Journal of Retailing*, 93(1), 1–6.

Herhausen, D., Binder, J., Schoegel, M., & Herrmann, A. 2015. 'Integrating bricks with clicks: retailer-level and channel-level outcomes of online–offline channel integration'. *Journal of Retailing*, 91(2): 309–325.

Kraaijenbrink, J., Spender, J.-C., & Groen, A. J. 2010. 'The resource-based view: a review and assessment of its critiques'. *Journal of Management*, 36(1): 349–372.

Levinthal, D. A., & Wu, B. 2010. 'Opportunity costs and non-scale free capabilities: profit maximization, corporate scope, and profit margins'. *Strategic Management Journal*, 31(7): 780–801.

Miller, D., & Shamsie, J. 1996. 'The resource-based view of the firm in two environments: the Hollywood film studios from 1936 to 1965'. *Academy of Management Journal*, 39(3): 519–543.

Neslin, S. A. & Shankar, V., 2009. 'Key issues in multichannel customer management: current knowledge and future directions'. *Journal of Interactive Marketing*, 23(1), 70–81.

Piotrowicz, W. & Cuthbertson, R., 2014. 'Introduction to the special issue information technology in retail: toward omnichannel retailing'. *International Journal of Electronic Commerce*, 18(4), 5–16.

Prahalad, C. K., & Hamel, G. 1990. 'The core competence of the corporation'. *Harvard Business Review*, 68(3): 79–91.

Rigby, D., 2011. 'The future of shopping'. *Harvard Business Review*, 89(12), 64–75.

Rusanen, O., 2019. 'Crafting omnichannel strategy: identifying sources of competitive advantage and implementation barriers'. In W. Piotrowicz & R. Cuthbertson (eds), *Exploring omnichannel retailing: common expectations and diverse realities*: 35. Springer.

Saghiri, S., Wilding, R., Mena, C., & Bourlakis, M. 2017. Toward a three-dimensional framework for omni-channel. Journal of Business Research, 77: 53–67.

Schmidt, J., & Keil, T. 2013. What makes a resource valuable? Identifying the drivers of firm-idiosyncratic resource value. Academy of Management Review, 38(2): 206–228.

Sirmon, D. G., Hitt, M. A., & Ireland, R. D. 2007. Managing firm resources in dynamic environments to create value: looking inside the black box. Academy of Management Review, 32(1): 273–292.

Sirmon, D. G., Hitt, M. A., Ireland, R. D., & Gilbert, B. A. 2011. Resource orchestration to create competitive advantage: breadth, depth, and life cycle effects. Journal of Management, 37(5): 1390–1412.

Teece, D. J., Pisano, G., & Shuen, A. 1997. Dynamic capabilities and strategic management. Strategic Management Journal, 18(7): 509–533.

Treadgold, A. D. & Reynolds, J., 2020. Navigating the new retail landscape: a guide for business leaders (2nd ed.). Oxford University Press.

Verhoef, P. C., Kannan, P. K., & Inman, J. J. 2015. From multi-channel retailing to omni-channel retailing: introduction to the special issue on multi-channel retailing. Journal of Retailing, 91(2): 174–181.

Wernerfelt, B. 1984. A resource-based view of the firm. Strategic Management Journal, 5(2): 171–180.

Wernerfelt, B. 2011. Invited editorial: the use of resources in resource acquisition. Journal of Management, 37(5): 1369–1373.

Winter, S. G. 2003. Understanding dynamic capabilities. Strategic Management Journal, 24(10): 991–995.

Wood, S., Lowe, M. and Wrigley, N., 2010. Conceptualising innovative customer-facing responses to planning regulation: the UK food retailers. The Service Industries Journal, 30(12), 1967–1990.

Zhang, J., Farris, P. W., Irvin, J. W., Kushwaha, T., Steenburgh, T. J., et al., 2010. 'Crafting integrated multichannel retailing strategies'. *Journal of Interactive Marketing*, 24(2), 168–180.

# 3

# New Business Models and the Transformation of Retailing

*Mikko Hänninen*

## Introduction

This chapter considers how business model innovation has risen through digitalization in the retail sector and how it has been accelerated during the Covid-19 pandemic. In the past couple of decades, advances in information and communication technologies have led to the rise of new competition and digital business models in the retail sector (e.g. Hänninen, Smedlund, & Mitronen, 2018). As the Chapter 2 has shown, this means that retail has largely entered a new era of a Red Queen Race where a huge gap is gradually forming between the traditional retailers heavily vested in a physical store presence and the digital competition embracing new digital marketing and sales channels. While information and communication technologies are, in itself, not new to retail, as the rapid growth of many retail chains such as Walmart in the 1990s and 2000s was based on the use of information and communication technology to optimize sourcing and distribution activities, what is new is the increasing application of technology at the customer end to optimize the front-end customer experience. This has made retail much more customer and service oriented, promising customers a fast, personalized customer experience with the ability to shop whenever and wherever they want. However, at the same time, this change is forcing traditional retailers to develop new competencies at a fast and unprecedented rate. The Covid-19 pandemic has accelerated this development.

Multi-sided digital platforms and marketplaces are one example of this business model innovation (e.g. Hänninen, Mitronen, & Kwan, 2019). Multi-sided digital platforms and marketplaces can be defined as intermediaries that connect people and organizations together to enable them to share information, or buy, share, and access a wide variety of both goods and services (e.g. Cusumano, Yoffie, & Gawer, 2019). By intermediating interactions and transactions between independent customers and complementors, that is third-party product and service providers, multi-sided digital platforms and marketplaces create online structures for a wide range of human activities (Kenney & Zysman, 2016). Therefore, by matching customers and suppliers together, these platforms arguably enable high volumes

Mikko Hänninen, *New Business Models and the Transformation of Retailing*. In: *The Red Queen Retail Race*. Edited by Richard Cuthbertson, Olli Rusanen, and Lauri Paavola, Oxford University Press.
© Mikko Hänninen (2023). DOI: 10.1093/oso/9780192862617.003.0003

and low prices combined with minimum transaction costs (e.g. Hänninen, Smedlund, & Mitronen, 2018).

As highlighted in the Chapter 2, the rules of the Red Queen Race have changed. These multi-sided digital platforms and marketplaces are here to stay and are radically challenging the competencies and business models of traditional retailers. At the same time they have significant implications on both customer and firm-level behaviour. For customers, these platforms promise access to services that are generally cheaper than and possess different qualities and features to those offered by traditional businesses, while for suppliers, the platforms promise access to a large demand side, in addition to minimum start-up costs, scheduling flexibility, and a stable income (e.g. Langley & Leyshon, 2017). Thus, multi-sided digital platforms and marketplaces enable many suppliers to reach a large, often global, demand side and to replace existing, incumbent, middlemen in the value chain (Reinartz, Wiegand, & Imschloss, 2019). As such, many businesses worldwide are increasingly dependent on multi-sided digital platforms and marketplaces as a channel to reach both new and existing customers.

In retailing, multi-sided digital platforms and marketplaces are still a novel research topic (Hänninen, 2020). Retailers have traditionally competed primarily with prices, location, and selection, but now through digitalization, creating concepts and services that add further value to customers has become a source of competitive advantage (e.g. Burt & Sparks, 2003). For example, in contrast to mass marketing and segmentation, targeting marketing efforts to individual customers has become more cost-effective through digital channels and tools (Bradlow et al., 2017). Digitalization in retail was accelerated through the introduction of e-commerce in the early 1990s, and multi-sided digital platforms and marketplaces have followed as the next step of this development. More specifically, in the early 1990s Internet technologies enabled firms to sell online to complement their offline business and open new marketing and sales channels; today these same, albeit more advanced, information and communication technologies are enabling customers and suppliers to bypass existing intermediaries in the value chain and are creating new markets in the process. Arguably multi-sided digital platforms and marketplaces transform the logic of exchange in retailing, as these platforms link end customers with the platform's supplier base, in other words the marketplace (e.g. Hänninen, Mitronen, & Kwan, 2019). In this logic, the platform owners, such as Alibaba Group, intermediate the transactions between independent buyers and sellers. The platforms orchestrate their retail ecosystem consisting of suppliers and end customers with information and communication technology, whereas supply chain integration has been the backbone of competitive advantage for many traditional retailers (e.g. Reinartz, Wiegand, & Imschloss, 2019).

This chapter proceeds as follows. The second section provides an introduction to retailing in the twenty-first century. The third section focuses on illustrating digital platforms and their platform logic. The fourth section presents a methodology used to study multi-sided digital platforms and marketplaces in the retail context, with the findings of the study presented in the fifth section, together with a case example of the business model development of Amazon.com. The example of Amazon.com is interesting, as it was able to successfully integrate a platform business model into its already successful retail business in the early 2000s with the launch of the Amazon Marketplace and is one of the most valuable companies in the world today, as well as one of the fastest growing retailers. To conclude, the sixth section discusses the academic, managerial, and public policy implications that some of the issues presented in this chapter pose for both practitioners and academics.

## Overview of platforms and platform logic

By definition, platforms are a 'set of stable components that support variety and evolvability in a system by constraining the linkages among the other components' (Baldwin & Woodard, 2009, p. 19). The initial discussion of platforms comes from the product development and innovation literature, in which a modular platform architecture enabled manufacturers to break components into interdependent and independent interfaces and thus reduce the complexity of new product development and production (e.g. Tiwana, 2014). Since the late 1990s, platforms have received a large amount of interest in the technology literature (e.g. McIntyre & Srinivasan, 2017). For example, Gawer (2014, p. 1240) defines digital platforms as a 'purposefully designed technology architecture' and Ghazawneh and Henfridsson (2015, p. 199) as a 'software-based system that provides core functionality shared by the modules that interoperate with it and the interfaces through which they interoperate'. Along these lines, digital platforms have been applied in many contexts as business models that enable firms to tap into the innovation capabilities of external firms that are not directly part of their supply chain (Gawer, 2014). For example, Alphabet, Apple, and Facebook have each leveraged a digital platform as part of their business model in order to enable third-party complementors to innovate and add their own products or services on top of the standardized technology interfaces.

While in the product development and innovation literature platforms refer to a particular architecture and design that enables firms to achieve economies of scope in the design and development of new products and services, lately platforms have been used to refer to a platform-driven business model, such as multi-sided digital platforms and marketplaces (Gawer, 2014). Multi-sided digital platforms and marketplaces, via an online digital interface, 'intermediate transactions among firms and/or individuals that may not be able to transact otherwise' (McIntyre & Srinivasan, 2017, p. 472). Such platforms are inherently multi-sided, meaning that they enable the direct interaction between two or more distinct sides of users

(Cusumano, Yoffie, & Gawer, 2019). Accordingly, such platforms 'bring together (or match) distinct groups, whereas the value for one group increases as the number of participants from the other group increases' (e.g. De Reuver et al., 2018, p. 127). Thus, multi-sided digital platforms and marketplaces have transformed how customers and suppliers interact in the twenty-first century (e.g. Hänninen, Mitronen, & Kwan, 2019).

So, what are the unique characteristics of multi-sided digital platforms and marketplaces? Multi-sided digital platforms and marketplaces have now created online structures for many human activities and have the potential to further revolutionize 'how we work, socialize, create value in the economy' (Kenney & Zysman, 2016, p. 61). Furthermore, such platforms now enable exchanges between the platforms' constitutive agents to be 'purely transactional, and where the pricing mechanism is the principal mode of coordination among platform agents' (Gawer, 2014, p. 245). In the context of multi-sided digital platforms and marketplaces, the value proposition is critical, as because of the presence of network effects the economic value of multi-sided digital platforms and marketplaces is measured in terms of the size of the platform's user base (Gawer & Cusumano, 2014), most critically the number of high-quality customers and suppliers using the platform (Haucap & Heimeshoff, 2014). Network effects, in which each new user increases the value of the multi-sided digital platform and marketplaces for other users of the platform (Rysman, 2009), arguably mean that the success of multi-sided digital platforms and marketplaces comes down to the ability of the platform to reach a critical mass of users (e.g. Ondrus, Gannamaneni, & Lyytinen, 2015). As such, scholars argue that network effects can trigger a continuous feedback loop of new users that drives a winner-takes-all situation to emerge in which one platform attains a dominant position in the market (e.g. Eisenmann, Parker, & Van Alstyne, 2006). The valuation of multi-sided digital platforms and marketplaces also depends heavily on network effects and the number of users, as the platform captures economic value primarily from sales commissions and the sale of value-adding services, such as digital marketing (Hänninen & Smedlund, 2019).

## Retailing in the twenty-first century

The retail sector is undergoing major transformations as new competition, in the form of multi-sided digital platforms and marketplaces, is winning over customers' minds and wallets. The retail sector has traditionally been, more or less, hierarchically coordinated (e.g. Mitronen & Möller, 2003). First, since the Second World War, retailers had followed a wholesale-retailer business model, in which the wholesaler and retailer were independent actors; they controlled and coordinated their own resources and activities and optimized independently their business resources and profits. Second, since the early 1990s large retailers had been, more or less, organized according to a chain organization model. In this centrally managed and controlled business model, the chain organization was responsible for the buying tasks and cooperation with suppliers, shifting responsibility from the individual stores to the central chain management. This model continues to be followed by most retailers around the world, where information technology has made cooperation with suppliers more efficient, for example, enabling the prediction and optimization of sourcing and distribution activities. Digitalization and multi-sided digital platforms and marketplaces, however, have brought about large changes to the prevailing retail business models used by traditional retailers, particularly by shifting the application of information and communication technology from the supply side to the customer side.

While large retail chains had been dominant during the past few decades, as the optimization of sourcing and distribution has often been the differentiating factor between success and failure, we are now witnessing increased disintermediation in the retail value chain as new entrants are applying advances in information and communication technology to create novel combinations of value for end customers (e.g. Hänninen, Smedlund, & Mitronen, 2018). This has been accelerated by the pandemic of Covid-19. For example, multi-sided digital platforms and marketplaces, such as the ones from Alibaba, Amazon, eBay, and Rakuten, are now raising the bar for the retail customer experience, aggregating supply- and demand-side data as well as merchandise, logistics, customer service, and payment information to create a harmonized customer experience across their platform (Hänninen, Mitronen, & Kwan, 2019).

Rather than competing with fixed assets, such as through a network of stores, the competitive power of multi-sided digital platforms and marketplaces comes from their ability to tap into a large group of end customers and suppliers as platform users (Hänninen, Smedlund, & Mitronen, 2018). However, the business models of multi-sided digital platforms and marketplaces are somewhat different from one another. Such platforms can be described as either pure play platforms, such as Alibaba's Tmall and Taobao, when all of the sales through the marketplace come from third-party providers, or hybrids, such as Amazon.com, when some of the sales come from third-party providers and the rest from their own inventory, including a growing share of private labels (e.g. Hagiu & Wright, 2015). This is a huge change in the retail sector where traditionally all of the products sold have come from a retailer's own inventory and its integrated wholesale activities (e.g. Mitronen & Möller, 2003).

By matching customers and suppliers with one another and having fewer fixed assets (e.g. a network of stores), multi-sided digital platforms and marketplaces have changed the prevailing earnings logic in the retail sector (Reinartz, Wiegand, & Imschloss, 2019). In the past, retailers' revenue came from their sales margin, the difference between the wholesale cost and the final sales price of the sold merchandise. Now, digital platforms earn revenue primarily from commissions rather than the sales margin as they only intermediate exchanges between buyers and sellers rather than bearing the inventory risk (Hänninen, Mitronen, & Kwan, 2019). Additionally, multi-sided digital platforms and marketplaces make money from a host of ancillary services such as advertising (Hänninen & Smedlund, 2019). This makes many platforms highly profitable, as they have fewer fixed assets and the margins are accordingly higher. For example, in 2019, Alibaba Group's net profit margin was over 33 per cent, a huge difference from retailers such as Walmart and Tesco with a net profit margin of approximately 3 per cent and 2 per cent respectively.

Therefore, what differentiates multi-sided digital platforms and marketplaces from traditional retail business models is that platforms must create added value for the individual customer to prevent customer transactions directly with the platform's suppliers or switching to a competing platform (Hänninen, Smedlund, & Mitronen, 2018). The platform leader in the market is arguably the one with the best technology platform and the best network of suppliers and customers. This is evident from the valuation of many platforms that correlate significantly with the size of their user base (Parker, Van Alstyne, & Choudary, 2016). In addition, the data assets provided by customers such as the accumulating purchase history, demographic information, preferences, and location make a large difference, as they are used by platforms to customize and personalize the customer experience (Hänninen, Smedlund, & Mitronen, 2018). This takes multi-sided digital platforms and marketplaces further away from the traditional supply chain-led view of retailing where customers are treated as a mass to one where all the activities of a platform are geared at optimizing the customer experience for the individual platform user (e.g. Bradlow et al., 2017).

## Research on multi-sided digital platforms and marketplaces

The foundation for this chapter lies in a research project on multi-sided digital platforms and marketplaces. Through 2016 and 2018, this research considered the digital transformation of the retail sector across the United States, Asia, and Europe, identifying key aspects of the platform business model in the retail context and the evolution of the retail sector altogether. It focused specifically on understanding ecosystem structures, earnings logics, and governance mechanisms of the leading multi-sided digital platforms and marketplaces.

Case study methods were employed to study leading multi-sided digital platforms and marketplaces. The focus of the research was on the four leading multi-sided digital platforms and marketplaces in the retail sector: Alibaba Group, Amazon.com, eBay, and Rakuten Group (see Table 3.1 for a comparison of these firms). The research drew primarily on a broad set of secondary data, including the full set of annual reports, analyst reports, SEC filings, prior academic articles,

**Table 3.1** Comparison of Alibaba Group, Amazon.com, eBay, and Rakuten Group

|  | Alibaba | Amazon | eBay | Rakuten |
|---|---|---|---|---|
| Year launched | 1999 | 1994 | 1995 | 1997 |
| Type of platform(s) | B2B, B2C, C2C platforms | B2C | B2B, B2C, C2C platforms | B2B, B2C, C2C platforms |
| Channel(s) | Online, offline | Online, offline | Online | Online |
| Headquarters | Hangzhou, China | Seattle, USA | San Jose, USA | Tokyo, Japan |
| Main markets | Asia, Europe | North America, Europe, Asia, Australia | North America, South America, Europe | Asia, Europe, North America |

Harvard Business School cases, books, business press articles, and other industry reports on the case companies as well as their public websites. In addition, three interviews were held with academic experts on multi-sided digital platforms and marketplaces as well as two interviews with practitioners working in the retail sector. Several informal discussions were also held with practitioners and academics on the topic.

Further data was also acquired through participation in a larger research project. One researcher was based in Japan (Tokyo) for approximately four months of the project, conducting interviews with several Japanese retailers, such as Rakuten executives, and another researcher was based in the United States (Silicon Valley) for approximately four months, conducting interviews with US-based retailers, such as Walmart executives. Throughout the project the researchers met, compared findings, and shared insights on how the findings related to the overarching research topic. In addition, throughout the research, workshops were held with the companies participating in the research project, which shed further light on the phenomena at hand. Furthermore, study visits were made to both Japan and the United Kingdom during the project with a specific focus on multi-sided digital platforms and marketplaces and the ongoing transformations related to them across the retail sector.

## A dominant business model

In this section, the key findings and overview from the research on multi-sided digital platforms and marketplaces in the retail context are presented. First, the relevance of the platform logic to retailers is explained. Then, one example of the multi-sided digital platforms and marketplaces that have emerged as a dominant business model in retailing is illustrated, describing how Amazon.com evolved from a pioneer in e-commerce to a leading global multi-sided digital platform and marketplace, which today connects consumers with millions of suppliers through the Amazon Marketplace.

## Platforms in retailing

A fundamental shift in retailing has occurred through the development and adoption of multi-sided digital platforms and marketplaces. Platform-based businesses, particularly, multi-sided digital platforms and marketplaces, challenge traditional retailers as the former do not generally own any fixed assets but simply orchestrate the exchanges and transactions taking place between customers and third-party suppliers; that is, the platform acts as a 'matchmaker' between supply and demand. As mentioned earlier, retailers have traditionally competed primarily with prices, location, and selection, but now through digitalization, creating concepts and services that add value to customers has become a source of competitive advantage.

The development of multi-sided digital platforms and marketplaces in retail started in the late 1990s. Though the dot-com boom brought the opportunities provided by the Internet to the attention of the masses, many small suppliers lacked an Internet presence, as they did not have the skills or capabilities to make the necessary leap to the Internet. This opened the door for new intermediaries, such as Alibaba and Amazon, who geared their businesses particularly towards small suppliers and promised them a cost-effective and easy way to sell products online. Therefore, small suppliers were connected through these platforms to a potentially global customer base, opening up new markets and earning opportunities. These marketplaces gained popularity throughout the 2000s and today have become one of the most popular forms of e-commerce in many markets, due to, for example, the added convenience for consumers of the vast selection that platforms provide compared to many traditional retail channels. In the United States, Amazon.com and eBay were the only two major e-commerce companies to survive the dot-com burst of 2001, with both companies following a platform business model today. In China Alibaba Group's Taobao and Tmall platforms and in Japan Rakuten Group's Rakuten Ichiba platform have allowed local retailers, and an increasing number of global brands, to connect with a growing amount of Internet users in their home countries. However, what makes Alibaba particularly unique is that it has both a wholesale platform, Alibaba.com, and a host of consumer platforms such as Taobao and Tmall, which means that small businesses in China can use Alibaba's platforms to both buy products directly from manufacturers through the wholesale platform and then sell them directly to customers globally.

The multi-sided digital platform and marketplace, therefore, brings several benefits to customers. Owing to the large number of suppliers on platforms such as

Amazon.com, customers arguably have a lot more choice in terms of selection when compared to other offline or online retail channels. Multi-sided platforms and marketplaces link customers with potentially millions of suppliers from around the world, making it easy to buy virtually anything from anywhere, with the platform acting as a mediator for these transactions. Customer centricity is also at the centre of the business model of multi-sided digital platforms and marketplaces, with convenience one of the key promises that these platforms make in their value propositions. Through network effects, maximizing the value of the end customer base is the main focus for the platform, as a loyal customer base attracts a large number of committed suppliers and vice versa. For example, the value promise of Amazon.com is 'low prices, large selection and fast shipping', implying that Amazon is a superior channel compared to other retailers. As a result of this customer centricity, multi-sided digital platforms and marketplaces are able to create several different value combinations for their customers through these digital means. Message boards and product reviews for instance foster social value, as customers are able to interact with other platform users as they switch from buyers of goods to content creators.

From the point of view of suppliers as well, there are many benefits from multi-sided digital platforms and marketplaces but also some threats that need to be considered. On multi-sided digital platforms and marketplaces, suppliers, from small suppliers to large multinational brands, have easy access to the platform and can decide what products they sell on the platform at their own discretion. This means that the platform can form either a primary or secondary sales channel for any supplier. For small businesses the platform is designed to be easy to use and for many suppliers it constitutes a primary online sales channel, while for large multinational brands the platform is often just one channel in their broader online and digital strategy. This is fundamentally different compared to traditional retail where it was the retailer who decided what products and at what quantity were sold from any given supplier. Now suppliers can decide themselves which products they sell and for what price, given that they comply with the rules and conditions set by the platform. As a cost to opening up access to the customer thus comes a new set of governance and control mechanisms. For example, by participating on a digital platform, suppliers must face the threat that a powerful platform owner will exploit its platform users, for example, by entering or threatening to enter successful spaces on the platform. Amazon, for example, may launch its own private label products that compete with its suppliers' successful product categories. When making the decision to join the platform, the supplier is also handing over data about its sales and performance on the platform to the platform owner.

So, what does this mean for the future of the sector? While many retailers are still attempting to catch up with the competitive advantage of the large multi-sided digital platforms and marketplaces, such as Alibaba, Amazon, eBay, and Rakuten, these platforms are proving dominant, as evident from their growing share of global e-commerce sales. This shift in competition is due to multi-sided digital platforms and marketplaces increasingly catering to the needs of more customers demanding convenience, by being able to create a more efficient one-click shopping experience combined with fast delivery and no-hassle returns. This comes from the integration of the back- and front-stage processes in the service system, enabling these platforms to deliver more holistic customer experiences that bridge the offline and online domain. In the platform economy, the customer experience is now click online (with all the aspects of price, selections, convenience), combined with the speed of receiving the product, the ability to shop whenever and wherever they want, and to return unwanted products at the customer's leisure. This, combined with an increased aggregation of both supply- and demand-side data to enrich the customer experience, makes the multi-sided digital platform and marketplace difficult for incumbents to catch up with, at least, without a fundamental transformation of their existing business model and competencies.

## Amazon.com

When talking about new business models and innovation in the retail sector, Amazon.com is one of the companies that come first to mind for many academics and practitioners. Since its foundation in Seattle in 1995 by Jeff Bezos, Amazon has grown from an online book retailer into a leading technology company and arguably the world's largest e-commerce company in the past couple of decades. One thing that has stood out from Amazon's strategy since the beginning is its customer focus, meaning that Amazon aims to offer the 'lowest prices, widest selection, and greatest convenience', which is difficult to match for any physical or digital competitor. Simultaneously, it has maintained a long-term focus, choosing to focus on long-term profits rather than short-term shareholder value, which has meant that Amazon's net profitability has been relatively low throughout its history, and only in recent years it has started to regularly make a profit (e.g. $11.6 billion in 2019, or approximately 4 per cent of revenue). Although initially Amazon followed a pure play online retail business model, where it only sold products sourced from wholesalers to customers, since the launch of the Amazon Marketplace in 2000, it has followed a hybrid platform strategy, meaning that Amazon.com combines its own inventory with the inventory from third-party suppliers.

Amazon.com's business model development over the past two decades can be characterized as a success. Originally, Amazon was founded as CEO Bezos was fascinated by the opportunities that the Internet could bring to businesses in a wide range of settings. Working in financial services at the time, Bezos saw an incorrect statistic in 1994 that stated that Internet usage was growing at a rate of 2,300 per cent per month, which sparked his interest in Internet businesses, especially e-commerce. After drawing up a list of around 20 products that he thought would sell well online, including books, movies, and music CDs, Bezos settled on books due to the millions of titles available as well as their sophisticated catalogue system; a regular bookstore, such as Borders, would be able to stock only a small percentage of the total amount of book titles available in the world, thus giving online businesses a competitive advantage. Amazon launched in May 1995, dubbed as the 'World's Biggest Bookstore', with sales initially growing at a modest 30–40 per cent during the first months. Taking advantage of the dot-com boom of the 1990s, Amazon.com decided to raise awareness by listing on the Nasdaq stock exchange in 1997 putting a value of $438 million on the company and raising in total $54 million of new share capital. It should be noted that $1,000 invested in Amazon in 1997 would have been worth around $350,000 at the end of 2015 (for a more detailed description on the background of Amazon.com and its early developments, read *The Everything Store* by Brad Stone).

As part of its 'Get Big Fast' strategy, Amazon had been growing at an impressive rate for much of its early years. However, it was still extremely focused on the US market, which meant that the next two natural steps for Amazon were to expand internationally and to diversify outside of the books category, for example, in order to better leverage its brand and expertise in e-commerce in other product categories as well. With the help of its fresh initial public offering capital, Amazon acquired leading online retailers in the United Kingdom and Germany, Bookpages.co.uk and Telebuch, in 1998, to start its global expansion. It also took the first steps in building a digital service ecosystem by acquiring Alexa Internet for $300 million—a company that specializes in gathering online user and browser behaviour analytics—which is still an important part of the Amazon.com ecosystem today.

After having grown outside of the books category and expanded globally, the most significant step in the development of Amazon's business model came with the launch of the zShops Marketplace in 1999 and later the Amazon Marketplace in 2000. Until the early 2000s, Amazon had been following a fairly traditional retail business model, selling products directly from its own warehouse and buying the inventory directly from suppliers or via distributors. However, as Amazon's vision was to become a self-dubbed 'Everything Store' catering to all the everyday needs of its customers, Bezos saw the potential of opening the Amazon platform to other suppliers as well, in order to cater for the huge number of small businesses that were not yet taking full advantage of the Internet.

The Amazon Marketplace was launched in 2000, initially with used books. On the Amazon Marketplace, sellers could sell their products directly on Amazon's own product pages and not only through a separate tab on the website, as had been the case with early versions of the marketplace, such as the zShops Marketplace. Thus, customers could choose whether to buy directly from Amazon or from a third-party seller, as well as being able to see a significantly wider selection of products in Amazon's product lists, now that the product lists included not only Amazon's but also third-party suppliers' inventory. Stone (2013) describes that the launch of the Amazon Marketplace provoked a lot of anger internally as Amazon category managers were struggling to understand how Amazon could now lose a sale to a competitor on its own website, to add to the increasing external competition. Amazon's suppliers were also worried about it allowing products to be paired up with unauthorized or sometimes even fake merchandise from third-party suppliers. However, all in all the marketplace was extremely successful with already 15 per cent of Amazon.com sales coming from the Amazon Marketplace by the end of the year in 2001, rising to over 50 per cent of Amazon.com's retail sales by 2017.

Unlike pure play multi-sided platform competitors, such as Alibaba Group, Amazon.com has also built an extensive supply chain capability consisting of over 1,100 logistics facilities (February 2020, MWPVL), globally, with delivery available to over 75 countries through the Amazon.com marketplace. Due to substantial investments in the supply chain, Amazon was able to introduce Free Super Saver Shipping in 2002, a move that revolutionized e-commerce—shipping costs had been rapidly increasing to shoppers, and as a result of Amazon's Free Super Saver Shipping programme, free shipping became the industry gold standard. In 2005, Amazon launched Amazon Prime, through which its customers gained access to free shipping and other services such as on-demand entertainment in exchange for a monthly subscription fee. In 2019, Amazon had over 150 million Prime subscribers, and it increased its free shipping from free two-day shipping to free same-day shipping for Prime members. Other Amazon subsidiaries and business units such as Amazon Web Services cloud computing, Whole Foods, Kindle e-readers and tablets, and the Zappos online shoe retail company were added to the Amazon ecosystem, including on-demand video and music, to name a few of the digital services offered.

Overall, this example shows how Amazon has successfully transformed its business model from a reseller to a platform and created much competitive advantage in the process. Today, it is already an established global player in the retail industry, sustaining its remarkable approximately 20 per cent yearly growth rate, with its annual net revenue exceeding $281 billion in 2019 and a net income of approximately $11.5 billion. Out of its revenue, around $141 billion is made from online product and digital sales, around $54 billion from third-party marketplace sales commissions, while sales through Amazon's physical stores make up around $17 billion. At the same time Amazon continues to face skyrocketing shipping and fulfilment costs, which now make up around $80 billion of all of Amazon's cost base. The future success of Amazon will, therefore, largely be dependent on how successful it is in optimizing its shipment and fulfilment network and, for example, succeeding in its plans to build a physical store network that would shift much of its home deliveries to a click-and-collect model. Given that US customers continue to prefer home delivery rather than click-and-collect, this will be easier said than done.

## Transformation in the retail business model

What this chapter has shown is that multi-sided digital platforms and market-places are challenging traditional retailers, as they are forcing retailers to develop new competencies and to rethink their business model. Today, through digitaliza-tion and the emergence of platform businesses, retail has shifted from a previously product-based business to a service-dominant logic, simultaneously making retail a truly global playing field, as through multi-sided digital platforms and market-places customers are now directly connected to global suppliers, whenever they want to and from wherever they are. This transformation in the retail business model means that there is a strong need for both practitioners and researchers to pay attention to the impact and implications that multi-sided digital platforms and marketplaces have for the industry structures and competitive dynamics of the retail sector. Without this wake-up call, it is possible that in the future retail will be governed by a few large global giants such as Alibaba Group, displacing traditional retailers who have based their competitive advantage on fixed assets, such as a network of physical stores.

As argued in the introduction, the retail sector has entered an era of a Red Queen Race where new competition, in the form of multi-sided digital platforms and marketplaces, is challenging traditional retailers. While traditional retailers need to run twice as fast in order to catch up with the business models of leading multi-sided digital platforms and marketplaces such as Alibaba, Amazon, eBay, and Rakuten, many of the platform companies are already gearing for the next transformation and investing heavily in the next technologies such as artificial intelligence (AI) start-ups. The Red Queen Retail Race is, therefore, very much ongoing and the winner still very much up for grabs. However, meeting the chal-lenge posed by this new digital competition is largely dependent on the ability of traditional retailers to develop more sustainable retail business models for the future and to renew their competencies for succeeding in the digital age.

While digitalization has provided several benefits to retailers, with more effi-cient back-end and front-end processes, this chapter has shown that it is especially business model innovation, for example, in the form of multi-sided digital plat-forms and marketplaces, that has the potential for transforming the structures and competitive dynamics of the retail industry in the twenty-first century. Changes in the retail business model are also rapid, as illustrated through the example of Amazon.com evolving from an online book retailer to one of the world's most valu-able companies on the Fortune 500 in a space of 20 years. It is, therefore, likely that with the adoption of AI and distributor ledger/blockchain technologies, we will continue to see further changes in the structure and organization of the retail sector in the next decade or so.

In the next section, the key learnings from the study of platform business mod-els are presented for (1) research and theory, (2) practitioners, and (3) public policy, discussing the impact of multi-sided digital platforms and marketplaces for customers, suppliers, and retail managers.

## Learnings for research and theory

Although multi-sided digital platforms and marketplaces have received increasing interest amongst practitioners and academics lately, the theoretical understanding of these developments is still one step behind (Hänninen, 2020). Thus, more research is needed to consider the effects of platforms on traditional businesses. The understanding of a platform business model is still at a very early stage, especially in the context of retailing. So far, research has confirmed that different multi-sided platform and marketplace business models exist in the context of retailing, but these business models have not been examined in detail. If platforms become the de facto organizing form of retail in future, more academic research is needed in this context as well.

Multi-sided digital platforms and marketplaces are theoretically interesting due to the implications they have for how value is created between customers and suppliers. Besides the obvious utilitarian benefits from the large selection that multi-sided digital platforms and marketplaces offer to customers, platforms also promote social exchanges, with Amazon often on top of national customer satisfaction surveys. Although traditional retailers such as John Lewis in the United Kingdom and Nordstrom in the United States have been able to respond to the threat of Amazon.com through their omni-channel strategy, other retailers such as Macy's have struggled to respond to the transformation of the retail industry. Succeeding in this new competition, therefore, is not just a question about downsizing physical stores but rather rethinking the role of the store in an overarching omni-channel strategy.

One factor that differentiates multi-sided digital platforms and marketplaces from traditional retailers is the deep customer understanding generated by these platforms. The data generated through all the transactions and interactions taking place on the platform will form an even greater competitive advantage in the future as platforms can combine interactions from both the offline and online channels automatically and in real time. If the pace of growth of multi-sided digital platforms and marketplaces, such as Amazon.com and Alibaba Group, continues in the same way as it has in the past decade, it is likely that in future consumers will be loyal to only a few digital service providers, due to the high levels of customer lock-in that multi-sided digital platforms and marketplaces are able to create. This is already true in markets like the United States, where over half of all e-commerce purchases begin on Amazon and the competition between suppliers is fierce within the Amazon ecosystem. Traditionally it has been assumed that online retailing lowers customer switching costs, but platforms challenge this claim as the digital service portfolio consisting of, for example, payment services in fact makes switching difficult. The same is true for the supplier side, where small and medium-sized enterprises are dependent on the policies set by platforms like Amazon.com, especially if they rely on these marketplaces as their only digital sales channel. At the same time, multi-sided digital platforms and marketplaces aim to engage with their users even more than in the physical realm, which poses a threat to traditional retailers. Good examples of this bridge between digital and physical are the Alibaba Hema grocery stores in China and the acquisition of Whole Foods by Amazon.com in 2017.

For suppliers using the platforms, the shift from traditional retail towards multi-sided digital platforms and marketplaces also has significant repercussions. According to the theory of network effects, a platform's value depends on the number of both customers and suppliers on the two sides of the multi-sided digital platform and marketplaces. However, the quality of the suppliers also matters significantly. Suppliers may also multi-home, that is, have a presence on multiple platforms simultaneously. This means that in future, multi-sided digital platforms and marketplaces will need to create more stringent engagement processes in order to make sure that the platform's suppliers fully integrate themselves into the platform, while also screening out potentially poorly performing suppliers. For example, on Amazon.com, suppliers that have high average product returns and low customer ratings below a pre-defined threshold are kicked off the platform, as it is generally expected that the poor performance of specific suppliers reflects poorly on customers' perceptions of the entire platform. At the same time suppliers need to be aware that on multi-sided digital platforms and marketplaces, the platform owner may place large pressure on its suppliers, especially as it has transparency over their full performance data on the platform and can use this data to exploit them, for example by raising prices or entering successful product or service spaces itself.

## Lessons for practitioners

Digital innovations challenge traditional retailers. These innovations, such as new business models, require new competencies from managers. In the retail sector, we are already seeing that hard discounters continue to profit around the Western world, despite the growing threat of multi-sided digital platforms and marketplaces such as Amazon.com, while higher end retailers, such as department stores, appear to have suffered more from the business model transformation in retail. The problem that department stores particularly face is that inventory-wise they can never compete with a marketplace like Amazon, with a selection of millions of products, and at the same time they do not have the same level of data about their customers that would enable them to truly tailor and personalize the customer experience. If the growth of platform-based business models continues in the same rate as it has recently, in future, competition may take place primarily inside platforms, rather than between different platforms.

Here, it is worthwhile mentioning the increasing move from players like Alibaba and Amazon to take over the physical store space as well, using their digital capabilities to make shopping altogether more efficient, regardless of the channel (e.g. Alibaba Hema and Amazon Fresh Supermarket grocery stores).

When looking at multi-sided digital platforms and marketplaces, I outline three managerial implications that platforms have for the retail business. First, new earning models shape the retail sector, as multi-sided digital platforms and marketplaces intermediate transactions without having the inventory risk or supply chain integration typical of traditional retailers. Traditionally efficiency in sourcing and distribution has been the winning formula for many retailers squeezing profits in a low-margin industry. Multi-sided digital platforms and marketplaces are, therefore, able to achieve a drastically higher profit margin than traditional retailers due to their unique earnings structure and fewer fixed assets.

Second, if multi-sided digital platforms and marketplaces become the dominant business model in retail, this will mean that traditional retailers are left with the decision to enter existing marketplaces or to establish their own platform. This first option has several potential problems, especially as entering established platforms such as Amazon.com means that the platforms' suppliers need to adhere to the platform owners' often stringent guidelines and commission models, with little room for negotiation. While some small suppliers may be able to find a niche with a unique brand and product range (e.g. Neusser Buch & Kunst Antiquiriat on Amazon), many others will succumb to high competition, particularly, as the presence of hundreds or even thousands of direct competitors within the same category will make it difficult to succeed. Suppliers should thus think carefully which platform they will enter, as there are significant differences between the type of control mechanisms and the type of processes in place, for example for helping suppliers to migrate to the platform. At the same time there is the risk of being exploited by the platform owner. This is not to say that retailers cannot set up their own platform and find growth through this way. Setting up an own platform enables retailers to experiment and gather data. There are many firms, such as Shopify, who now provide all the tools and infrastructures necessary for any firm to set up online. While an important and viable alternative for many, it nevertheless requires a careful strategy and strategic fit before any level of investment into an own platform is made.

Finally, responding to the threat posed by multi-sided digital platforms and marketplaces will require new competencies from retail managers. Topics such as big data and predictive data analytics are emerging in retail, and the leading multi-sided digital platforms and marketplaces are already ahead of traditional retailers in their customer data and analysis, due to the high volumes of customer transactions they facilitate each day. The high number of daily customer transactions and interactions allows platforms to gather an understanding of customer behaviour, as data analysis is built into their business model. Although many traditional retailers have high volumes of transactions as well, and collect data, for example through loyalty cards, the main difference is the operationalization of this data. For multi-sided digital platforms and marketplaces, customer data use is a part of their DNA, and they apply the insights from their customer data in real time to customize and personalize the customer experience, making this a competitive advantage at a scale not seen before in the sector.

## Learnings for public policy

From the public policy angle, multi-sided digital platforms and marketplaces are especially interesting as it is generally acknowledged that platforms reorganize industries (cf. Parker, Van Alstyne, & Choudary, 2016). As platforms like Uber and Airbnb were launched from outside the European Union, the less restrictive US legislation upon which they have been based created friction when these Silicon Valley start-ups imported their business models to Europe, often with little room for compromise to fit in with the local legislative environment. As a result, public policy has had to react to business models imported from elsewhere, rather than drafted policy that will make it easier for similar platforms to be launched in Europe, respecting the local legislation. For example, in its May 2016 communication over the opportunities and challenges of online platforms for Europe, the European Commission stated that despite platforms like SkyScanner and BlaBlaCar originating from Europe, only 4 per cent of the total worldwide market capitalization of online platforms is European based.

In the retail context, the public policy considerations related to multi-sided digital platforms and marketplaces are related primarily to questions about privacy and competition. Each of the major platforms introduced in this chapter, Alibaba Group, Amazon.com, eBay, and Rakuten Group, has built a vast digital service portfolio on top of its retail platform, which complicates the competitive situation. Compared to traditional retailers, multi-sided digital platforms and marketplaces are able to combine customer data from a wide range of interactions and transactions across the platform ecosystem, which is unprecedented in the industry.

The first public policy issue considered here is privacy. The possibility to combine payment data (e.g. Alibaba Group through payment affiliate Alipay) and retail data (e.g. from Alibaba's retail platforms) is something that is virtually impossible for traditional retailers to do, for example when considering the privacy laws in place in many European countries. This is something that public policy needs to pay attention to, especially if this equates to an unfair competitive advantage when data is owned by companies based in other legislative environments.

The second is the issue related to competition. Through the billions of dollars of investments into start-ups and new technology, platforms as a result of their different cost structure have an edge over other retailers and have been able to start to pilot future technologies and also increase the size of their ecosystem. For example, consider Alibaba Group's and Rakuten Group's investments in Silicon Valley–based start-ups during the past few years. The large amount of cash available makes competing against platform-based businesses difficult for traditional retailers. At the same time, the mentality is different, as multi-sided digital platforms and marketplaces, such as Amazon.com, are open about their long-term focus, meaning that there is no need to make short-term profits. Instead, platforms prefer to invest money in growing their customer base, in order to create high levels of customer lock-in that will hopefully translate to more business in the long run. This 'start-up' mindset sets apart traditional and digital businesses.

The final issue is related to the rights and responsibilities of a platform over the products sold by third-party suppliers. As multi-sided digital platforms and marketplaces simply intermediate transactions, there is a question about how strictly the platform should control the suppliers and who is responsible for possible fraud taking place on the platform. With a large amount of cross-border transactions taking place through multi-sided digital platforms and marketplaces, customers may have difficulty understanding that the customer protection rights in their home country may not apply to a platform based in another continent, even if the user interface was translated to their native language. Another topic that has received a lot of coverage is that of counterfeit goods. In 2008, eBay was famously sued by the French fashion giant LVHM over the sales of counterfeit products on its platform. The case was later settled out of court in 2014. Although the leading multi-sided digital platforms and marketplaces insist that they are doing everything they can to eliminate counterfeit products from their marketplace, there is a big question about who in the end has responsibility and who should monitor such platforms. Is it up to the brands, the platform itself, or the governments?

## The Red Queen Retail Race is a reality

This chapter has shown that now that the transformation brought on by multi-sided digital platforms and marketplaces have been realized across the retail sector, and accelerated during Covid-19, it is time for retailers to start believing in the viability of this new competition and to start developing the competencies and businesses to respond to this digital competition. This chapter has discussed in detail one type of innovation that has emerged from digitalization in the retail sector, illustrating how new digital business models, such as multi-sided digital platforms and marketplaces, challenge traditional retailers.

Overall, digitalization has allowed retailers, both traditional and new, to create more efficient customer-centric processes and become more sustainable. But when looking at business model innovation in particular, the diffusion of innovation has progressed slowly and the benefits of digitalization have been received only by a few companies that were early to react to changes in customer behaviour and customer expectations during the dot-com boom. Amazon.com started out as an online books retailer and Alibaba as a business directory for Chinese suppliers, but now both are among the most valuable companies in the world. This transformation has been due to timing and being at the right stage of development at the right time. Changes in the retail business model, therefore, can happen fast, as the impact of the Covid-19 pandemic has shown. Now is the time for traditional retailers to develop and design the competencies for the new Red Queen Retail Race.

So, the Red Queen Retail Race is very much on across the sector. It is true that there is still much that traditional retailers need to do in order to catch up with the benchmark set by the leading multi-sided digital platforms and marketplaces. For example, fast shipping, vast selection, and personalized customer experience are now very much the new rules of the game. However, retailers are only beginning to realize the full benefits of digitalization and the next transformations are just around the corner. For example, big data and predictive data analytics are just two examples of sources of potential future transformation in the retail sector, which will put further pressure on all types of retailers to take advantage of the associated new business models and opportunities. Perhaps, there is still some hope at the end of the tunnel and the race is not over yet?

## Acknowledgement

This research was supported by the Finnish Funding Agency for Innovation (Business Finland, formerly Tekes) under the GlobaMa project, together with the partner companies. Professor Arto Lindblom, Professor of Practice Lasse Mitronen, Dr Anssi Smedlund, and I were part of the team of researchers gathering data on the business models of platforms in retailing, between 2016 and 2018.

## References

Baldwin, C. Y. & Woodard, C. J., 2009. 'The architecture of platforms: a unified view'. *Platforms, Markets and Innovation*, 32, 19–44.

Bradlow, E. T., Gangwar, M., Kopalle, P., & Voleti, S., 2017. 'The role of big data and predictive analytics in retailing'. *Journal of Retailing*, 93(1), 79–95.

Burt, S. & Sparks, L., 2003. 'E-commerce and the retail process: a review'. *Journal of Retailing and Consumer Services*, 10(5), 275–286.

Cusumano, M. A., Yoffie, D. B., & Gawer, A., 2019. *The business of platforms: strategy in the age of digital competition, innovation, and power*. HarperCollins.

de Reuver, M., Sørensen, C., & Basole, R. C., 2018. 'The digital platform: a research agenda'. *Journal of Information Technology*, 33(2), 124–135.

Eisenmann, T. R., Parker, G., & Van Alstyne, M., 2006. 'Strategies for two-sided markets'. *Harvard Business Review*, 84, 92–101.

Gawer, A., 2014. 'Bridging differing perspectives on technological platforms: toward an integrative framework'. *Research Policy*, 43(7), 1239–1249.

Gawer, A. & Cusumano, M. A., 2014. 'Industry platforms and ecosystem innovation'. *Journal of Product Innovation Management*, 31(3), 417–433.

Ghazawneh, A. & Henfridsson, O., 2015. 'A paradigmatic analysis of digital application marketplaces'. *Journal of Information Technology*, 30 (3), 198–208.

Hagiu, A. & Wright, J., 2015. 'Multi-sided platforms'. *International Journal of Industrial Organization*, 43, 162–174.

Haucap, J. & Heimeshoff, U., 2014. 'Google, Facebook, Amazon, eBay: is the Internet driving competition or market monopolization?' *International Economics and Economic Policy*, 11(1–2), 49–61.

Hänninen, M., 2020. 'Review of studies on digital transaction platforms in marketing journals'. *The International Review of Retail, Distribution and Consumer Research*, 30(2), 164–192.

Hänninen, M., Mitronen, L., & Kwan, S. K., 2019. 'Multi-sided marketplaces and the transformation of retail: a service systems perspective'. *Journal of Retailing and Consumer Services*, 49, 380–388.

Hänninen, M. & Smedlund, A., 2019. 'On retail digital platforms suppliers have to become responsive customer service organizations'. *Strategy & Leadership*, 47(1), 37–43.

Hänninen, M., Smedlund, A., & Mitronen, L., 2018. 'Digitalization in retailing: multi-sided platforms as drivers of industry transformation'. *Baltic Journal of Management*, 13(2), 152–168.

Kenney, M. & Zysman, J., 2016. 'The rise of the platform economy'. *Issues in Science and Technology*, 32(3), 61.

Langley, P. & Leyshon, A., 2017. 'Platform capitalism: the intermediation and capitalisation of digital economic circulation'. *Finance and Society*, 3(1), 11–31.

McIntyre, D. P. & Srinivasan, A., 2017. 'Networks, platforms, and strategy: emerging views and next steps'. *Strategic Management Journal*, 38(1), 141–160.

Mitronen, L. & Möller, K., 2003. 'Management of hybrid organizations: a case study in retailing'. *Industrial Marketing Management*, 32(5), 419–429.

MWPVL (February 2020), https://www.mwpvl.com/html/amazon_com.html

Ondrus, J., Gannamaneni, A., & Lyytinen, K., 2015. 'The impact of openness on the market potential of multi-sided platforms: a case study of mobile payment platforms'. *Journal of Information Technology*, 30(3), 260–275.

Parker, G. G., Van Alstyne, M. W., & Choudary, S. P., 2016. *Platform revolution: how networked markets are transforming the economy and how to make them work for you*. WW Norton & Company.

Reinartz, W., Wiegand, N., & Imschloss, M., 2019. 'The impact of digital transformation on the retailing value chain'. *International Journal of Research in Marketing*, 36 (3), 350–366.

Rysman, M., 2009. 'The economics of two-sided markets'. *Journal of Economic Perspectives*, 23(3), 125–143.

Stone, B., 2013. *The everything store: Jeff Bezos and the age of Amazon*. Random House.

Tiwana, A., 2014. *Platform ecosystems: aligning architecture, governance, and strategy*. Newnes.

# 4

# Physical Retail Spaces in a Digital World

*Lauri Pulkka and Richard Cuthbertson*

## Introduction

Given the increasing importance of digital resources (Chapter 3) within the Red Queen Retail Race, this chapter considers the new meaning of physical space. There is no denying that digitalization is disrupting physical retail spaces, but exactly how? The Covid-19 pandemic may be considered to have provided an extreme version as to where this aspect of retailing is heading, but what are the key competences of the future, which physical spaces will emerge most used, and which will fail to find shoppers?

This chapter looks at different perspectives of the impact on retail real estate of the developing digital revolution. We examine how different organizations perceive different futures for retailing in general and for shopping centres in particular. In addition to teasing out the various perceptions, we attempt to discern what they may mean for the firm, consumers, and the business ecosystem that exists today and which may exist in the future.

The structure of this chapter is twofold. First, we describe prior applications of the scenarios methodology as an approach to better understand and prepare for an uncertain retail future. Companies and other organizations can follow these steps to create their own scenario narratives regarding the future of retailing. We build on the work by Mukherjee and Cuthbertson (2016) conducted in China, India, Norway, Singapore, the United Kingdom, and the United States, which, although with distinct national contexts, all converge on four broad contrasting scenarios of future retailing. Second, we employ these four broad scenarios in three focus groups to explore the implementation and operational implications for the future of physical retail space, the shopping centres in particular.

## Building future retail scenarios

The purpose of using a scenarios approach in this chapter is to identify how the uncertain contextual environment of retail real estate may affect the development of the sector. According to Van der Heijden (1996), we cannot predict what will

Lauri Pulkka and Richard Cuthbertson, *Physical Retail Spaces in a Digital World*. In: *The Red Queen Retail Race*. Edited by Richard Cuthbertson, Olli Rusanen, and Lauri Paavola, Oxford University Press. © Lauri Pulkka and Richard Cuthbertson (2023). DOI: 10.1093/oso/9780192862617.003.0004 happen in the future, as the recent pandemic outbreak amply demonstrated. However, we can make useful statements about the future by reducing complexity and discovering common elements in such uncertain situations. Scenario planning is an appropriate tool to use for such an exploration, as it accepts structural uncertainty with multiple interpretations and multiple futures. It can help managers and policymakers better understand a current situation by developing multiple views of what the current situation might imply for the future. It does this by working through how a variety of different possible interpretations of the future could change the business environment. While scenario planning cannot take away the uncertainty in a situation, it can help reduce it and thus enable managers to come to a reasonable judgement on the degree of robustness of a specific decision across a range of uncertainties.

Scenario building supports more informed sensemaking of the immediate transactional environment. It sensitizes stakeholders to the underlying assumptions of a situation. This enables the stakeholders to reframe the context and lens through which they visualize the contextual landscape and so helps to develop links between external and internal factors in a more informed way. Mukherjee, Ramirez, and Cuthbertson (2020) explain how the scenarios methodology enables this process to work by initially disconnecting the macro long-term drivers of change from the micro day-to-day operations of the individual stakeholder, before 'jumping into the future' to reconnect the macro and the micro in a perceived future environment and then returning to the present to explore the current relationship between the macro and the micro. The scenarios approach also challenges current group thinking and encourages more diverse viewpoints to be taken into consideration. In challenging current thinking, scenarios can provide a completely new platform and point of reference for stakeholders to engage with one another. This may result in cultural change and indeed may create new collaborative positions from which to prepare for the future.

Scenarios can be built in eight stages (Van der Heijden, 1996): formulating the central question, identifying the driving forces that will influence the development of the central issue, considering the critical uncertainties, constructing the scenario frameworks, developing the scenario stories, evaluating stakeholder implications, determining strategic options for stakeholders, and identifying key metrics and signposts (see Figure 4.1).

So, in order to understand the impact of the Red Queen Retail Race on physical space, the scenarios approach is employed in this chapter to consider the following question:

– What types of customer experiences will take place where in the future?

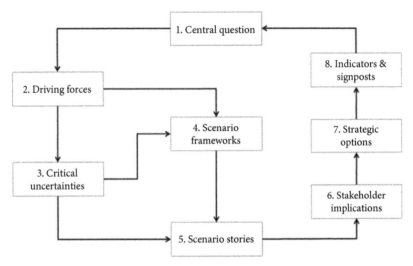

**Figure 4.1** The stages in scenario building (after Van der Heijden, 1996)

This then leads to implications for the following sub-questions:

- What type of physical space will be in demand in the future, and why?
- What will the balance of investment be between online and physical spaces in the future?
- What type of infrastructure will need to be developed, and what will need to be managed into decline?

An assessment of the main forces contributing to the sector's historical transformation and future trends is a necessary starting point in this process. This is referred to as 'mapping the strategic environment' in scenario analysis. Mapping the strategic environment of a sector enables the identification of the driving forces of change. In this chapter, we examine those aspects of the retail sector's latest emerging economic, socio-demographic, technological, and regulatory trends that both secondary research and primary research with stakeholders considered useful in contextualizing potential future developments in the sector. We then take this initial analysis and combine it with wider, relevant secondary data and specific primary data to identify the key issues pertinent to the future development of retail real estate. The secondary research comprises a review of previous and projected future trends in economy, politics, regulation, and technology that have a significant impact on retailing in general and shopping centres in particular. The primary data was collected from senior retail practitioners and other stakeholders, such as product suppliers, market researchers, technology providers, and policymakers, in the light of their own experience where they sought to consider the implications for the future of retailing. The data collected from the primary and secondary research was subsequently analysed using a scenario building methodology. An important principle of these discussions was that each individual had their his/her valid view dependent upon his/her own experience, preferences, store profile, locality, and so on.

## Critical uncertainties

The critical drivers were identified and evaluated. In particular, the importance and uncertainty of these drivers in the near future were assessed. These assessments could then be plotted on an Impact-Uncertainty matrix (see Figure 4.2).

It is important to recognize the impact of the major driving forces, which in Figure 4.2 above were a combination of demographic, digital, and global issues. Changing lifestyle as well as an ageing economy suggests a diversity of consumer needs in the future. Despite the high impact of these trends, the implications for the retail sector could be assessed with appropriate segmentation techniques, thereby minimizing uncertainty regarding their outcome. Digital innovation is happening and will continue into the future, and therefore there is less ignorance of its general impact but a diversity of views on the nature of any specific innovation.

Retail policymaking was suggested as a high-impact driving force, the unpredictability potentially arising from a specific law at any given point that companies have no choice but to implement. Such impactful policy changes may not be restricted to retailing directly. For example, commercial transportation taxes may encourage or discourage bulk movements (important for store-based retailing) compared to parcel delivery (important for digital retailing). Consequently, public policy is often seen as a driving force when exploring future scenarios.

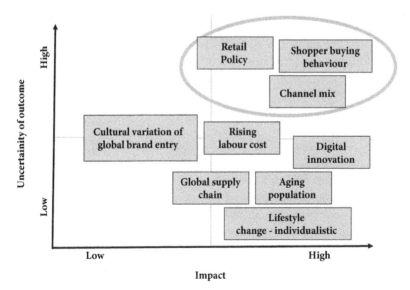

**Figure 4.2** An example of an Impact–Uncertainty matrix (see Mukherjee & Cuthbertson, 2016 for more details)

Common critical drivers involved the impact of technology on channel mix, alongside the impact of public policy or consumer expectations on shopper buying behaviour.

Shopper behaviour and the ability to pre-empt (or encourage) trends are central to the success of any retail business that wants to be successful and so remain relevant to a target market. The impact of changing shopper behaviour is therefore very high. The unpredictable nature of future shopper buying behaviour can translate into a number of possibilities surrounding their choices in the future. Will consumers be value seeking for some product categories and luxury seeking for others? Will they shop differently for themselves and for their families? Will they shop online for some products and offline for others? Will they eventually go back to the basics of shopping and abandon technology with the increased threat of cybercrimes and monitoring by outside parties? With increased individualization, how will this translate into overall shopping behaviour?

The interplay between the digital and physical platforms for retailers has been game changing within the sector and has given new meaning to the term 'shopping experience', as Chapter 5 will explore further. A number of questions however point to the uncertain nature of how this will develop. Will the digital shopping experience occur inside the store or shopping centre, and on which device? Will digital shopping primarily develop inside the home or office, away from the store setting? Will digital media be used mainly for browsing or buying? Will stores and malls become delivery and pick up points for products? Will in-store shopping remain more relevant for older shoppers while digital shopping becomes the preferred choice of youth? Will shopping malls focus on entertainment and high-service shopping activities while the digital channels become the preferred choice for everyday shopping?

This interplay between the changing nature of shopper behaviour and the various permutations across the digital-physical spectrum results in four thought-provoking future scenarios for retailing.

## Future scenarios for retailing

Following the identification of the critical and uncertain driving forces by Mukherjee and Cuthbertson (2016), this chapter focuses on two extreme outcomes of two critically uncertain driving forces.

At one extreme of the outcomes for shopper buying behaviour was 'consistent shopper buying behaviour', where shoppers were always going to buy the same products/brands, from the same places using the same channel. At the other extreme, 'diverse shopper buying behaviour' would stem from shoppers buying across diverse product/brand groups, under different consumption contexts making use of the diversity of channels available.

The extreme outcomes for channel mix could be summarized as hi-touch, where physical channels and customer service staff enabled the entire shopping experience, and hi-tech, where digital innovation using automated and mobile channels provide the entire shopping experience and human contact with customer service staff is negligible.

Combining these extreme outcomes results in the creation of four distinct scenarios for retailing, as identified by Mukherjee and Cuthbertson (2016) and shown in Figure 4.3.

In the 'Reliable World' scenario, the consumer retail experience would be largely in stores and malls, where shoppers would seek interaction with service staff for pre-purchase, purchase, and aftersales service. Consistency in the consumer experience would stem from familiarity and trust in the brands, and consumers would seek a familiar experience in the purchase and consumption of these brands on every occasion. Services would be geared towards building relationships with consumers to secure their long-term custom by developing loyalty to the service experience, as well as to product brands.

In the 'Craft World' scenario, the retail experience would not be limited to shopping transactions but also extend to the entertainment value of the physical space. There may be a blended mix of indoor and outdoor retail space. There would be greater and more varied interactions between consumers and service staff involving the co-creation and co-design of products and services to meet diverse and personalized consumer needs. The service system would be geared to a large extent towards attracting consumers, such as street performances, entertainment shows, on-site craftsmanship, and a plethora of services to enhance a greater feeling of community public space.

In the 'App World' scenario, diverse consumer retail experiences would be provided through personalized apps on mobile devices. Consumer interaction with

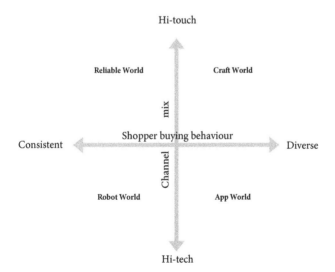

**Figure 4.3** Future scenarios for retailing (see Mukherjee & Cuthbertson, 2016 for more details)

actual service staff would be minimal and possibly non-existent, with bots helping to perform such roles. Personnel may be required to create new apps though back-end functions such as data management and analysis would be automated wherever possible, for example, by employing artificial intelligence. In such a hi-tech environment, state-of-the-art technological solutions would enable all retail experiences, and any physical infrastructure involved would have to be geared towards enabling this hi-tech interaction with shoppers. Digital developments would aim to stimulate the human senses and motivate consumers to buy.

In the 'Robot World' scenario, consumers would seek consistency, efficiency, and reliability in their interaction with a hi-tech environment, and usually at a low price. Scope for creativity and customized services would be limited. The service system would be geared towards mass delivery via technology-based transportation, such as drones. Robotics technology would be employed to provide precision and consistency. Automation would provide a seamless service to customers.

These scenarios are summarized in Table 4.1. It should be noted that these are neither exclusive nor predictive. These scenarios could co-exist for different

Table 4.1 Scenario outlines

| Reliable World | Craft World |
|---|---|
| **Dominant retail format:** stores, malls, departmental stores | **Dominant retail format:** indoor and outdoor stores/malls/departmental stores, fairs, exhibitions |
| **Customer experiences:** personalized, emotive, consistent, meeting expectations, familiarity | **Customer experiences:** personalized, emotive, creative, surprise element, entertainment |
| **Service characteristics:** labour intensive, value addition from interpersonal interaction, humane aspect of service fundamental, motivated and empowered staff | **Service characteristics:** labour intensive, value addition from interpersonal interaction, skilled and multitasking staff, engaging consumers, co-creation of value with consumers |
| **Robot World** | **App World** |
| **Dominant retail format:** self-help kiosks, click & collect kiosks/vaults, drone delivery, physical stores as showrooms, if at all | **Dominant retail format:** state-of-art, connected hi-tech stores with interactive gadgets to customize experience |
| **Customer experiences:** efficient, impersonal, convenient, empowered, precision based | **Customer experiences:** personalized, innovative, informative, real time, relevant, instantaneous & empowered |
| **Service characteristics:** interactive technology driven, technological singularity, robotic precision, virtual payment systems, state-of-art supply chain & distribution management, dark warehouses, interconnectivity across all channels | **Service characteristics:** appropriate infrastructure to enable hi-tech/mobile/digital interaction with consumers, big data management, information management systems, interconnectivity, interactivity at every touch point with consumer |

consumer segments, different geographies, different products, different retail brands, different timings, and so on, with varying degrees of similarity to those outlined.

## The impact on real estate

This section discusses data collected through focus groups between 2015 and 2017 (i.e. pre-pandemic). The focus group method differs from group interviews as it gives more attention to interactions between participants (Kitzinger, 1994). The facilitator plays an active role, encouraging interaction between participants. Exercises or other activities (e.g. videos, stories, or games) can be employed to focus the attention of the group on the subject, direct attention from the facilitator to other participants, and structure cross-group comparison.

Things to consider in forming the groups are group size, homogeneity, and segmentation (Morgan, 1996). Our rules regarding group size were simple. The group should be large enough that exercises can be performed in pairs or subgroups. Since one subgroup can discuss one or two scenarios in a session, and there are four scenarios, the minimum size for the group is four participants. There is no fixed upper limit; it depends on group dynamics. The main limiting factor is that individual participants have less time to contribute to the group discussion as group size increases.

The rule of thumb regarding internal homogeneity of focus groups is that the participants should be similar, so there is common ground for a fruitful discussion, but not identical, so there is variance in opinions. There are two sides to having groups consisting of participants from one firm. Possible benefits include greater trust among participants and the ability to discuss business cases openly. Possible disadvantages include narrowness of vision and conflict averseness. Therefore, we invited both intra- and interfirm groups to participate in this research.

The research population covered firms involved in retail real estate to understand their views on the possible role of retail real estate in the scenarios under consideration. Variables for creating segments included the firm's place or role within the value chain, the individual participant's position within the firm, and relevant geographical aspects, such as the urban–rural context. The data consists of three focus groups with 30 participants in total, representing such stakeholders. The groups are described in Table 4.2. Based on the professional background of the participants and the content of the discussions, we have labelled the groups as 'digital', 'physical', and 'mixed' to reflect the main perspective from which the participants viewed their business.

All three focus groups were provided with the generic scenarios described in Table 4.1. They then followed similarly structured sessions, combining the result of the scenarios approach with a discussion around the three core elements of

**Table 4.2** Information about the focus groups

| Label | Participants | Description |
| --- | --- | --- |
| Group A: 'Digital' | 6 | Customer experience management consultants from a digital services company and one participant from their restaurant-services client company |
| Group B: 'Physical' | 7 | Retail real estate managers and commercial managers from a company that owns and operates multiple shopping centres |
| Group C: 'Mixed' | 17 | Participants of a professional course on retail real estate management, ranging from shopping centre operators to real estate developers, consultants, and lawyers |

the Service Innovation Triangle (Furseth & Cuthbertson, 2016): customer experiences, the service system providing those customer experiences, and the underlying business model allowing all parties to gain value. The Service Innovation Triangle was utilized as it highlights the result of moving from a product-centric world based on resources to a service-centric world based on what you do with those resources, as described in Chapters 1 and 2.

## The Service Innovation Triangle

The Service Innovation Triangle (Furseth & Cuthbertson, 2016) was developed to provide a framework highlighting the major elements for innovation within a service firm. In particular, the model differentiates between resources, such as real estate and technology, what is done with those resources by the management, and the value created by what is done with those resources, as illustrated below. This is a useful framework to consider what the management would do differently to maximize value with the same resources under different scenarios.

In terms of these particular focus groups who were considering the impact on real estate under different scenarios, real estate resources are included as Tangible Assets (bottom left), while digital resources are included under Technology. The discussions of the focus groups were deliberately directed towards what the management might do with such resources (the middle layer) under the four different scenarios described previously. This helped move the discussions away from the existing resources of organizations today towards a future focus on what a manager would do regardless of today's situation. Hence, the groups were directed towards discussing future customer experiences, a future service system to deliver such experiences, and a future business model to provide the necessary financial returns.

## Challenging past assumptions

After an introduction to the overall approach of combining the scenarios methodology with the Service Innovation Triangle, the participants were divided into
pairs or subgroups. Each subgroup was then provided with a written and illustrated one-page description of each future scenario: Reliable World, Robot World,
App World, and Craft World. The first task was to discuss any scenario-specific
characteristics of the customer experiences, the service system, and the business
model and to write them onto post-it notes. For example, what type of experiences
might a customer want in the Reliable World scenario? What type of processes
and facilities would be needed to provide them? And how does it change from the
way firms do business today? In addition to writing the issues identified on post-it
notes, the subgroups were instructed to discuss the scope of change compared to
the status quo. Two facilitators went around the groups to listen in and to provide
prompts and answer questions as required.

The participants were then required to place the post-it notes on a two-by-two
matrix whose quadrants represented the four scenarios, with different coloured
notes representing customer experiences (green), the service system (yellow), and
the business model (red). The instructions were to place the note closer to the
centre of the matrix if the issue was perceived as easy to implement or compatible with existing practices and further from the centre if the issue was difficult to
implement or disruptive to existing practices. Figure 4.4 shows an example of the
output of this second assignment. Everyone in the focus group was encouraged to
comment and to ask questions during the task.

Each focus group was analysed to provide a summary and preliminary analysis
of the discussions. This was shared with the participants of each focus group to
confirm any points of interpretation. After discussions of the third focus group

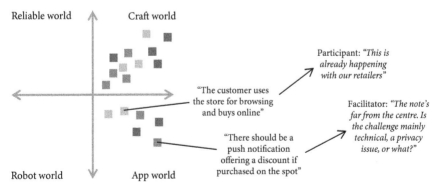

**Figure 4.4** Example analysis from focus group

were summarized, a cross-group analysis was conducted. In the analysis, we focused on similarities and differences between the four scenarios as well as between the three focus groups.

## Positive customer experiences, technical challenges, and financial implications

We set out to explore how individuals and organizations perceive the future of retail real estate under different scenarios and how they would respond under those different conditions. The results of these focus groups are presented in three steps. First, we summarize the discussions on each of the four future scenarios. Second, we identify the main similarities and differences between the scenarios on how customer experiences, the service system, and the business model might be approached from a management perspective. Third, we compare the main challenges associated with each of the different scenarios.

The focus group discussions are summarized in Table 4.3. The table contains selected, central issues on customer experiences, the service system, and the business model under the different scenarios. Many issues came up in all three focus groups, although there was some variation in how they were expressed. Differences between groups are highlighted where relevant.

In each focus group, the presentation of the Reliable World scenario began with the subgroup contemplating whether the scenario describes a future world at all, because it feels so similar to the current or even past forms of retailing. As one participant put it: 'We had the boring scenario.' We see from Table 4.3 that only incremental changes or additions were thought to be needed to the service system and the business model to provide the envisioned customer experiences. The need for technological development was perceived as virtually non-existent. In fact, we observed difficulties with the groups in coming up with uses for digital technologies at all in this scenario.

Discussions on the Craft World scenario were animated, and the participants were comfortable with discussing such a future scenario as it seemed to fit with many future plans of the firms participating. Increasing the share of entertainment, restaurants, and services in shopping centres seemed to be on the real-world agenda of most of the participants. Fully transitioning into the Craft World was argued to require changes to the service system. More specifically, it demands spaces that are more flexible so that retailers, service providers, and content creators can come and go without disrupting the overall operations of the centre. The continuously changing offering is an integral part of the perceived customer experiences. One subgroup suggested an 'experience manager' to coordinate changing content such as pop-up stores, performances, and courses. Digital technologies were viewed more as an add-on (e.g. virtual reality experiences) than a substitute for the physical space.

Table 4.3 Summary of the focus group discussions on the four future scenarios

| | Reliable World | Craft World | App World | Robot World |
|---|---|---|---|---|
| **Customer experiences** | Human interaction, customization, and emotions | Entertainment, participation, and variety | Convenience, personalization, and exclusiveness | Convenience, selection, and efficiency |
| **Service system** | Builds on existing elements: in-store personnel, long-term tenants, and identification of customers through loyalty programmes | Builds on flexible spaces and greater coordination and deeper integration of retailers' concepts into the shopping centre | Builds on information about the activities of customers inside and outside the shopping centre, requiring advanced ICT infrastructure | Builds on automated click & collect and return points, showrooms, and shared logistics spaces |
| **Business model** | Traditional model of long revenue-based lease agreements is complemented with new revenue streams from services | The shopping centre is a platform for outside service providers; entertainment drives footfall, which compensates for lost sales due to online shopping | Online sales eat into the profitability of revenue-based leases; selling data on visitors to the retailers becomes a significant source of revenue | Revenue-based leases still work with restaurants and services; with goods retailers, leases are based on the shopping centre's function as a distribution centre |
| **Summary** | 'Business-as-usual' scenario: very similar to retail real estate of today and considered mainly as unexciting | 'Entertainment' scenario: shopping centres and city centres compete as a destination and service platform | 'Information' scenario: physical retailing competes against e-commerce players with its own strengths | 'Threat' scenario: retail real estate embraces online shopping and assumes a central role in the supply chain, rather than as a shopping destination |

App World is a high-tech scenario, which was reflected in the discussions. Participants focused on the digitalization of the service system. More specifically, on what kind of information and communications technology (ICT) infrastructure would be required to allow the customer to interact with the retailer not only physically but also digitally. Some individuals discussed the issue through their firm's current experimentation with smartphone apps, indoor positioning, and digital services. Although the term 'omni-channel' was used a lot, a common sentiment was that e-commerce is primarily a threat to retail real estate and that digital elements are integrated into the physical offering primarily to defend against the threat of losing sales to online retailers rather than to enhance customer experiences per se.

Robot World was labelled as a 'threat' scenario because the participants viewed it as the scenario in which retail real estate retains least control over the shopping experience. To provide the desired customer experiences, shopping centres were seen to have to implement a service system that is subservient to online retailing: for example showrooms and click & collect points, rather than shops. Transitioning into this scenario was seen as costly, especially for existing centres, because of the required changes to physical structures. Revenue-based leases work with restaurants and other services, but it was unclear how a shopping centre can profit from acting as a distribution centre.

Based on the focus group discussions, three themes of consensus became apparent: the balance between people and technology within customer experiences, the level of innovation required to develop the appropriate service system, and the diversity of revenue sources required to move towards a new business model. We can illustrate these through three continuums in customer experiences, service system, and the business model. The continuums and the placement of the scenarios on them are illustrated in Figure 4.5. This summarizes our analysis of the similarities and differences between the scenarios. It should be kept in mind that the scenario narratives are based on different combinations of two dimensions, channel mix (hi-touch/hi-tech) and shopper buying behaviour (consistent/diverse), and so there is obviously some overlap between these concepts.

The first continuum in customer experiences ranges from social to automated. Social customer experiences are created through human interaction, automated customer experiences are created through human–machine interaction, and in between are experiences facilitated by a combination of people and technology. The connection to the channel mix dimension behind the scenario narratives is obvious. Social customer experiences were considered hi-touch, whereas automated customer experiences were considered hi-tech.

Craft World was perceived as dominantly social, with the physical retail space hosting participatory events like cooking courses. Digital tools were mainly seen as a way to enhance and expand the experience of the physically based activity. Customer–customer and customer–employee interactions were thought to form

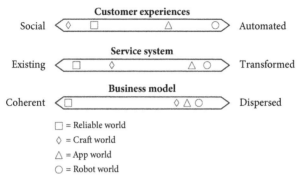

**Figure 4.5**  The four future scenarios placed on continuums in customer experiences, service system, and business model

the essence of this scenario. Reliable World was also seen as social, with most inter-actions taking place between customers and employees. Digital experiences and automation were acknowledged, but participants had difficulties in seeing their relevance to the scenario. For example, Group A talked about how digitalization is supposed to enable personalization, but in this scenario, 'it has failed. That is, dig-ital services have not succeeded in personalization, and one reason can be that … the algorithms and technologies are simply not sophisticated enough to respond to the human need and situational awareness.'

Within App World, there was a mix of human and digital elements in the dis-cussions. Digitalization was perceived to be much more pervasive, but digital tools were also used to improve human interactions between retailers and customers.

At the other end of the continuum, discussions on Robot World were character-ized by a lack of other human elements besides the individual customer—with an emphasis on the word 'individual'. For example, none of the participants' notes or presentations on Robot World mention families or friends shopping together.

Overall, it is very important to recognize that customer experiences in all four scenarios could be considered 'good' customer experiences. Both social and auto-mated customer experiences were seen as relevant, and it was easy for participants to come up with examples in all scenarios. In other words, the social–automated continuum of customer experiences does not describe the desirability of any particular scenario over another by itself.

The second continuum is from an existing to a transformed service system. Overall, in terms of the service system, it seems that retail real estate is cur-rently better geared towards the hi-touch scenarios. Participants saw little need for changes in Reliable World. In Craft World, shopping centres were thought to benefit from spaces that are more flexible. Flexibility facilitates shorter leases and a deeper integration of a combination of retailers' own concepts into the shopping mix, which in turn requires the offering of the retail real estate to be more dynamic.

The required changes to the service system were considered more extensive in the hi-tech scenarios. Retail real estate in App World was seen to revolve around collecting, analysing, and using information. While the participants talked about experimenting with business analytics, conducting it at scale and in real-time, this was seen to require large investments in information technology (IT) software and hardware, as well as the necessary digital skills. Robot World was seen as requiring similar investments into ICT infrastructure but also greater modifications to the existing physical structure and layout of retail spaces. Among the diversity of focus group participants, shopping centre managers in particular highlighted the physical incompatibility of their current physical space with that envisaged as required for entering a Robot World.

The third continuum is from a coherent to a more dispersed business model. By coherent, we emphasize having a single critically important revenue stream that is controlled, at least to some extent, through the retail real estate—for example, through rental payments. A dispersed business model means having multiple significant revenue streams that contribute to the value of retail real estate. Revenue-based leases, whereby rent is determined as a fixed share of the retailer's monthly sales, were seen as the backbone of the business model of retail real estate today. Therefore, the current situation is best described as coherent on our continuum.

The participants did not suggest any radical changes to the business model in Reliable World. Revenue-based leases were seen as the main revenue stream here.

In Craft World, it was felt that leases would continue to be an important source of revenue for retail real estate providers but that they would not cover new customer experiences, and so new revenue streams would need to be found. The issue of fees as a source of revenue came up in all three groups. The costs of activities and entertainment at a retail location might be covered with customer participation or even entrance fees.

In the hi-tech scenarios, the business model becomes even more dispersed. In both scenarios, the rise of e-commerce was seen to erode the basis of revenue-based leases. In App World, the shopping centre would generate business from collecting information on the consumers and selling it to retailers, product suppliers, and other interested parties. It was argued that retailers know only their own customers and that the shopping centres or high streets could be seen as a platform to collect data on all visitors to that space.

Robot World seemed to be the most difficult scenario for the participants to understand and agree on the role of physical space. They saw many ways in which their existing business model would simply not work but also doubted the long-term viability of any substitute revenue streams suggested. This is discussed in more detail later in the chapter.

Finally, we turn our attention to the different challenges associated with the four future scenarios (see Table 4.4). The discussions around them were helpful for understanding whether the participants found the scenarios realistic and in which timeframe changes are expected. They also uncovered more examples of ideas that organizations in the retail real estate are currently experimenting with.

In general, the hi-touch scenarios, Reliable World and Craft World, were seen as relatively easy to transition into, whereas the hi-tech scenarios, App World and Robot World, would require functions and activities whose implementation was considered very problematic given current organizational capabilities.

The comparison of the challenges emphasized by different groups is also interesting; the main issue was often the same but it was approached from different perspectives. All three groups expressed a similar challenge concerning Reliable World. It was not seen as a realistic future scenario, because it is too low-tech and organizations are already taking steps in other directions. Reliable World was seen as a niche, perhaps for luxury brands, but in mass competition with e-commerce players, the human-centric offering was considered too expensive to appeal to the masses at a financially sustainable price. Group A even argued that the only way Reliable World could be prevalent in the future is if 'the experience of giving up private data has somehow broken—there has been a privacy catastrophe or crisis that has caused the consumers to draw the line. The digital world is more a threat and people want to return to safer human interaction.'

Craft World posed a tough challenge for all groups: activities and entertainment are expensive to provide, and although they drive footfall, retailers are not willing to share the costs and the fees would deter consumers. Group B also voiced their concern regarding extensive refurbishments to provide more flexibility and to increase the attractiveness of shopping centres and high streets as destinations: 'We have to fade out the shopping centre from the shopping centre.' Groups B and C thought the challenge is relevant today and discussed examples of experimentation that are already taking place, for example allocating previously underutilized spaces such as hallways for pop-up stores and other services that enable a centre to continuously refresh its offering.

We observed maximum divergence between the groups concerning the challenges in App World. Group A approached the scenario from the perspective of servitization—using digital tools to turn the retail experience into a service experience, for example, at a basic level, by offering bundles across stores based on purchases or by creating shopping lists based on recipes. The group argued that historically the producer has been responsible for the accuracy of product information, but when the retail real estate provider and retailers start to offer services that combine multiple products, they become responsible. Integrating product information into the software systems of shopping centres and retailers was seen as an enormous challenge.

**Table 4.4** A comparison of the main challenges associated with different scenarios by different groups

| Group | Reliable World | Craft World | App World | Robot World |
|---|---|---|---|---|
| **A: Digital** | This world will cease to exist: all current developments in technology and business are pointing in a hi-tech direction | It is easy to envision consumers enjoying entertainment, surprises, and liveliness but impossible to see them paying for it | Responsibility for the accuracy of product information shifts from producers and service providers to retailers and shopping centres | Developments in the supply chain and logistics can eliminate the role of the shopping centre as a distribution centre |
| **B: Physical** | Customer experiences are not appealing enough to the masses to sustain the traditional business model | The shopping centre cannot look or feel like a shopping centre, yet the customer experiences require a central orchestrator | Intangible assets such as customer data are difficult to prioritize, because current business revolves around tangible assets | There are currently not enough people with the right competences to manage the transition from low- to high-tech |
| **C: Mixed** | Human interaction and digitalization are incompatible; digital customer experiences are highly problematic for the service system and business model | The costs of having entertainment and events at the shopping centre should be shared by the retailers, but they do not pay for more footfall but sales | Seamless customer experience calls for an 'app of retail apps', which works across centres, and heavy investments into the ICT infrastructure | The required new infrastructure is expensive and the business model works only as long as the last mile is expensive for retailers, and so shoppers require a distribution point |
| **Summary** | Providing the customer experiences of the Reliable World are not seen as viable or realistic in the future | There are many beneficiaries but few payers for the new customer experiences | Managing apps, customer data, and product information are not traditional strengths of shopping centres | The transformation of the shopping centre into a distribution or logistics centre is difficult and the benefits short-lived |

Group C did not mention product information but saw that the implementation of the required ICT infrastructure would be arduous. How to get enough shoppers to adapt to the technology to justify the investments required was seen as a major issue. It was thought that location-specific smartphone apps or other user interfaces would not be attractive enough and that what would be needed is an 'app of apps' that works across shopping centres and high streets, which could be (and are being) 'developed by the likes of Google and Amazon'. Group B highlighted another problematic issue concerning digitalization. The required development of some emerging assets, such as customer data, is not prioritized currently by retail real estate providers, as it is not seen as part of the core business but is seen more as an add-on that may enhance but not secure a physical offering.

In addition to being labelled the 'threat' scenario due to retail real estate being seen as replaced by warehousing and logistics real estate, Robot World was perceived as challenging for two other reasons. First, all groups saw transitioning into the Robot World as expensive and difficult. It was seen to require investments into ICT as well as the physical infrastructure. Moreover, Group B in particular highlighted that the skills required from people are very different in Robot World compared to today's retail focused real estate. Second, assuming a role in the e-commerce players' supply chain as the 'last-mile distribution centre' was considered risky in the long term. Developments in technology (e.g. drones) threaten to make that role obsolete as well.

## The reality of implementation in the Red Queen Retail Race

Underlying this study is a seeming discrepancy between discourse and action in retail real estate firms. The idea that retail is facing unprecedented change is being touted from many directions, but many seem unwilling to change the approach despite this disruption rhetoric. It certainly has not stopped the development of new shopping centres.

We set out to investigate how organizations perceive the future of retail real estate. In addition to uncovering perceptions about the future, our aim was to discern what they mean for the firm, shoppers, and the overall business ecosystem, today and in the future.

The main finding is that retail real estate firms are largely geared for business as usual, even though it is not seen as viable in the future. The possibility of long-term success with the prevailing customer experiences, service system, and business model is questioned, but there is a reluctance to transform. Organizations invested in retail real estate see its future as threatened and constrained.

The perceptions of threat associated with the future come mainly from the technological nature of the disruption. New technologies are seen to benefit e-commerce players more than retail real estate. Digital technologies can be used in retail environments in many ways. For example, they can enable new services, provide customer data for analysis and promotion, and manage dynamic pricing. However, digital technologies are typically developed by technology firms and online retailers, rather than real estate firms. Moreover, e-commerce platforms like Amazon were conceived and raised in the digital world. Retail real estate firms were not. It became apparent in the focus group discussions that most organizations in retail real estate do not have the relevant resources to take advantage of digitalization. This applies not only to owners and operators but also to developers and even regulators. Referring back to the Service Innovation Triangle, while retail real estate firms generally have good tangible, financial, and intangible assets, they do not generally possess enough people and technology relevant to a digital age. Moreover, the large asset base may be seen as a drag on any innovation within this space.

A limited ability to innovate in this increasingly digital environment often leads to suboptimal implementation (see Chapter 9 of this book) as well as extensive outsourcing, relying on others to provide what is increasingly a core capability. Perhaps the most blatant example of this was a discussion of a vision of the future facilitated by a general shopping centre app that all the participants thought should be developed by Google, Apple, or the like—and certainly not by any real estate firm. It is difficult to say which was more concerning: the perceived inability to develop an app or the readiness to surrender such an integral part of a future business to competitors.

Organizations also perceived the future of shopping centres and high streets as constrained, meaning that they have limited agency over their own future direction. This manifests itself in three ways. First, there is the issue of 'wrong people', which is discussed above. It seems that future scenarios that are incompatible with current organizational structure and strategy are not given equal weight in organizational decision-making. Second, there are institutionalized practices that discourage risk-taking and change. Again, these taken-for-granted rules and ways of working are not limited to real estate owners and operators but concern the entire business ecosystem. For example, the concept of 'anchor tenant' was used often but never questioned in the focus group discussions, although it is not necessarily compatible with the Craft World scenario, in which the offering is in constant flux. Another typical example that came up in the discussions is a practice by investors to commit to a new development only when there are signed lease agreements for 60 per cent of the spaces for the first three to five years—arbitrary numbers, which are solely grounded on practice. Third, it is difficult to let go of the existing business model when business is going fine, or at least okay. For example, Citycon, an owner, operator, and developer of shopping centres in the Nordic and Baltic region, has recently studied the financial performance and changes in the tenant mix of selected shopping centres (Metsi, 2017). Despite a recent eco-nomic recession and hype about the ever-growing market share of e-commerce, the numbers gave little reason to panic as the following case description illustrates.

## Restraining reality: the case of Citycon

Citycon is one of the largest owners, operators, and developers of shopping cen-tres in the Nordic and Baltic region. Tenant mixes in Citycon's shopping centres have remained relatively stable for a long time. There has also been little varia-tion between the centres. Consistency of the offering has worked well for Citycon in the past in the markets it operates. However, with the rise of online shopping and all else that comes with the digital revolution, Citycon, alongside other firms in the shopping centre industry, has been facing the new reality of omni-channel shopping that threatens business as usual, and even more so following the coron-avirus pandemic from 2019 onwards. So, how are tenant mixes in shopping centres changing as a result of these external pressures?

Citycon has recently explored this question in five selected Nordic shopping centres (Metsi, 2017). The study suggests that changes so far have been small, but trends are emerging. The three measures are: (1) number of stores, (2) share of leasable area, and (3) share of rental income of different tenant categories (e.g. clothing stores, department stores, cafes, and restaurants). In addition, the opera-tional performance of each centre was analysed. The main years of comparison vary slightly from centre to centre but are focused on one to five years up to 2017. The impact of coronavirus on these results is still an ongoing investigation; however, the main findings from the initial study are clear.

The main finding is that the changes correlate with the online resiliency of different tenant categories. The largest growth was in cafes and restaurants, ser-vices and offices, and specialty stores—tenant categories that are less threatened by online shopping. The share of home and leisure and department stores, categories under more pressure, decreased. Interviews with the managers of the shopping centres provided support to this trend. According to the managers, more changes in the same direction are likely across shopping centres in the future. Despite find-ing such trends, it is well to keep in mind that the observed changes in tenant mixes were small, measured in single digits. The operational performance of the centres was analysed using four metrics: sales, footfall, rents, and occupancy during the same period. Overall, there was a small decline in the operational performance across all metrics. Sales and footfall dipped slightly more than rental income and occupancy. But, again, the observed changes were minor. Moreover, the inter-viewed shopping centre managers were aware of the numbers but not concerned by them.

Based on the numbers, it is easy to conclude that online shopping has not managed to shake the foundations of the shopping centre business and that incremental, rather than fundamental, change is taking place. But the numbers do not paint the whole picture. The study uncovered another interesting perspective as to how tenant mixes in shopping centres are changing and, more precisely, into the process of how changes in tenant mix take place.

It turns out that the process is connected to the physical development of the centres. This finding arises from a preliminary analysis that was conducted to determine which centres to include in the main study. The preliminary analysis suggested that in the centres that have not gone through a redevelopment project, the changes in tenant mixes were negligible. A recent redevelopment project thus became a criterion for including shopping centres in the study. Moreover, the extent of the redevelopment project correlated with the size of the changes to the tenant mix. This finding implies that the ability to manage tenant mix is hindered by the (changing) physical properties of the shopping centre.

Overall, changes in the tenant mixes of Citycon's shopping centres have been small. The link between physical development and changes in tenant mix increases the discontinuity of the process. However, it is not the only factor slowing down the pace of change. Long lease agreements, for example, are another well-recognized issue that constrains changes in tenant mix. While Citycon has taken steps to react to the increase in online shopping, there may be underlying pressures for much greater changes to tenant mixes in multiple centres that have not surfaced due to the built-in constraints to tenant mix management. The identified constraints cast uncertainty on how quickly shopping centres are able to adapt to sudden shifts in the retail landscape.

This case study can be read as a warning against the dangers of sticking to a business-as-usual approach for too long amidst transformational sectoral change, even if the current business model is profitable for now and substantial changes require investment and are time-consuming. The long timeframes for change are largely the result of the physical nature of the retail real estate business.

Tenant mix refers to the variety of stores and their layout within a location (Dawson, 1983). It is an integral part of the overall customer offering of a retail location and a major means of differentiation from competitors, but the Citycon case casts doubt over how quickly the tenant mix can change. The connection between measurable changes in the tenant mix and the physical redevelopment is particularly noteworthy. It implies that existing shopping centres and high streets are not flexible enough to be able to react quickly to future scenarios, which may call for a constantly changing offering. The same issue applies to new developments as well, if they are not designed to be flexible. The Citycon case highlights the importance of the first tenant mix in new shopping centres, because changes can be hard to implement afterwards.

## Restraining reality: the wider context

The case of Citycon is part of a wider discussion regarding urban development. For example, in Finland, the typical timeframe from planning to first use is well over 10 years. In line with Rajakallio et al. (2018), we argue that there is a chasm between the development and use, or the supply and demand, of commercial real estate development. The demand-side actors include shopping centre operators, retailers, citizens, and consumers. The supply side includes urban planners, developers, and real estate investors. Sometimes different business units or functions of the same organization can be on different sides. For example, Citycon is a developer and operator, and municipalities are responsible for urban development but also business-support services. Furthermore, we argue that due to the success of business-as-usual and the pervasive institutionalized practices, the supply side of retail real estate has become insensitive to changes on the demand side. Herein lies a risk. If growing e-commerce, increasing development of new shopping centres, changes in consumer behaviour, or any combination thereof makes existing generic shopping centres obsolete, what happens to the value of those properties and the businesses? There is overwhelming faith, as illustrated in the focus group discussions, that the newest shopping centres and locations with the latest offering and in the best locations will attract consumers and turn a profit, while the old and remote retail locations will struggle. The success of new retail centres may encourage the supply side to continue to pour money into the development of new locations, while old ones are left to sink into oblivion.

How can the chasm between the supply and demand be bridged? The dominant, traditional approach to urban development is linear (e.g. Rydin, 2010). The development process is split into sequential phases—planning, investment, design, construction, use—whereby responsibility is handed from organization to organization like a baton in a relay race. The linear model has little interaction between demand and supply side actors. Moreover, it does not encourage coordination between different developments within the same region. The linear model may be efficient, but the long timeframe of development becomes a problem during turbulent times, as witnessed by the recent coronavirus outbreak since 2019, as well as the ongoing growth in online retailing. Planners and designers tend to focus on the 'first use' of the development and assume that the 'first use' will essentially last for 20 years or more. The ongoing digital transformation increases the risk that retail development plans and designs are no longer the best ones by the time the construction phase is completed.

Rajakallio et al. (2018) suggest a platform ecosystem model of urban development might be a better approach to close the gap between retail real estate development concepts and their subsequent operation. Based on a survey of organizations involved in retail real estate development projects, they conclude that new developments are led by developers, who have a limited interest in the use phase beyond the first few years, and that municipalities are in a key position to integrate both demand and supply side actors as well as to coordinate different development projects within a region. Active participation by municipalities and retail real estate operators from planning to the use phase is argued to shift the focus from 'first use' to sustainable use. The platform ecosystem model of urban development encourages the consideration of different future scenarios and creating spaces that are more flexible. Compared to the linear model, the platform ecosystem is also more sensitive to external factors such as e-commerce, existing spaces, and other developments.

The four generic future scenarios used in this analysis are not an exhaustive description of what the future of retailing will look like. The future is unpredictable, but the platform ecosystem model and other ways of integrating the supply and demand sides of the shopping centre business can be used to more readily prepare for different eventualities. Today, existing and new developments adhere to traditional views on retail real estate development and operation even though everyone involved recognize that such traditional views are coming to an end and must change. The recent success of business as usual may decrease the impetus to change, but action should be taken now before organizations currently investing in retail real estate lose the initiative to disruptors from other and new industries. The original 'child' of retailing, real estate, now has to play a more grown-up role, interacting with the new sibling of online retailing, in order to keep ahead in the Red Queen Retail Race.

## Digital regulations lag physical regulations

In this chapter, we have considered how the ongoing digital retail transformation is affecting physical retail space. Our aim was to uncover how organizations in retail real estate perceive their future and what it implies for those organizations, consumers, and the business ecosystem. The main conclusion is that retail real estate firms are geared for business as usual, even though it is not seen as a viable business model in the future. This applies to both existing centres and new developments.

We encourage practitioners to utilize and adapt the methodology employed in this chapter to address other wild problems, which have multiple possible outcomes. The steps from mapping driving forces and critical uncertainties to building the scenario stories and frameworks have been outlined in the beginning of this chapter and provided in more detail by Ramirez et al. (2017). The scenario narratives are an effective means of communicating desirable futures and are therefore useful for managing change proactively. This chapter also presents an opportunity for companies and other organizations to reflect whether they identify the same challenges, how they would deal with the different scenarios, and what steps they are taking to shape their own future.

The policy implications of this chapter are twofold. First, the participants in our study, from retail real estate backgrounds, felt that the playing field is tilted in favour of the e-commerce players, partly due to flawed regulation. Online retailing was perceived to be a decisive element in how the scenarios play out. Platform retailers are able to circumvent local rules and regulations that shopping centres and high streets with their physical presence find harder to avoid, especially in terms of taxation. Policymakers should consider how their regulations skew the market in favour of one form of retailing over another. Without radical changes, the relationship between e-commerce and retail real estate will continue to be conflicted, which may not be in the consumers', and society's, best interests. Second, it is uncertain what retail real estate should look like in order to successfully compete in the Red Queen Retail Race. Given the long timeframes of urban development, there is a need to increase the sensitivity of the development of physical spaces to changes in consumer and retailer behaviour. The platform ecosystem model of urban development outlined can be used to create flexible spaces and to bridge the gap between the development and use phases of commercial real estate development (Rajakallio et al., 2018). In order for it to function, however, the model would require much greater investment and focus on retail development and use by the public sector in many markets. These changes in the mix of physical and digital resources in the Red Queen Retail Race have an impact on customer experiences (Chapter 5) and the resulting customer loyalty (Chapter 6).

# References

Dawson, J. A., 1983. *Shopping center development*. Longman.

Furseth, P. I. & Cuthbertson, R. W., 2016. *Innovation in an advanced consumer society*. Oxford University Press.

Kitzinger, J., 1994. 'The methodology of focus groups: the importance of interaction between research participants'. *Sociology of Health and Illness*, 16, 103–121.

Metsi, S., 2017. 'Changes in tenant mixes in Nordic shopping centers'. Thesis, Aalto University.

Morgan, D. L., 1996. 'Focus groups'. *Annual Review of Sociology*, 22, 129–152.

Mukherjee, M. & Cuthbertson, R. W., 2016. 'Capturing the uncertainties of retail development in emerging marketing using the scenarios approach'. *The International Review of Retail, Distribution and Consumer Research*, 26(3), 323–346.

Mukherjee, M., Ramirez, R., & Cuthbertson, R. W., 2020. 'Strategic reframing as a multi-level process enabled with scenario research'. *Long Range Planning*, 53, 5.

Rajakallio, K., Pulkka, L., Cuthbertson, R., & Junnila, S., 2018. 'Creating urban platforms—opportunities and challenges for innovation in commercial real estate development'. *Cities*, 77, 92–103.

Ramirez, R., Churchhouse, S., Hoffman, J., & Palermo, A., 2017. 'Using scenario planning to reshape strategy'. *MIT Sloan Management Review*, 58(4), 31.

Rydin, Y., 2010. 'Planning and the technological society: discussing the London plan'. *International Journal of Urban and Regional Research*, 34(2), 243–259.

Van der Heijden, K., 1996. *Scenarios: the art of strategic conversation*. John Wiley & Sons.

# 5

# Digitalization of the Retail Servicescape

*Jussi Nyrhinen and Outi Uusitalo*

## Introduction

A combination of rapid technological development, a shift into digital environments, the disappearance of traditions, and alienation from nature has evoked a longing for authenticity and human contact for many people, while consumption has simultaneously become a culturally accepted means of seeking happiness, well-being, and a better quality of life (Wilmott & Nelson, 2003). Perhaps, more than ever in recent history, the Covid-19 pandemic reminded us of this enduring feature of humanity. Consequently, our contemporary, digitalized consumer society has given rise to a growing demand for real-life events and artefacts and genuine human interaction. These trends are connected with the increasing importance of experience, which is widely recognized among marketing practitioners and scholars (e.g. Pine & Gilmore, 1999).

Customer experiences are a key issue in the retail sector because the retail landscape is evolving rapidly due to the emergence of technology-enabled channels and business models as well as rapidly changing patterns of consumption (Rigby, 2011). Customers now interact with firms through numerous touchpoints in multiple channels, and customer experiences are more social in nature (Lemon & Verhoef, 2016). Technology, digitalized services, and smartphones are no longer used solely by young, urban diginatives and early adopters; rather, they are also increasingly being used by the diverse and heterogeneous consumer majority, including elderly people and those living in non-metropolitan areas. The needs, preferences, and desires of different customers are still poorly understood. Thus, the Red Queen's Race (cf. Carroll, 1871) is an effective metaphor to describe the need for retailers to continuously adapt to consumers' changing needs and perpetually adopt new technologies to retain the expected level of service. Therefore, deep insight into various customer groups' shopping behaviours and service experiences in omni-channel environments is necessary so that channel integration can create value for both customers and retailers.

An omni-channel service experience takes place when a customer interacts with a retailer through multiple channels, which they often utilize simultaneously (i.e. a physical store and digital channels, such as websites, social media, and in-store

Jussi Nyrhinen and Outi Uusitalo, *Digitalization of the Retail Servicescape*. In: *The Red Queen Retail Race*. Edited by Richard Cuthbertson, Olli Rusanen, and Lauri Paavola, Oxford University Press. © Jussi Nyrhinen and Outi Uusitalo (2023). DOI: 10.1093/oso/9780192862617.003.0005 technologies). Various studies have shown that a satisfying omni-channel experience leads to increasing purchases and stronger customer loyalty due to increased interaction with customers and the customers' active role (see Verhoef, Kannan, & Inman, 2015). Omni-channel retailing integrates both online and offline channels that are pursuing a seamless customer experience across multiple channels. This augments the retail offering and enables customers to achieve their shopping goals more efficiently (e.g. Kumar & Venkatesan, 2005; Verhoef, Kannan, & Inman, 2015; Wallace, Giese, & Johnson, 2004). Despite documented success stories, several companies in industries with products and services that have been either partially or entirely digitized have encountered challenges while trying to expand their services online. For instance, entertainment retail companies, such as HMV and Blockbuster, have enhanced their offline record stores with online streaming services; however, they have not been as successful as online-only players such as Spotify and Apple iTunes. This is evidenced by the bankruptcy of Blockbuster in 2013 and HMV being placed under administration in 2018. To avoid such failures in implementing omni-channel concepts, further understanding is required regarding how customers' successful omni-channel experiences are formed.

Service experiences occur in servicescapes that have been re-evaluated due to digital disruption. The servicescape is a combination of customer service and environment that defines both the physical and digital environments in which customer experiences are created (Normann, 2001; Rafaeli & Vilnai-Yavetz, 2004). Since the emergence of e-tailing, both customer service and the retail environment have become experienced in both the physical and virtual forms, often simultaneously. The retail landscape in its entirety in all channels, including the physical, digital, social, and symbolic aspects, is an essential element in the formation of a customer's experience. A consumer's preference to either shop online or utilize digital technology while shopping is affected not only by the adoption of technologies but also by various lifestyle factors, such as the appreciation of social interaction and seeking personal indulgence (Dholakia et al., 2010). Moreover, consumers who are living in different geographic areas face different supply conditions in terms of access to stores and availability of different chains and brands. These conditions lead to different possibilities for conducting shopping in general, which is often overlooked because retail chains target their omni-channel offerings predominantly to the niche segment of technology-savvy pioneers and early adopters. Moreover, earlier omni-channel studies have drawn their conclusions from hypothetical future examples (Rigby, 2011), managerial interpretations of consumption patterns (Piotrowicz & Cuthbertson, 2014), and survey-based analyses that were conducted in both US and UK metropolitan areas. However, through the wide adaptation of Internet technologies, omni-channel retailing has become important for many consumers in different regions, and current research tends to ignore the majority, who are not regarded as early adopters of new technologies.

For instance, this is evidenced by earlier research conducted by OXIRM (Oxford Institute of Retail Management at the University of Oxford's Saïd Business School) across 20 European nations (Treadgold & Reynolds, 2020). This study confirmed that consumers in all of these geographies were comfortable with shopping across a range of channels. Thus, more understanding is needed regarding how people with various backgrounds interpret omni-channel retail environments and how their service experiences in these environments are constructed.

This chapter provides increased understanding of the challenges of omni-channel retail environments by focusing on the rarely addressed perspective of consumers living in non-metropolitan areas. We support the theoretical discussion with empirical evidence that was collected from consumers of different socio-demographic and socio-economic backgrounds in a provincial town that is a commercial centre of a rural region. We seek to identify the challenges in current omni-channel services and delineate the potential for further developing the services and enhancing service experiences. The results suggest guidelines for practitioners to integrate digital and physical channels and develop omni-channel servicescapes.

In this chapter, we examine how the service experience is constructed in servicescapes that are comprised of both online and offline stores. We first discuss the constituencies of service experience in the digitalizing retail context. Then, we outline the major dimensions of the omni-channel retail servicescape. Apart from rational and cognitive factors, affective and social elements of the customer experience are highlighted because previous studies have emphasized the significance of emotions in shopping behaviour (see, e.g., Sheth, Newman, & Gross, 1991). We also examine the integration of the digital and physical servicescapes as well as the roles of social and contextual factors in the retail service experience. Finally, we discuss the consequences of service experience construction in the retail servicescape and suggest avenues for enhancing customers' retail service experiences in the digitalized retail servicescape.

Subsequently, Chapter 6 will further examine the interplay of the cognitive and emotional aspects of the service experience to loyalty in the omni-channel retail system. We also study cross-channel loyalty behaviours between online stores (e-store) and brick-and-mortar (B&M) shops. To illustrate this phenomenon, we use survey data that was collected in Finland in 2016.

## Experiencing a digitalized retail servicescape

This section addresses customer service experience construction in digitalizing the retail servicescape. Consumers' shopping behaviours take place in retail spaces and places, which can be conceptually defined as servicescapes (Bitner, 1992; Booms & Bitner, 1981). Per Bitner (1992), a servicescape consists of three types of stimuli: ambient condition, spatial layout, and signs, symbols, and artefacts. This environmental psychology approach has emphasized that objective physical and measurable stimuli influence customers' and employees' internal cognitive, emotional, and physiological responses as well as their overt behaviours, which manifest as either approach or avoidance reactions. Moreover, social interactions both between and among customers and employees can result from servicescape variables. The augmented servicescape concept emphasizes interactions and emotions in addition to the physical and cognitive aspects of the servicescape (e.g. Johnstone, 2012; Rosenbaum & Massiah, 2011). Likewise, these servicescapes acknowledge customers' active role in interpreting environmental cues and forming experiences.

A well-known example of the successful implementation of an omni-channel servicescape is the US department store Nordstrom. It has optimized both its digital and physical store spaces to provide customers with a consistent service experience across both channels. In addition to focusing on its B&M stores' customer service and store designs, Nordstrom has augmented its selection and service to online and mobile stores so that both browsing and shopping can be done with ease in all channels. In addition, interaction between customers has been brought online via various social media platforms to enhance the customer community. A servicescape highlights the important elements of a retail environment and clarifies how customers interact with various physical, social, and symbolic cues therein. The retail service experience is—in this section—regarded as either customers' subjective response to or their interpretation of the elements of the service. This experience emerges during the patronage process, and it is influenced by the retail servicescape cues as well as a customer's previous knowledge and emotions (Jaakkola et al., 2015). The retail service experience in the digital-physical servicescape emerges in a context where different, old, and new channels intersect and customers both interpret and use various cues and elements of these channels (see Table 5.1).

## Cognitive and emotional experiences

Service experience is in this chapter regarded as an interactive process wherein customers construct experiences by merging services within their own life processes (see Heinonen et al., 2010; Heinonen, Strandvik, & Voima, 2013; McColl-Kennedy et al., 2015; Tax, McCutcheon and Wilkinson, 2013). Therefore, service experience is personal and subjective in nature and it reflects on how a customer thinks or feels about the company or its products or brand (see Meyer & Schwager, 2007). Customers interact with service personnel and other customers within the retailer's environment while shopping at both the online and offline stores. This type of customer experience is shaped by the retail servicescape cues

**Table 5.1** Key concepts and how they are related

| Author | Term/Dimension | Definition |
|---|---|---|
| Heinonen et al., 2010 | Customer experience | A process wherein customers construct experiences by merging services within their own life processes |
| Babin, Darden, & Griffin, 1994 | Emotional experiential state | An affective relation with the company, which involves one's affective system through the generation of moods, feelings, and emotions; seeking positive emotions from consumption |
| Frow & Payne, 2007 | Cognitive experiential state | Connected with thinking and conscious mental processes, using creativity or in situations of problem solving; meeting shopping goals |
| Bitner, 1992 | Servicescape | A built environment that affects both consumers and employees in service encounters and examined as the combination of ambient condition, spatial layout, and functionality as well as the signs, symbols, and artefacts of a store setting |
| Ballantyne & Nilsson, 2017 | Physical realm of servicescape | Physical setting of the servicescape, atmosphere, physical objects, processes, and equipment within the offline store |
| | Digital realm of servicescape | Digital setting of the servicescape, audio-visual stimuli, interface, functionalities, and processes of the online store |
| | Social realm of servicescape | Interaction with other customers and/or service personnel both online and offline |
| Verhoef et al., 2015 | Omni-channel | Retailing where retailers combine multiple online (digital) and offline (physical) channels in a convergent manner to provide a unified customer experience during the purchase process |
| Chiu et al., 2011 | Cross-channel integration | Mutual support and interchangeability between online and offline channels in terms of availability, information, and customer service; depicted as a prerequisite of seamless omni-channel customer experience in terms of consistency of service and complementary channel. |
| Miller, 2001 | Social capital | In the retailing context, the networks and relationships among customers as well as between customers and a retailer and its personnel |

as well as customers' previous knowledge and emotions (Jaakkola, Helkkula, & Aarikka-Stenroos, 2015, p. 186). The concepts 'customer experience' and 'service experience' are often used as synonyms in literature. However, from the customer's perspective, the service experience is affected by the direct interaction between service providers, customers, and/or other actors involved in service encounters (McColl-Kennedy et al., 2015; Tax, McCutcheon, & Wilkinson, 2013). Therefore, social factors are the central element in the service experience formation in the retail context.

Because the customer experience consists of one's personal feelings and thoughts about the retailer, it can be divided into the cognitive and emotional experiential states (Mosteller, Donthu, & Eroglu, 2014; Rose, Hair, & Clark, 2011) The cognitive experiential state refers to the functional/goal-oriented aspects of shopping such as fulfilling the daily chores of consumers and households (Babin, Darden, & Griffin, 1994), which involves rational processing of information (Frow & Payne, 2007). The emotional experiential state is associated with consumers' participation, meaning generation and agency when feeling and/or sensing an environment, and they create a memorable, unique experience (Borghini et al., 2009). Thus, the shopping experience is not only an instrument that is used to obtain needed products, it is also an end that is valued for its own sake (Babin, Darden, & Griffin, 1994; Hirschman & Holbrook, 1982; Rintamäki, Kuusela, & Mitronen, 2007), which emphasizes the roles of store environment and personal service (Turley & Milliman, 2000).

## Knowledgeable and rational consumers

A considerable portion of consumers' shopping activities occur in the realm of necessary purchases, which are made to fulfil daily needs (see, e.g., Bagozzi & Dholakia, 1999). Consumers are also pursuing tangible, extrinsic benefits from shopping. Rational choices are usually connected with successful purchases of necessary products and gaining monetary value via either low prices or price discounts. Therefore, customer experience includes the attainment of goals (Keiningham et al., 2017; Novak, Hoffman, & Duhachek, 2003). The cognitive dimension of the service experience entails fulfilling functional goals by completing the shopping task or purchase in a reasoned and efficient manner. In this type of shopping, consumers prefer (above all) hassle-free processes during the shopping journey. Smooth channel integration implies the elimination of barriers and delays and ensures security and trust (see, e.g., Chiu et al., 2011). The success of Amazon is largely based on the streamlining of cognitive factors. In addition to its low prices and superior selection, which are provided by its online platform business model, Amazon often ships merchandise to customers within two days for free. Moreover, it is currently opening distribution centres in major cities that enable shipping in mere hours rather than days. All steps in the purchase process that involve search costs are being minimized and replaced with automatization by launching applications such as Dash Button, which enable repeat purchases with one click of a device. Therefore, these large online retailers have been able to disrupt retail trade by relying on the cognitive factors.

## Consumer emotions, feelings, and enjoyment

Although functionality and 'shopping as everyday task' drive consumer shopping behaviours, emotions and pleasurable experiences remain a strong shopping motivation. This implies that shoppers are seeking intrinsic and personal pleasure as well as emotionally rewarding experiences (Babin, Darden, & Griffin, 1994). The experiential aspect of consumer behaviour is well established (Hirschman & Holbrook, 1982), and the trends of intangibility, pleasure seeking, servitization, and increasing leisure time are boosting consumers' interest in and demand for products, services, and retail channels that provide them with enjoyable experiences. Enjoyment can be present in mundane shopping experiences in retail stores that feature many forms of sensory stimuli. The crucial role of physical store atmospherics is widely understood (Kotler, 1973); yet, the future potential of digital channel integration lies in the incorporation of various cues and symbols to facilitate omni-channel shopping. Music, lights, colours, and layouts affect customers' reactions, such as the length of time in the store, the amount of money spent, and the pace of movement. The effects of sensory stimuli are typically unconscious and can be traced by observing customers and/or measuring their behaviour (Turley & Milliman, 2000).

Retail servicescapes are sometimes designed to offer enjoyable or extraordinary experiences in spectacular retail landscapes, such as at Disneyland, the flagship Niketown, Starbucks Reserve, or Apple Stores. Besides being a convenient online store, Apple provides authentic and educational experiences in its B&M shops. Apple Stores can be regarded as places for entertainment and interaction where consumers enjoy spending time and learn about the benefits of Apple products, which they will share with their community. Retailers can also evoke emotion by utilizing shared values of their customer community. These social encounters may transform into shared emotions such as a sense of belonging (see, e.g., Gunawardena & Zittle, 1997; Jahn et al., 2011). For instance, the sportswear company Patagonia is fostering retail experiences by using emotional appeals. Its campaigns emphasize sustainability as its core value by using slogans (e.g. 'Buy less!' and 'If it's broke, fix it!') to support its message. Further, it is engaging customers in environmentally conscious consumption by providing them with a platform for re-selling their used garments. These emotionally involving experiences are associated with customers' active participation, meaning generation and agency when feeling and/or sensing an environment, and they create a memorable, unique experience (Borghini et al., 2009). Online-only retailers that excel in the rational aspects of experience have not been appealing to experiential consumption to the same extent as B&M shops. However, by establishing physical outlets former omni-channel retailers have been able to enhance their emotional experiences with real-life human contacts and in-store atmosphere as Apple has done with its B&M stores.

## Customer experiences across the physical and digital servicescapes

The physicality of retail places is a focal issue in retail management, especially the idea of the retail environment as a collection of stimuli that evoke customers' cognitive, affective, and behavioural responses. However, consumers and locations are intertwined and should therefore be considered a coherent whole. In addition to commercial activities that occur within the servicescape, consumer patronage choices are also affected by the interaction between customers and service personnel. A servicescape can form a platform that supports activities and interactions with customers; thus, it acts as a link between people through its symbolic meanings (Johnstone, 2012). However, the dimensionality of the servicescape is not restricted to the physical and social realms; it extends to the digital dimension as well. This integration of the physical, social, and virtual environments is referred to as a blended servicescape (Bolton et al., 2018). In a retail environment that consists of multiple channels, consumers form their experiences by choosing elements from each realm, including what channels they use and with whom they prefer to interact (Bolton et al., 2018). Innovative servicescapes capitalize on physical landscapes and digital technologies, which simultaneously play important roles in omni-channel retail experiences.

## The retail servicescape as both a physical and social setting

Traditionally, retail spaces have mainly been regarded as locations that consist of physical stimuli that influence customers and employees and lead to various emotional responses and overt behaviours (Kotler, 1973). Physical, objective, and managerially controllable factors, such as layout, products, and prices, affect customers' service quality perceptions and satisfaction. However, consumption sites of today comprise subjectively perceived stimuli, including social and emotional phenomena, which influence consumers' behaviours in different, even unpredictable, ways (Rosenbaum & Massiah, 2011). Customers perceive and interpret servicescape stimuli in various subtle ways and end up in meanings that are idiosyncratic, emotional, and contextual. Thus, consumers are viewed as active and autonomous constructors of their own meanings and interpretations. Retailers influence customers' experiences with their design of retail servicescapes. When customers interpret and use these servicescapes, they form their own experiences (Jaakkola et al., 2015).

The role of social interaction in the servicescape has been highlighted during the last few decades. Rosenbaum and Massiah (2011) proposed that physical, social, socially symbolic, and natural dimensions in a servicescape may either enhance or constrain employee and customer approaches and/or avoidance decisions in their social interaction behaviours. Carú and Cova (2015) illustrated how service experiences can be fundamentally social. Some customers in servicescapes provide support in the form of rewarding personal interaction, assistance, and/or feedback. A sense of belonging to a community is one outcome of social relationships in service settings.

## Transforming the conceptions of place and time

The digital disruption that is occurring in the retail sector is transforming retail servicescapes; yet only a few academic studies have addressed the changes and their consequences. For example, the digital space transforms the understanding of the dynamics of time and place. Instead of being restricted by linear time and physical place, consumers can move from one place to another at any time and in any place. The digital servicescape is accessible at all times, and the shopping process, from pre-sale to post-sale service, is open ended in terms of time (Ballantyne & Nilsson, 2017, p. 229). Because retail spaces and places are evolving due to digitalization and servitization, novel interpretations of the servicescape are in place. Consumption environments are increasingly combining physical and virtual places to form contemporary physical-digital servicescapes (Ballantyne & Nilsson, 2017). Digitalization is modifying retail servicescapes in multiple ways. For instance, interactive communication and dialogue have become established due to information transmission. Additionally, the roles of retailers and customers are more active, with new applications and sites facilitating their engagement and immersion. Finally, active customers obtain more power; thus, the retailer's position becomes less dominant. The servicescape has to address the requirements of multiple touchpoints to provide a smooth service experience (Ballantyne & Nilsson, 2017; Jaakkola et al., 2015).

In the digital retail servicescape, technologies facilitate new services and new ways of browsing, shopping, and interacting. Previous studies have indicated that e-servicescapes and online cues have the potential to contribute to positive attitudes, emotions, and purchase intentions (see Mari & Poggesi, 2013). An important managerial issue concerns designing a digital servicescape that aptly supports the correlating physical servicescape. An innovative omni-channel servicescape combines and intertwines the advantages of the physical place and digital space. Importantly, digitalizing a servicescape provides novel opportunities for service experiences that encourage social interaction and dialogue. To achieve the benefits of the synergy that is provided by an omni-channel servicescape, the customer should perceive that the channels are seamlessly integrated (Payne & Frow, 2004). Channel integration is defined as the mutual support and interchangeability between online and offline channels in terms of availability, information, and customer service (see, e.g., Chiu et al., 2011). The more positive the customer evaluations of the channel integration are, the more beneficial the entire retail channel system is considered to be to the customer (Schramm-Klein et al., 2011).

## Human contacts, relationships, and communities

Social aspect of retail shopping is in a state of flux when digitalizing retail servicescapes because face-to-face (F2F) contacts offline are either replaced by or paired with virtual contacts online (Rose, Hair, & Clark, 2011). Especially social media has increased the role of other consumers in service experience, because consumers communicate about their shopping with their wide social network. Mobile technology has enabled this interaction in the B&M channel as well and simultaneously when service experiences occur (Piotrowicz & Cuthbertson, 2014). The increased role of sociality and co-creation of services has manifested in areas such as customer engagement, brand communities, word of mouth (WOM), and services created by communities. Therefore, service experience co-creation is no longer limited only for frontline service management but has implications for a broad range of marketing activities such as branding, promotion, innovation, and stakeholder relationships (Jaakkola et al., 2015). This chapter examines interpersonal relationships, social networks, and customers' involvement in relation to the customer experience in the servicescape. In the literature, these phenomena are referred to as social capital in the sociological theory (see Lin, 1999). In the retailing context, social capital is examined as reciprocal actions between customers and retailers that represent both interpersonal and institutional levels of reciprocity (Miller, 2001) (i.e. networks and relationships among customers as well as between customers and a retailer and its personnel).

The social aspect of retail shopping manifests in multiple forms. For example, social interaction between customers and sellers as well as among customers is a basic characteristic of traditional physical retailing. Even transactional exchanges and the emergence of self-service have not repressed the importance of human interaction in the retail sector. The social dimension of the servicescape is present even when individual consumers purchase everyday products and brands. This is because consumers develop and imagine relationships when making purchase decisions; the products purchased are used to create and maintain important social ties (Miller, 1998). For instance, Swedish furniture and houseware retailer Ikea provides an in-store social experience that has been labelled as a shopping day with friends and family. Large stores that are often located far from city centres provide play areas for children and family restaurants.

Further, the importance of social ties as part of the customer experience stems from consumers' quest for communities in which they can share common experiences, values, feelings, knowledge, rituals, and habits. The significance of communities with respect to consumer behaviour has been emphasized by Cova (1997), who developed the concept of the 'linking value' of either a product or a service. The linking value has strategic importance because, as a matter of survival, products and services must contain this communal value, which implies their capacity to connect people. The communities of today are frequently formed around consumption-related issues, such as brands, hobbies, and leisure activities. They are being held together through shared emotions, lifestyles, new moral beliefs, senses of injustice, and consumption practices (Cova, 1997). For instance, in order to engage its customers and to gain deeper understanding about their preferences, Danish toy retailer Lego has enhanced its brand with social experience by establishing the Lego Ideas online community, where building block enthusiasts can share their design ideas. Customers are also participating in the co-creation of products; if a design receives more than 10,000 likes, it might be considered an official building set that will be sold by Lego. The designer is rewarded with commissions from sales to reinforce the community.

Brand communities are based on social ties and activities, and community activities online are potential enhancers of customer experiences. Communities are characterized by a shared understanding of the brand, its rituals and traditions, and its sense of moral responsibility (Muniz & O'Guinn, 2001). While the members of brand communities are involved in certain social activities because of those brands, social connections and sharing between community members sustain the communication and practices that are related to the brands. The practices of community members are constructed based on the members' explicit knowledge of the brands, their tacit knowledge and know-how, and the emotional bonds between members. Importantly, communities and their practices create value for their consumers, and that value extends beyond the value created by companies and products. By building and supporting the community aspects of their brands, retailers can foster value co-creation both among consumers and between consumers and brands (Schau, Muniz, & Arnould, 2009).

## Customer experiences are co-created through interaction

Although services always encounter social interactions in retail environments, the importance of these encounters in physical, virtual, and omni-channel servicescapes is increasing, along with an experiential turn in consumer behaviour. Consumers today assume an active role when interacting with companies. This also implies that consumers collaborate with companies and, within those co-creative processes, shape their own experiences. In addition, how a physical store space is designed is vital to managing encounters between companies and consumers (Pecoraro & Uusitalo, 2014). Digital channels offer non-personal feedback possibilities and chat forums. Ultimately, it is the complex network of service encounters and interactions with different products and channels that are important to consumers. Thus, the focus of retail experiences is shifting from individual, dyadic encounters towards viewing consumers' retail experiences as being constructed through their active participation in social servicescapes via multiple possibilities for interaction with other customers, brands, and retailers (Carú & Cova, 2015). The term 'co-creation' refers to the company and the customer creating value in interactions and collaborations either with or without the influence of other actors, and it is typically conceptualized as occurring through the exchange and integration of resources (Jaakkola et al., 2015). In the consumer service context, customers themselves can be that resource for the retailer as well as for other customers. A retail service encounter (i.e. commercial exchange) is a crossing point of a company's and a customer's 'spheres', where the value that the retailer delivers merges with the value that is created by the consumer through usage of the service (cf. Grönroos & Voima, 2013).

## Social interaction and emotional experiences

Omni-channel servicescapes can provide rich and multifaceted sets of meanings that consumers can draw upon when either fulfilling their rational shopping goals or engaging in more hedonic leisure shopping. Social aspects, relationships, and interactions both between and among customers and employees are important for consumers, regardless of whether they are shopping in either a physical store or a digital environment.

While the social dimension of a servicescape is considered important in the retail and other service domains (Aubert-Gamet & Cova, 1999; Johnstone, 2012; Mari & Poggesi, 2013; Rosenbaum & Massiah, 2011), several cases have illustrated how the servicescape facilitates the construction of emotional service experiences. Digital shopping is usually depicted as a goal-oriented activity, and emotional and social experiences in digital servicescapes were initially considered more common in the field of online and video games than retail. However, customer service chat applications and online customer communities are facilitating human contact in a digital environment. Formerly online-only retailers, such as French fashion retailer Spartoo, are also beginning to enhance their emotional customer service experiences by establishing physical outlets where customers can receive F2F customer service and experience the merchandise with multiple senses instead of only audio-visually.

The servicescape of retailing influences customers' construction of service experiences. In omni-channel servicescapes, digital technologies can radically disrupt conventional methods of shopping. This utilization of both digital and physical shopping channels is no longer the consumption style of only the young and technologically advanced consumers in urban metropolitan areas but is adopted by a wide range of consumers with different socio-demographic backgrounds and in various geographies (see, e.g., Treadgold & Reynolds, 2020) Understanding retail servicescapes' potential as an omni-channel service experience is important for successful retail management. This review has demonstrated how the functional, emotional, and social aspects of service experience are linked to the designs of both the physical and digital servicescapes. Therefore, all the described aspects are relevant in terms of understanding consumers' experiences in omni-channel retail settings.

## Experience formation in an omni-channel servicescape

In this section, we further elucidate how consumers construct service experiences in an omni-channel servicescape using the empirical data that was collected during the Red Queen research project in Finland in 2016. The data provides examples that illustrate how consumers' service experiences are formed through the service environment cues and social interaction in both the physical and digital servicescapes. Moreover, it highlights why and how cross-channel integration is valued by customers. Importantly, the data depicts how omni-channel experiences manifest for consumers from various socio-economic backgrounds in non-metropolitan shopping context.

### Understanding shared interpretations of service experiences

Interviews were conducted with the members of four focus groups, each group comprising 3 to 7 participants, with a total of 17 participants, who were recruited from the personal networks of students via snowball sampling (see Noy, 2008). The criterion for interviewees was their experience as an omni-channel consumer; all participants had visited both the e-store and a B&M shop of a certain retailer either simultaneously or during the purchase process. Each group was mixed in terms of the participants' socio-economic background. To enhance discussion in the focus groups, the participants were divided into demographically concordant groups between men and women and between different age groups (ages 18 to 35 years and over 35 years). The purpose of this sampling was to reach omni-channel consumers other than only young males with higher education in metropolitan areas, which population is typically perceived as the early adopters of new technologies (Venkatesh, 2003) and thus regarded as typical omni-channel consumers. The background information of the participants in each group is listed in Table 5.2.

The interviewees were recruited from a provincial town of less than 140,000 inhabitants that is in the centre of a rural municipality in Finland. A town that is located outside the metropolitan area is an interesting setting for a study of omni-channel retailing because the shopping distances are often long and only a limited number of retailers have established physical outlets in a provincial town. Thus, existing B&M outlets are often the initial and most convenient places to shop for many consumers. Conversely, the digital retailer is often an attractive (if not the only) alternative shopping outlet in certain product and price categories. Finland is a post-industrial, affluent society; however, it is rather young as a consumer society. Urbanization and consumption-oriented lifestyles emerged there between the 1960s and the 1980s, which is rather late compared to many other Western European societies (see, e.g., Autio & Heinonen, 2004; Wilska, 2002). However, Finland has an extensive communication technology infrastructure, and the use of both the Internet and e-commerce (including mobile) has been widely adopted among Finnish consumers: 90 per cent of the Finnish population aged 16–89 years use the

**Table 5.2** List of participants

| Group | Age | Occupation | Education |
|---|---|---|---|
| *18-30 years old* | | | |
| Women | 20 | Student | Upper secondary education |
| | 21 | Student | Upper secondary education |
| | 24 | Student | Upper secondary education |
| | 24 | Student | Upper secondary education |
| | 25 | Researcher | MSc |
| | 29 | Unemployed | MA |
| | 29 | Translator | BA (Hons) |
| Men | 26 | Student | BSc |
| | 27 | Student | Upper secondary education |
| | 27 | Student | Upper secondary education |
| *Over 30 years old* | | | |
| Women | 34 | Customer service specialist | BA |
| | 34 | Salesperson | Vocational education |
| | 34 | Student | MSc |
| | 36 | Exhibition builder | BA |
| Men | 33 | Student | Upper secondary education |
| | 41 | Student | Vocational education |
| | 64 | Attending physician (retired) | Specialist degree in medicine |

Internet, and 50 per cent had purchased either products or services online within a span of three months in 2017 (OSF, 2019). This extensive adoption of information technology has enabled online and omni-channel shopping in rural and provincial areas; thus, these forms of digital consumer behaviour cannot be expected to be exclusive to metropolitan areas. Moreover, the rural context should not be disregarded when examining the digital disruption of retail trade. In many developing countries, for instance in India where 69 per cent of the population lives outside urban areas, rural consumers are becoming wealthier as well as more aspirational (see, e.g., Treadgold & Reynolds, 2020). The use of the Internet is also increasing rapidly with expected 627 million Internet users in 2019 and this growth is driven by rural Internet usage (*The Economic Times*, 2019). One should neither ignore the emerging trends of counter-urbanization nor decrease in car use in the mature markets such as the United Kingdom and Japan (Treadgold & Reynolds, 2020). Consumers are seeking residency outside metropolitan areas and drive less or give up car use either for financial reasons or for sustainable lifestyle choice. These developments create demand for home delivery and for services produced near where consumers actually live.

Focus group methodologies are effective for elaborating the interactive dynamics through which people negotiate various discursive positioning (Daymon & Holloway, 2002). Hence, focus group interviews are utilized to understand how shared interpretations and meanings of service experiences are constructed among consumers. In our study, the focus group technique allowed the discussion and sharing of the meanings among group members, which yielded accounts of various aspects of service experiences, including functional, emotional, and social experiences. Discussion between the interviewees may also enrich the data because the participants complement one another's views, which can bring out aspects that would not occur otherwise.

The data analysis was based on a qualitative content analysis, which implies a systematic reading of texts that enables inferences to be made from the data (Krippendorf, 2004; Wilkinson, 2004). Both authors of this chapter contributed to the analysis by individually reading the transcriptions of the focus group's recordings and comparing their interpretations. From an analysis of the literature, the data was categorized into themes. These are presented in the model shown in Figure 5.1 to depict how retail experiences are formed in the omni-channel servicescape (also see Guba, 1981).

We embarked on a detailed analysis by scanning through the data and identifying major themes that emerged in each focus group. We first examined how social and emotional experiences were formed intertwined through service environment and interaction in the omni-channel retail servicescape. Then we depicted how digitalization of the servicescape enhances social and emotional service experiences and how positive experiences may manifest as affection towards a retailer. We also illustrated how sensory and cognitive experiences were constructed in a

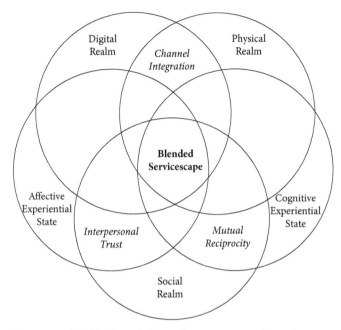

**Figure 5.1** Model of omni-channel customer experience in a
blended servicescape

convergent manner in the omni-channel shopping context. Subsequently, we analysed the role of digitalization for sensory and cognitive service experiences and
how these experiences manifested in customer decision-making. Finally, we summarized the findings by depicting how channel integration enhanced consistent
and convenient service experiences.

## Information and sensory cues across the digital
## and physical servicescapes

Cognitive experiences are linked to ideas, inspirations, or certainties that
were provided by information and sensory cues of the servicescape, such as
in-store product displays and audio-visual elements of the online store. The importance of sensory stimuli (sight, hearing, touch, taste, and smell) for cognition
emerged from the data. Despite the availability and the amount of information in
the e-store, consumers often complemented digital information with the tangible
cues of the B&M store environment and audio-visual elements of the e-store. Conversely, the unavailability or inaccuracy of information can result in frustration,
uncertainty, inconvenience, and disappointments. These negative experiences

were described especially as inconsistency of information between the e-store and the B&M store and lack of information during the purchase process as illustrated in the following quotation.

> What causes me to leave disappointed is when online and offline stores do not complement each other or are not even aware of each other's offerings. (Male, 41 years)

Even though information and sensory stimuli of both digital and physical retail environments were mainly associated with cognitive experiences, interaction with the service personnel and other customers in the e-store and the B&M shops was also depicted as an important source of information. Besides relying on the expertise of the shop assistants, the participants acknowledged observing other customers in the B&M store space to seek inspiration. Thus, the online servicescape augmented the cognitive experiences through product reviews by other customers and easily accessible online customer service. Such scenarios are illustrated in the following quotations.

> Occasionally when I am looking for a new shirt or such, I see another customer looking at a certain shirt and get an urge to try on the same shirt. Sometimes this has an impact (on the purchase decision). (Female, 25 years)

> I enjoy the ability to 'like and share' in an online store as well as read product recommendations by other customers, which tempts me to buy, especially if I can relate to the recommender. (Female, 21 years)

Cognitive experiences can be seen to manifest as a seemingly rational decision to continue with the retail chain based on an assessment of the information and sensory cues. The availability and accuracy of product information and certitude that service was delivered correctly and constantly convinced them that future experiences would be satisfying. For instance, the knowledge that the retailer was either able to deliver service close to the customer or had certain items in its selection was mentioned as an example of retention based on cognition. However, this type of relationship was considered easily broken. This occurred when there were either inconsistencies in service quality or if the customer discovered a more interesting alternative, as the following quotation illustrates.

> I have moved often within the past couple of years, and I have acknowledged that loyalty (toward a grocery store) is engendered by the location (i.e. what grocery store happens to be closest to me). Also, the selection constitutes loyalty; I choose to visit a store that I know to have local foods that I prefer in its selection. (Female, 24 years)

The digital and physical servicescapes were expected to complement each other in terms of the information they provided. However, the type of favourable cognitive experiences differed between the channels. Evidently the digital servicescape provided instant and convenient access to an extensive amount of information and audio-visual cues. The search and comparison engines enhanced cognitive decision-making. In the physical servicescape, the sensory cues of retail environment were especially described as being central to cognitive experiences as depicted earlier. These sensory cues and the instant availability of merchandise and service in a B&M store compensated the inconveniences, uncertainties, and risks related to intangible online shopping. The physical servicescape as a source of sensory information was considered crucial for products that are difficult to evaluate solely based on the description that is provided by digital channels. Thus, for certain product categories (e.g. food, cosmetics, and also some high-involvement products), physical stores have a lower purchasing barrier because many customers require sensory information when buying. The following quotations show how the role of the B&M store as a source of information was emphasized when shopping for cosmetics and sports equipment.

> Cosmetics are something that I must try before I purchase. For instance, the actual colour of a lipstick can differ from the package, and you can't know that if you are buying online. (Female, 25 years)

> There is certain sports equipment that is difficult and risky to shop for online. I must test their features to evaluate the quality. (Male, 36 years)

The interplay of the digital and physical shopping environments enhanced cognitive experiences when sensory information from the B&M complemented the information that was provided by the e-store and vice versa.

## Emotional experiences across the digital and physical servicescapes

Emotional experiences in the specialty retail shopping context were primarily connected to social interaction with other customers and store personnel in our data. The positive emotions related to shopping were often depicted as feelings of trust, enjoyment, belonging, or being looked after. On the contrary, negative emotional experiences were often related to feelings of being let down or being neglected, that is negative inconsistencies in service interactions. Thus, emotional and social aspects of the service experience seem to be intertwined in the specialty retail context, as reflected in the following quotations.

> I think the most important role of a physical store is to provide face-to-face customer service. More attention should be paid to the traits of service personnel,

such as helpfulness and expertise, because those things can have a huge impact on the customer's experience. (Male, 41 years)

In-store shopping can be considered a social activity as it is something you do with friends or family. (Female, 25 years)

The role of the shopping environment can be considered a physical setting or a digital platform (such as an online customer community) for the social interaction. In-store service technologies were often perceived as exciting novelties, and the participants did not feel that existing applications, such as touchpads, significantly enhanced convenience, emotions, and/or social interactions during their shopping journeys. Even though emotional experiences were primarily related to social interaction, the atmosphere in both the physical and digital retail environments provided clues regarding what to expect from the interaction as depicted in the following quotation.

I reckon that if the general appearance (of an online store) is clear and assuring, it enhances trust. (Female, 25 years)

Favourable emotional experiences manifest as affection towards the retailer. This interpretation was not based on seemingly rational assessment; rather, it was formed through social interaction. The focus group discussions indicated that trust in something cannot be felt towards an inanimate object such as the store environment or an abstract retail brand; it must be earned by another person or group of people such as the store personnel. Also the feeling of belonging to a customer community of a retailer enhanced the affection towards the retailer (e.g. shared shopping experiences with familiar people). However, a feeling that either an individual customer servant or an entire team of service personnel is committed to looking after the customer evoked emotions that reflected on the entire retail chain/brand, including its e-stores and other outlets. Such interpretation is depicted in the following quotations.

For me, loyalty equals trust; I know 'these fellows' will do their job well. I will receive good service and find what I am looking for. (Male, 27 years)

I consider that sales personnel have a significant impact on brand image and the way the customer is encountered in the (service) environment. At least I form the perception of a retail store or a chain based on these interactions. (Female, 21 years)

Notably, feelings of belonging and/or being looked after could be delivered digitally through virtual customer service and online customer communities. If B&M shops or the e-store of the same retailer is not able to deliver an impression of similar personal service, trust can be either broken or limited to an individual salesperson. Therefore, trust is earned via a uniform retail experience that is consistent across all channels. However, the form of preferred social interaction was depicted to differ between digital and physical servicescapes. Even though the actual purchasing process of other customers is more visible and observable in a physical setting, which provides a sense of belonging, a proper dialogue with other customers in a B&M store is uncommon. However, social media has augmented the service experience with dialogue and a sense of community between customers online. Due to the intangible nature of online shopping and the perceived uncertainty in e-commerce, the presence of other customers and sales personnel, which was augmented online through social media applications, was also appreciated as a source of information and reliance. The following quotation illustrates this.

> The availability of online customer service in an e-store is important to me. The support should be available in all phases of the purchase process, from shopping to payment and shipping. Many trust issues are involved in tracking the order. (Male, 36 years)

These interpretations indicate that favourable service experience is defined by not only convenience but also social ties. Besides the importance of the service personnel, the role of other customers was emphasized in the data. In addition to being a source of trust, this interaction with store personnel and other customers can be regarded an experience in itself.

## Cross-channel integration

Regarding shopping in an e-store and B&M shops, expectations towards these two channels varied based on the shopping context (e.g. generic versus highly specialized products or whether the consumer was shopping pragmatic goods or looking for experimental service). Retail experiences were formed in different manners in digital and physical channel contexts. Table 5.3 shows the roles of digital and physical servicescapes in the construction of service experience based on the data.

Convenience and consistency were reoccurring themes in the focus groups that were related to the channel integration. These themes describe the interplay of digital and physical servicescapes and the removal of barriers and delays as well as the reliance towards a retailer as the following quotation summarizes.

> I was glad to see how convenient it was to return a dysfunctional product that I bought online to a local outlet of this same retailer. They were even able to provide me with a compensatory product instantly. (Male, 27 years)

**Table 5.3** How congruency among digital, physical, and social realms of servicescape impact on customer experiences and relationships

|  | Cognitive experience | Affective experience |
|---|---|---|
| Digital realm | Digital text and audio-visual information complement sensory cues | E-store atmosphere; graphic elements and audio-visual stimuli; platform for online customer community |
| Physical realm | Sensory cues, trying and testing the merchandise in B&M complements digital information | Emotional associations engendered by atmosphere in B&M; platform for F2F human contacts |
| Social realm | Online customers and product reviews enhance available information<br><br>Service personnel and other customers as source of information; convenient in-store returns and pick-ups | Online communities and access to customer service via e-store complement<br><br>B&M provides F2F customer service, real-life interaction with other customers |
| Congruency among the realms | Channels are complementary in terms of information they provide<br><br>⬇ | Channel integration enhances human interaction<br><br>⬇ |
| Relationship outcomes | Mutual reciprocity based on relationship benefits | Interpersonal trust based on emotions |

The risks and inconveniences were related to lack of information and certitude encountered during the omni-channel shopping journey. Inconveniently arranged payment, poor shipping and return policies and processes, and waiting for the order to arrive were described as barriers to shopping online. Mutually, if B&M shopping required travelling or extensive comparison of alternatives, it was described inconvenient. These inconveniences illustrated in the quotations below are especially relevant in provincial and rural areas, where delivery times may be longer and the offering in B&M shops may be fewer than in more densely populated areas.

> I prefer to shop online, where I can browse through the selection. When I go shopping in a brick-and-mortar store, I have to consider all the travel arrangements and such. (Male, 41 years)

> When I encounter a need to buy something, I first browse the assortment and prices online. I only shop brick-and-mortar if I have to test or try the product I

am looking for. Usually, the prices are also cheaper in online stores than in local brick-and-mortar shops. (Male, 61 years)

As illustrated in Figure 5.1, e-stores complement the B&M stores with convenient access to service and information for customers via computers and mobile devices. Consequently, B&M stores were said to both bring omni-channel retailers closer to their customers and enhance service via personal human contact. Even though, in the data, the channels were described to serve different roles, the service experience appeared unified. Also, the manifestations of the omni-channel experiences, such as affection or retention, reflected towards the entire retail brand, not a separate channel. This phenomenon is encapsulated in the following quotation.

It is difficult for me to separate an online store from a brick-n-mortar store. It is the same brand behind them after all. Experiences in both channels co-effect how I perceive them. (Female, 36 years)

Within the focus group data, failures in service delivery were often linked to inconsistencies in prices, misinformation about merchandise, or customers being unnecessarily obligated to switch between channels during shopping. Hence, the channel interaction can be regarded rather as a prerequisite for satisfying customer experience than something luxurious or novelty, even for consumers outside metropolitan areas.

## The kaleidoscope of customer experiences in a blended servicescape

To conclude, in this chapter, we illustrate the service experience construction in a blended servicescape where the digital and physical spaces, emotions, cognitions, and people involved in service together shape the overall experience (Figure 5.1). The digitalization of the retail trade augments the physical servicescape with digital features and touch points. Consumers construct service experiences by utilizing different channels and even using them simultaneously sometimes (Ballantyne & Nilsson, 2017; Jaakkola et al., 2015). Thus, instead of taking place exclusively in one channel service, experiences are often formed by an entirety of clues in the digital and physical servicescapes. Again, experiences in different channels tend to be interconnected; if a service is perceived as satisfying in a specific B&M shop, consumers expect it to be consistent in that brand's e-store and vice versa (e.g. Piotrowicz & Cuthbertson, 2014). However, experience manifests in different ways in both the physical and digital servicescapes, as depicted in our empirical illustration.

Consistency and convenience can be seen as manifestations of a smooth channel integration, which was considered as a prerequisite for a satisfying customer experience for consumers from different socio-economic backgrounds and also outside metropolitan areas. Therefore aiming for more seamless channel integration does not initially guarantee competitive advantage in itself but rather helps retailers to retain their level of service and keep up with the Red Queen Race of digital disruption of the retail industry. Initially convenience and consistency are linked to cognitive experiences, because they remove barriers for information retrieval and goal-oriented shopping (e.g. Kumar & Venkatesan, 2005; Verhoef, Kannan, & Inman, 2015; Wallace, Giese, & Johnson, 2004). However, this chapter illustrates how social interaction is expected to be consistent across the omni-channel servicescape, even though the form of human contact varies between digital and physical channel contexts. The findings of this study contribute to the understanding of connectivity across the digital, physical, and social realms of the servicescape (Bolton et al., 2018) by illustrating how channel integration facilitates customer experience co-creation.

In cognitive experience formation, sensory cues (touch, taste, and smell) of the physical realm of the servicescape complement audio-visual information of the digital servicescape. The importance of sensorial cues for decision-making is emphasized especially in certain product categories where products are linked to physical factors such as eating (foods), appearance (fashion, cosmetics), or athletics (sports gear). For these product categories physical servicescape can still be an irreplaceable part of the experience. This interpretation is in contrast to some prior studies that associate sensory experiences mainly with fun and play while shopping rather than with cognitive processing (Hirschman & Holbrook, 1982). These cognitive experiences manifested as seemingly rational decisions based on an assessment of the available information and sensory cues to commit with a specific retailer for an expected good in return. However, unlike emotional affection, this type of retention was often replaced, if these situational factors favoured an alternative retailer.

Emotions and social interaction are often intertwined in service experiences (see Gunawardena & Zittle, 1997; Jahn et al., 2011). Our empirical illustration elucidates how emotions are targeted to the people involved in service formation (i.e. service personnel and other customers) rather than to places, artefacts, or abstract factors such as shop brands, even though the store atmosphere sets expectations towards social interaction (see also Pecoraro & Uusitalo, 2014). Moreover, the digital-physical environment serves as a platform for human contacts, interpersonal relationships, and social networks. Thus, both digital and physical servicescapes are linked to emotional experiences in our model through atmosphere and social interaction. In the omni-channel era, the purpose of B&M stores is often depicted to provide these emotional experiences through personal customer service (e.g. Rigby, 2011). However, online, particularly mobile, shopping has enhanced the importance of dialogue with other consumers for service experience in the form of online WOM.

People are a defining element of the service experience, because retail service is experienced in the interactions with service personnel and other customers in the service encounter (McColl-Kennedy et al., 2015; Tax, McCutcheon, & Wilkinson, 2013). The availability of information and better achievability of retailers through digital technologies have emphasized rational factors in decision-making, but our empirical illustration highlights how consumers are still social and emotional beings. If perceived favourable, emotional experiences engender interpersonal trust towards the service personnel or a feeling of belonging to a customer community. As depicted in prior studies, these feelings that are based on personal emotions and human contacts may also reflect as affection towards the retailer (see, e.g., Oliver, 1997; Schwarz, 2000) This type of relationship can be considered more committed because emotion and human contact cannot be easily replaced (Chaudhuri & Holbrook, 2001).

## Implications for design

From the perspective of the design of a servicescape, consumers expect consistent interaction, information, and atmosphere across both online and B&M stores. Thus, the atmosphere and customer service in both digital and physical servicescapes should reflect the values and brand of the retailer in a convergent manner. The servicescape is not necessarily expected to be symmetric between the e-store and B&M as long as the channels complement each other. In order to achieve this, the customer service and shopping environment may be optimized individually for both the e-store and B&M to utilize the full potential of an omni-channel servicescape. For instance, in-store and mobile shopping technologies could be embedded so that they enhance the actual human contacts by automatizing the manual processes (e.g. payment, browsing), not the social interaction or the sensations in a store space.

Online and omni-channel retailers may also enhance their presence in potential, but remote, market areas by investing in physical outlets, which could give them an advantage over their competitors that have focused their B&M retailing in metropolitan areas. For instance, Swedish furniture retailer Ikea has utilized this strategy by establishing a simplified store concept for provincial and rural markets that mainly serves as a pick-up outlet for their e-store and offers F2F customer service. Similarly, specialty retailers that operate in the small boutiques in the city centres or shopping malls could enhance their service experience by investing in e-store and in-store technologies as their resources are often limited in terms of the service personnel and store space. Digital augmentations of service can also engender cost efficiency as virtual space is often more affordable than acquiring more store space or service personnel. This is made evident by British catalogue retailer Argos, which operates small shops along with its e-store, often within the markets of its owner, Sainsbury's. As the store space and staff are limited, customers browse the selection though the in-store displays or pick up their online purchases from the physical shops of Argos.

## Future research

Although this chapter illustrated how the digital and physical servicescapes are associated with service experience and customer loyalty, more evidence is needed to show how the effects of a servicescape's elements on customer loyalty are mediated through both cognitive and emotional experiences and how channel integration can enhance loyalty across online and offline channels. In addition, further understanding of the joint effect of digital and physical servicescapes on customer experience is needed to fully understand the dynamics of omni-channel experience formation. These issues will be discussed in Chapter 6 of this book.

The empirical part of this chapter illustrated interpretations of omni-channel service experiences in specialty retail in a provincial context utilizing focus group methodology. In order to achieve broader understanding of customers' expectations and interpretations of servicescapes and customer experiences, more studies in different cultural and shopping contexts could be conducted. Focus group interviews provide insights into how service experiences are interpreted in relation to other consumers, but in-depth interviews and ethnographies could enhance the understanding of consumers' idiosyncratic meanings and actual behaviours in the servicescape.

## References

Aubert-Gamet, V. & Cova, B., 1999. 'Servicescapes: from modern non-places to postmodern common places'. *Journal of Business Research*, 44, 37–45.

Autio, M. & Heinonen, V., 2004. 'To consume or not to consume? Young people's environmentalism in the affluent Finnish society'. *YOUNG*, 12(2), 137–153.

Babin, B. J., Darden, W. R., & Griffin, M., 1994. 'Work and/or fun: measuring hedonic and utilitarian shopping value'. *Journal of Consumer Research*, 20, 644–656.

Bagozzi, R. & Dholakia, U., 1999. 'Goal setting and goal striving in consumer behavior'. *Journal of Marketing*, 63, 19–32.

Ballantyne, D. & Nilsson, E., 2017. 'All that is solid melts into air: the servicescape in digital service space'. *Journal of Services Marketing*, 31(3), 226–235.

Bitner, M. J., 1992. 'Servicescapes: the impact of physical surroundings on customers and employees'. *Journal of Marketing*, 56, 57–71.

Bolton, R. N., McColl-Kennedy, J. R., Cheung, L., Gallan, A., Orsinger, C., et al., 2018. 'Customer experience challenges: bringing together digital, physical and social realms'. *Journal of Service Management*, 29(5), 776–808.

Booms, B. H & Bitner, M. J., 1981. *Marketing strategies and organization structures for service firms*. American Marketing Association, Chicago.

Borghini, S., Diamond, N., Kozinets, R. V., McGrath, M. A., Muñiz Jr., A. M., & Sherry, Jr., J. F., 2009. 'Why are themed brandstores so powerful? Retail brand ideology at American girl place'. *Journal of Retailing*, 85(3), 363–375.

Carroll, L. 1871. *Through the Looking-Glass*. New York: Macmillan Publishers Ltd.

Carù, A. & Cova, B., 2015. 'Co-creating the collective service experience'. *Journal of Service Management*, 26(2), 276–294.

Chaudhuri, A. & Holbrook, M. B., 2001. 'The chain of effects from brand trust and brand effect to brand performance: the role of brand loyalty'. *Journal of Marketing*, 65, 81–93.

Chiu, H. C., Hsieh, Y. C., Roanc, J., Tseng, K. J., & Hsieh, J. K., 2011. 'The challenge for multichannel services: crosschannel free-riding behavior'. *Electronic Commerce Research and Applications*, 10(2), 268–277.

Cova, B., 1997. 'Community and consumption: towards a definition of the "linking value" of product or services'. *European Journal of Marketing*, 31(3/4), 297–316.

Daymon, C. & Holloway, I., 2002. *Qualitative research methods in public relations and marketing communications*. Routledge.

Dholakia, U. M., Kahn, B. E., Reeves, R., Rindfleisch, A., Stewart, D., & Taylor, E., 2010. 'Consumer behavior in a multichannel, multimedia retailing environment'. *Journal of Interactive Marketing*, 24, 86–95.

Frow, P. & Payne, A. J., 2007. 'Towards the "perfect" customer experience'. *Journal of Brand Management*, 15(2), 89–101.

Guba, E. G., 1981. 'Criteria for assessing the trustworthiness of naturalistic inquiries'. *Educational Communication and Technology Journal*, 29, 75–91.

Gunawardena, C. N. & Zittle, F. J., 1997. 'Social presence as a predictor of satisfaction within a computer-mediated conferencing environment'. *American Journal of Distance Education*, 11(3), 8–26.

Grönroos, C. & Voima, P., 2013. 'Critical service logic: making sense of value creation and co-creation'. *Journal of the Academy of Marketing Science*, 41(2), 133–150.

Heinonen, K., Strandvik, T., Mickelsson, K-J., Edvardsson, B., Sundström, E., & Andersson, P., 2010. 'A customer dominant logic of service'. *Journal of Service Management*, 21(4), 531–548.

Heinonen, K., Strandvik, T., & Voima, P., 2013. 'Customer dominant value formation in service'. *European Business Review*, 25(2), 104–123.

Hirschman, E. C. & Holbrook, M. B., 1982. 'Hedonic consumption: emerging concepts, methods and propositions'. *Journal of Marketing*, 46, 92–101.

Jaakkola, E., Helkkula, A., & Aarikka-Stenroos, L., 2015. 'Service experience co-creation: conceptualization, implications, and future research directions'. *Journal of Service Management*, 26(2), 182–205.

Jahn, S., Drengner, J., Gaus, H., & Cornwell, T. B., 2011. 'Connected consumers: the influence of temporal sense of community, socio-emotional experience, and satisfaction on event loyalty'. *Advances in Consumer Research*, 39, 556–558.

Johnstone, M.-L., 2012. 'The servicescape: the social dimensions of place'. *Journal of Marketing Management*, 28(11–12), 1399–1418.

Keiningham, T., Ball, J., Benoit, S., Bruce, H. L., Buoye, A., et al., 2017. 'The interplay of customer experience and commitment'. *Journal of Services Marketing*, 31(2), 148–160.

Kotler, P., 1973. 'Atmospherics as a marketing tool'. *Journal of Retailing*, 49, 48–64.

Krippendorf, K., 2004. *Content analysis. An introduction to its methodology*. SAGE.

Kumar V. & Venkatesan, R., 2005. 'Who are multichannel shoppers and how do they perform? Correlates of multichannel shopping behavior'. *Journal of Interactive Marketing*, 19, 44–61.

Lemon, K. N. & Verhoef, P. C., 2016. 'Understanding customer experience throughout the customer journey'. *Journal of Marketing*, 80(AMA/MSI Special Issue), 69–96.

Lin, N., 1999. 'Building a network theory of social capital'. *Connections*, 22(1), 28–51.

Mari, M. & Poggesi, S., 2013. 'Servicescape cues and customer behavior: a systematic literature review and research agenda'. *The Service Industries Journal*, 33(2), 171–199.

McColl-Kennedy, J. R., Gustafsson, A., Jaakkola, E., Klaus, P., Radnor, J. Z., et al., 2015. 'Fresh perspectives on customer experience', *Journal of Services Marketing*, 29(6/7), 430–435.

Meyer, C., & Schwager, A. 2007. Understanding customer experience. *Harvard Business Review*, 85(2), 117–126.

Miller, D., 1998. *A theory of shopping*. Cornell University Press.

Miller, N. J., 2001. 'Contributions of social capital theory in predicting rural community in shopping behavior'. *Journal of Socio-Economics*, 30, 475–493.

Mosteller, J., Donthu, N., & Eroglu, S., 2014. 'The fluent online shopping experience'. *Journal of Business Research*, 67(11), 2486–2493.

Muniz, A. M. & O'Guinn, T. C., 2001. 'Brand community'. *Journal of Consumer Research*, 27(4), 412–432.

Normann, R., 2001. *Reframing business: when the map changes the landscape*. John Wiley & Sons.

Novak, T. P., Hoffman, D. L., & Duhachek, A., 2003. 'The influence of goal-directed and experiential activities on online flow experiences'. *Journal of Consumer Psychology*, 13(1–2), 3–16.

Noy, C., 2008. 'Sampling knowledge: the hermeneutics of snowball sampling in qualitative research'. *International Journal of Social Research Methodology*, 11(4), 327–344.

Official Statistics of Finland, 2019. Retrieved on 3 February 2020 from https://www.stat.fi/til/sutivi/2019/sutivi_2019_2019-11-07_kat_001_fi.html

Oliver, R. L. 1997. Whence consumer loyalty?. *Journal of Marketing*, 36, 33–44.

Payne, A., & Frow, P. 2004. The role of multichannel integration in customer relationship management. *Industrial marketing management*, 33(6), 527–538.

Pecoraro, M. & Uusitalo, O., 2014. 'Exploring the everyday retail experience: the discourses of style and design'. *Journal of Consumer Behavior*, 13(6), 429–441.

Pine, J. & Gilmore, J., 1999. *The experience economy. Work is theatre & every business a stage*. Harvard Business School Press.

Piotrowicz, W. & Cuthbertson, R., 2014. 'Introduction to the special issue information technology in retail: toward omnichannel retailing'. *International Journal of Electronic Commerce*, 18(4), 5–16.

Rafaeli, A. & Vilnai-Yavetz, I., 2004. 'Emotion as a connection of physical artifacts and organizations'. *Organization Science*, 15(6), 671–686.

Rigby, D. 2011. The future of shopping. *Harvard Business Review*, 89, 64–75.

Rintamäki, T., Kuusela, H., & Mitronen, L., 2007. 'Identifying competitive customer value propositions in retailing'. *Managing Service Quality*, 17(6), 621–634.

Rose, S., Hair, N., & Clark, M., 2011. 'Online customer experience: a review of the business-to-consumer online purchase context'. *International Journal of Management Reviews*, 13, 24–39.

Rosenbaum, M. S. & Massiah, C., 2011. 'An expanded servicescape perspective'. *Journal of Service Management*, 22(4), 471–490.

Schau, H. J., Muniz, A. M., & Arnould, E. J., 2009. 'How brand community practices create value'. *Journal of Marketing*, 73, 30–51.

Schramm-Klein, H., Wagner, G., Steinmann, S., & Morschett, D., 2011. 'Cross-channel integration—is it valued by customers?' *The International Review of Retail, Distribution and Consumer Research*, 21(5), 501–511.

Schwarz, N. 2000. Emotion, cognition, and decision making. *Cognition and Emotion*, 14(4), 433–440.

Sheth, J. N., Newman, B. I., & Gross, B. L., 1991. 'Why we buy what we buy: a theory of consumption values'. *Journal of Business Research*, 22(2), 159–170.

Tax, S. S., McCutcheon, D., & Wilkinson, I. F., 2013. 'The service delivery network (sdn): a customer-centric perspective of the customer journey'. *Journal of Service Research*, 16(4), 454–470.

*The Economic Times*, 2019, March 6. 'Internet users in India to reach 627 million in 2019: report'. Retrieved on 3 February 2020 from https://economictimes.indiatimes.com/tech/internet/internet-users-in-india-to-reach-627-million-in-2019-report/articleshow/68288868.cms

Treadgold, A. & Reynolds, J., 2020. *Navigating the new retail landscape—a guide for business leaders*. Oxford University Press.

Turley, L. W. & Milliman, R. E., 2000. 'Atmospheric effects on shopping behavior: a review of the experimental evidence'. *Journal of Business Research*, 49(2), 193–211.

Venkatesh, V., Morris, M., Davis, G., & Davis, F. 2003. User acceptance of information technology: toward a unified view. *MIS Quarterly*, 27(3), 425–478.

Verhoef, P. C., Kannan, P. K., & Inman, J. J., 2015. 'From multi-channel retailing to omni-channel retailing'. *Journal of Retailing*, 91(2), 174–181.

Wallace, D. W., Giese, J. L., & Johnson, J. L., 2004. 'Customer retailer loyalty in the context of multiple channel strategies'. *Journal of Retailing*, 80(4), 249–263.

Wilkinson, S., 2004. *Analyzing focus group data. Qualitative research* (3rd ed.) (ed. by D. Silverman). SAGE.

Wilmott, M. & Nelson, W., 2003. *Complicated lives: sophisticated consumers, intricate lifestyles and simple solutions*. Wiley.

Wilska, T-A., 2002. 'Me—a consumer? Consumption, identities and lifestyles in today's Finland'. *Acta Sociologica*, 45, 196–210.

# 6

# Impact of the Retail Service Experience on Cross-Channel Customer Loyalty

*Jussi Nyrhinen and Heikki Karjaluoto*

## Introduction

It is widely acknowledged that customers are increasingly interacting with retailers through a variety of touchpoints in both online and offline channels. In this fragmented channel environment, managing these multiple touchpoints with reduced control has become the focus of both multi-channel and omni-channel retailing strategies (Lemon & Verhoef, 2016). Marketing through multiple channels is also a discipline that outperformed against expectation as an opportunity (8 per cent predicted vs 10 per cent actual); many companies continue to benefit from a more integrated approach to their marketing activities across a scope of digital and online channels (Econsultancy, 2018). The emergence of omni-channel retailing has enabled an increase in purchases and interactions between customers and retailers. In addition, there are more opportunities for additional sales at multiple touchpoints, and the retailer can enhance customer service through complementing channels (e.g. Kumar & Venkatesan, 2005; Verhoef, Kannan, & Inman, 2015; Wallace, Giese, & Johnson, 2004). Developments to marketing platforms and an increased understanding of a single customer's perspective have made it possible for many companies to benefit from well-coordinated marketing campaigns that offer a more consistent and synchronized experience for customers (Econsultancy, 2018). On the other hand, online retailing has increased competition and minimized switching costs for consumers, which is making customer loyalty increasingly difficult to sustain (Srinivasan, Anderson, & Ponnalovu, 2002; Wallace, Giese, & Johnson, 2004). Moreover, the retailers face challenges in providing an exceptional omni-channel experience because of the difficulty of mapping out customers' complex paths to purchase through multiple channels (cf. e.g. Herhausen et al., 2015; Lemon & Verhoef, 2016). These developments show that shopping across channels does not only provide opportunities for the retailers. It has also made it more difficult for retailers to retain their customer relationships and obtain or exceed the anticipated customer experience (CX), which holds up with the Red Queen Race metaphor 'in a fast world you must run just to stay still' (cf. Carroll, 1871).

Jussi Nyrhinen and Heikki Karjaluoto, *Impact of the Retail Service Experience on Cross-Channel Customer Loyalty*.
In: *The Red Queen Retail Race*. Edited by Richard Cuthbertson, Olli Rusanen, and Lauri Paavola, Oxford University Press.
© Jussi Nyrhinen and Heikki Karjaluoto (2023). DOI: 10.1093/oso/9780192862617.003.0006

Retailers continue to focus on CX, as well as the content required to facilitate this. Companies committed to CX are shown to outperform their peers. When asked about the single most exciting opportunity for the year ahead, optimizing CX (19 per cent) comes first, before data-driven marketing that focuses on the individual (16 per cent) and creating compelling content for digital experiences (14 per cent) (Econsultancy, 2018). Although research on CX has grown recently, only a few attempts have been made to understand the interplay between online and offline channels. Therefore, the objective of this chapter is to firstly examine how a customer's overall service experience is affected by the experiences that are gained from the servicescape in both online (e-store) and brick-and-mortar (B&M) stores. We focus on examining how CX is formed in the retail servicescape because it includes sensory cues, social actors, and social interactions with other customers and/or service facilitators (Ballantyne & Nilsson, 2017). Today, this consumption setting often simultaneously combines physical places (B&M stores) and virtual spaces (e-stores) to form physical-digital (i.e. omni-channel) servicescapes.

Initially the servicescape may seem remote for a retailer's performance and sound like 'nonsense' to a practitioner, but this chapter illustrates how the servicescape is 'as sensible as dictionary' (cf. Carroll, 1871) by showing its importance from customers' perspective and linking the servicescape to performance management measurements. Therefore, this chapter secondly examines how a customer's overall service CX is related to customers' willingness to share information (WSI) with a retailer and how that affects customer loyalty in terms of share of wallet (SOW) and positive word of mouth (WOM). WSI can be considered a crucial antecedent to loyalty because customers who are likely to have WSI with the company can be considered familiar with the relational benefits that the company offers and thus WSI to receive those benefits in the future (Leppäniemi, Karjaluoto, & Saarijärvi, 2017; Palmatier et al., 2006. Previous studies have examined WSI as an outcome of factors such as satisfaction and trust, while we are among the first to consider obtaining consumers' consent to disclose personal information as an outcome of both cognitive and emotional processing of a previous experience.

SOW has become a primary indicator of loyalty through the emergence of the customer relationship/management paradigm because a sole expenditure does not reflect the share of purchases in relation to a customer's purchase power and expenditures in comparison to competitors (see, e.g., Du, Kamakura, & Mela, 2007). Recommendations can also be regarded as a manifestation of loyalty; satisfied customers become advocates for the brand by sharing positive WOM (Hennig-Thurau et al., 2004). The emergence of social media has emphasized the role of WOM as a loyalty metric because the retailer has no direct influence on social networks that fall outside a brand's control. Thus, the importance of a one-to-one relationship between a retailer and a customer has increased. The customer serves as a medium between himself/herself and the wide social network, and this relationship is maintained (even in the in-store environment) via mobile devices (Piotrowicz & Cuthbertson, 2014).

The evaluation of one channel affects how an entire omni-channel system is perceived (Schramm-Klein et al., 2011), as depicted by co-founder and co-CEO Dave Gilboa of Warby Parker: 'We also see a halo effect, where stores themselves become a great generator of awareness for our brand, drive a lot of traffic to our website, and accelerate our e-commerce sales'. The former online-only retailer eyeglass brand Warby Parker opened its first B&M flagship store in 2013. It now has 20 stores and plans to add another 20 in the United States. Previous studies have focused on examining these antecedents and outcomes of WSI either in online or B&M contexts (e.g. Leppäniemi, Karjaluoto, & Saarijärvi, 2017; Metzger, 2004, 2006), but we are among the first to examine the cross-channel effects of WSI, SOW, and WOM.

More specifically, this chapter investigates how the positive evaluation of the omni-channel retail servicescape affects loyalty responses through customers' positive cognitive and emotional service CXs. Both rational, cognitive processing and emotional, affective processing constitute part of the experience formation (Frow & Payne, 2007). Previous studies have shown that especially emotional processing leads to long-term associations in the memory (Edvardsson, 2005). Therefore, CX is a key driver of customer affection (e.g. Keiningham et al., 2017). However, research that has examined the joint effects of emotions and cognitions on CX is scarce.

In the omni-channel context, social interaction in the form of human contact (e.g. customer service personnel and shopping with friends) and experiential elements, such as sensory factors (e.g. touch-and-feel, trying, and testing), are often depicted as a competitive advantage of omni-channel retailers when compared to online-only retailers (see, e.g., Rigby, 2011). In addition, retailers that are also operating in B&M channels have the advantage of building deeper interpersonal relations and CXs, which are connected to affection towards the retailer and have been evidenced by multiple B&M store openings by former online-only retailers, such as Amazon, Vista Print, Warby Parker, Athleta, and clothing retailer Bonobos. In Bonobos' B&M shops, customers can make an appointment with a stylist, try on outfits, and set up a style profile. The purposes of this physical store environment are to provide personal face-to-face (F2F) customer service and build customer community. Notably, affection towards a retailer is considered a deeper manifestation of customer loyalty (see, e.g., Oliver, 1997; Schwarz, 2000).

This chapter develops and tests a conceptual framework with a sample of 880 omni-channel retail consumers. The findings of the study confirm the majority of the hypotheses and show that a physical servicescape has a stronger effect on both aspects of CX, which emphasizes the experiential role of B&M stores. Further, we elucidate how these positive experiences with a retailer enhance customers'

WSI and loyalty. Finally, we illustrate the effect of cross-channel loyalty in terms of
SOW and WOM. We conclude the chapter with a discussion on the findings from
both the academic and managerial perspectives and offer suggestions for future
research. The key concepts and their definitions of this chapter are presented in
Table 6.1.

**Table 6.1** Key concepts of the chapter

| Authors | Concept | Definition |
| --- | --- | --- |
| Bitner, 1992 | Physical servicescape | The setting (atmosphere, sensory cues) and interaction with other customers and/or service facilitators that constitute the service experience |
| Ballantyne & Nilsson, 2017 | Digital servicescape | Digital space (website layout, audio-visual elements) and virtual interactions with other customers and/or service facilitators that constitute service experiences |
| Schramm-Klein et al., 2011 | Perceived cross-channel integration | Integration of channels eases the cross-channel movement of customers by connecting digital and physical servicescapes. Favourable evaluation of channel integration is expected to positively affect how an entire retail channel system is perceived. |
| De Keyser et al., 2015 | CX | The cognitive, emotional, physical/sensorial, and social elements that mark either the customer's direct or indirect interaction with market actors |
| Keiningham et al., 2017 | Loyalty | The attitudinal component of consumer loyalty is developed after an experience (or experiences) with a brand. These encounters with products, brands, and employees can lead to intense emotions, which can influence key customer outcomes, such as WOM and SOW. |
| Schoenbachler & Gordon, 2002 | WSI | A critical prerequisite for understanding changing customer needs; satisfied customers are more willing to share information to obtain relationship benefits. Customers who manifest high levels of loyalty intentions and behaviour towards a company are familiar with the relational benefits and thus willing to share information. |
| De Wulf, Odekerken-Schröder, & Iacobucci, 2001 | SOW | A customer's proportion of overall spending that is allocated to a particular firm or to a particular retail channel in the omni-channel context |
| Zeithaml et al., 1996 | WOM | WOM with positive valence (i.e. the likelihood that a customer will recommend and say positive things about a company to others). |
| Piotrowicz & Cuthbertson, 2014 | | The customer serves as a medium between himself/herself and the wide social network, and this relationship is maintained even when experiences occur. |

## Antecedents and consequences of omni-channel retail service experience

To illustrate how a satisfying CX in the omni-channel retail servicescape enhances loyalty across channels, a survey study was conducted during the Red Queen Effect project in 2016. Based on a literature review, we developed a conceptual model of cross-channel loyalty in the omni-channel retail context and tested the following hypotheses. In this section, we first examine the interplay between the digital and physical retail servicescapes and the overall service CX. Subsequently, we discuss how service CX enhances WSI and how WSI is related to customer loyalty. We finally explore cross-channel loyalty in omni-channel shopping by examining the interaction between online and offline loyalty.

### Joint effect of digital and physical servicescapes on service CX

Multiple channels have a joint effect on customers' purchase routes. The customer service and retail environments are experienced in a combination of physical and virtual places (Ballantyne & Nilsson, 2017). Thus, the evaluation of individual channels affects how the entire retailer is perceived (Schramm-Klein et al., 2011; Verhagen & van Dolen, 2009). Because the evaluation of one channel influences the evaluation of the other channels in an omni-channel environment, the joint effect of the digital and physical servicescapes should be examined when measuring satisfaction towards an omni-channel service (Neslin & Shankar, 2009).

As consumer decision-making in online shopping is initially based on cognition and rational factors (Rose, Hair, & Clark, 2011), comparison engines, such as Google Shopping and Nextag, have automatized this assessment and found that online loyalty can often be considered situational and thus relatively weak. However, online retailers have disrupted the retail trade by excelling in this situational and seemingly more rational loyalty, while B&M-only retailers have faced challenges when competing with these rational factors, which include prices and availability.

Conversely, moods and emotions can also profoundly influence decision processes. Consumers may use their apparent affective response to a target as the basis of a decision by essentially asking themselves the following: 'How do I feel about this?' (Schwarz, 2000). If the available information is limited, spontaneous affective reactions rather than cognitions tend to have an especially greater effect on consumer choice. In this situation, consumers are more likely to choose the alternative that is superior in the emotional dimension but inferior in the cognitive dimension (Shiv & Fedorikhin, 1999). This notion has created further interest in CX because experiences may be designed by combining functional and emotional benefits to achieve a competitive advantage (Mascarenhas, Kesavan & Bernacchi, 2006). Hence, the following hypotheses were developed:

- Satisfaction towards a digital servicescape is expected to positively affect a shopper's cognitive CX and emotional service CX (H1a & H2a).
- Satisfaction towards a physical servicescape is expected to positively affect a customer's cognitive CX and emotional service CX (H1b & H2b).

## Perceived cross-channel integration enhances service CX

Per Schramm-Klein et al. (2011), in addition to the assessment of individual channels, evaluating the integration of all individual retail channels in a multi-channel system is particularly relevant. The more positive a customer's evaluation of channel integration, the more positively the entire retail channel system is perceived. Alongside availability that is enhanced by channel integration, we have measured the perceived cross-channel integration of both customer service and product information (see Jiang, Xu, & Bao, 2015). Therefore, channel integration can be assumed to be positively associated with both the cognitive and emotional aspects of CX. This chapter proposes the following additional hypothesis:

- Satisfaction towards cross-channel integration is expected to positively affect a customer's cognitive and socio-emotional service CX (H3a &H3b).

## Associations between service CX, WSI, and SOW

A business executive's interest in CX results from a general perception that enhancing CX will result in greater loyalty to the firm and/or brand (Keiningham et al., 2017). Previous studies on social exchange theory have argued that consumers' WSI is based on their assessment of the costs, risks, and benefits (Andrade, Kaltcheva, & Weitz, 2002; Laufer & Wolfe, 1977). Evidently, consumers are more willing to build customer relationships with organizations that are familiar to them and that they believe are seeking mutual benefits in relationships (Phelps, Nowak, & Ferrell, 2000; Szmigin & Bourne, 1998). Perceived benefits are known to enhance customers' WSI (Dinev & Hart, 2006; Xu, Peak, & Prybutok, 2015). Therefore, a positive previous experience with a retailer enhances the likelihood of a customer consenting to provide data for a retailer (Leppäniemi, Karjaluoto, & Saarijärvi, 2017); as such, the following hypotheses are examined:

- Emotional CX is expected to positively affect WSI (H4).
- Cognitive CX is expected to positively affect WSI (H5).

As depicted earlier, SOW is an effective loyalty metric because it measures customer loyalty in comparison to competitors (Du, Kamakura, & Mela, 2007). In this survey, the relative share of overall expenditure is measured within specific categories of specialty retail and in specific shopping channels. To further understand the effects of emotion in relation to cognition on customer loyalty formation in the omni-channel context, the following hypotheses are proposed:

- Emotional experience is expected to positively affect SOW in both e-stores and B&M shops (H6a & H7a).
- Cognitive experience is expected to positively affect SOW in both e-stores and B&M shops (H6b & H7b).

Although there is limited evidence on the effects of customers' WSI on loyalty, customers who manifest high levels of loyalty intentions and behaviours towards a company are familiar with the relational benefits that the company offers (Palmatier et al., 2006). Conversely, being a member of a loyalty programme does not necessarily enhance loyalty because these programmes usually reward already loyal customers. Thus, consumers often enrol in multiple loyalty programmes to take advantage of all available offers and reward schemes (Bellini, Cardinali, & Ziliani, 2011). However, prior studies suggest a connection between WSI and loyalty in the context of specialty retail (Leppäniemi, Karjaluoto, & Saarijärvi, 2017), even though these effects are considered rather weak. Hence, the following hypothesis is studied in this chapter in the context of cross-channel shopping behaviour:

- WSI has a positive effect on SOW in both e-stores and B&M shops (H8a & H8b).

## Impact of SOW on WOM across the channels

Shopping that crosses a merchant's different channels can be regarded as a central characteristic of omni-channel customer behaviour. Retailers whose customers engage in this cross-channel shopping are most likely expected to profit from the possibility of differentiation that is provided by an omni-channel strategy in terms of customer loyalty (Wallace, Giese, & Johnson, 2004). Companies are increasingly interested in observing customer loyalty behaviour rather than loyalty intentions because the former is more directly connected to revenue and profitability (Chandon, Morwitz, & Reinartz, 2005; Keiningham et al., 2017; Kumar, Pozza, & Ganesh, 2013; Leppäniemi, Karjaluoto, & Saarijärvi, 2017). Therefore, the cross-channel effects of these two metrics of behavioural loyalty are tested in this study.

As a loyalty outcome of a positive CX, the SOW can be assumed to engender WOM with positive valence. We hypothesize that there are positive cross-channel effects between these two constructs because digital media not only enable omni-channel shopping but customers also share their experiences through social media (even simultaneously) when they are experiencing a retail service (Piotrowicz & Cuthbertson, 2014). The previously described halo effect of B&M store openings to e-stores indicates this phenomenon. Thus, the following hypotheses are considered:

- SOW in an e-store is expected to positively affect the WOM of a B&M store (H9).
- SOW in a B&M store is expected to positively affect the WOM of an e-store (H10).

## Moderating effect of perceived cross-channel integration

In the omni-channel retail system, the main benefit for customers is the synergy that emerges from channel integrations (see, e.g., Rigby, 2011; Verhoef, Kannan, & Inman, 2015). Thus, alongside having a direct effect on CX (Schramm-Klein et al., 2011), channel integration can be expected to enhance the effect of individual channels. More specifically, we are focusing on the effect of perceived asymmetric channel integration, where channels are not uniform in terms of information and variety but are rather complementary (e.g. 'one channel carries all the items of the other channel as well as additional merchandise', see Verhoef, Kannan, & Inman, 2015). Therefore, it can be expected that a customer's perception of how well the shopping channels complement each other moderates the effects of both physical and digital servicescapes on an overall CX. On this basis, we propose the following hypotheses:

- The effects of the digital servicescape on the emotional CX and the cognitive CX are moderated by the evaluation of perceived channel integration (H11a & H11b).
- The effects of the physical servicescape on the emotional CX and the cognitive CX are moderated by the evaluation of perceived channel integration (H12a & H12b).

We have depicted these components and hypotheses for the conceptual model in Figure 6.1, where the hypotheses are illustrated as arrows. The model was controlled by age (in years), living area (metropolitan vs provincial), and gender because previous research suggests that socio-demographic factors affect both consumer channel adaptation and cross-channel behaviour (see Verhoef,

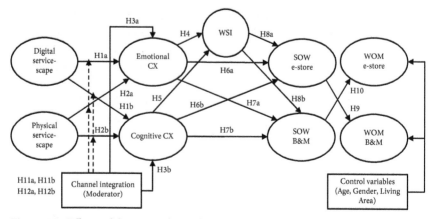

**Figure 6.1** Effects of the omni-channel servicescape on cross-channel loyalty through service CX and WSI

Kannan, & Inman, 2015). A consumer's age and gender are known to affect technology adoption (Venkatesh et al., 2003), while densely populated metropolitan areas often have a broader variety of shops and a more advanced technology infrastructure in comparison to rural and provincial regions. Previous studies have also shown that female consumers generally give and receive social support through the Internet more than men (Fan & Miao, 2012; Gefen & Ridings, 2005).

## Case study data and analysis

The data was collected by surveying 880 Finnish omni-channel consumers who were aged between 18 and 75 years via a structured Internet panel. Finland is a post-industrial, affluent society (see, e.g., Autio & Heinonen, 2004; Wilska, 2002) with extensive communication technology infrastructure, and the use of both the Internet and e-commerce has been widely adopted among Finnish consumers nationwide, which makes Finland an adequate setting for an omni-channel study. As evidenced by Official Statistics of Finland (OSF, 2019a), 90 per cent of the Finnish population aged 16–89 years use the Internet, and 50 per cent had purchased either products or services online within a span of three months in 2019 (OSF, 2019b). The respondents were instructed to choose 1 specialty retailer from 15 popular specialty retailers from multiple categories such as books, fashion, cosmetics, do-it-yourself, sporting goods, home electronics, general merchandise, furniture and home decoration, animal supplies, and pet accessories. Both Finnish and international retailers were included in the survey. To capture consumers who are regarded as omni-channel shoppers, the requirement was that the respondents had visited this store in both the online and offline channels. The sample characteristics are depicted in Table 6.2.

Table 6.2  Sample characteristics

| Variable | | N | % |
|---|---|---|---|
| Gender | Male | 423 | 48.1 |
| | Female | 457 | 51.9 |
| Living area | Provincial or rural | 724 | 82.3 |
| | Metropolitan Capital Region | 156 | 17.7 |
| Age group | 20–29 | 93 | 10.5 |
| | 30–39 | 188 | 21.4 |
| | 40–49 | 182 | 20.7 |
| | 50–59 | 185 | 21.1 |
| | 60–69 | 181 | 20.6 |
| | 70 or older | 51 | 5.8 |

The questionnaire was then completed per the respondents' experiences of this specific retailer. Respondents evaluated 37 statements on a 7-point Likert-type scale (1=strongly disagree to 7=strongly agree). The marker variable approach was used to assess the effects of the common method bias (e.g. Lindell & Whitney, 2001; Malhotra, Kim, & Patil, 2006). A single, theoretically unrelated item ('How frustrated did you feel while completing this survey?') was measured on a 7-point semantical differential scale that was anchored by 'not at all' to 'extremely frustrated', which served as a marker variable. The highest correlation between the marker and the latent variables ($r = -0.236$) was below the level that would significantly affect the studied structural relations (Malhotra, Kim, & Patil, 2006). Thus, we consider that common method bias should not be a concern in our data set.

## Measurement model

Both the digital and physical servicescapes were modelled as reflective-formative type second-order factors (the first order was reflective and the second order was formative). The digital servicescape consisted of CX and the service environment in an e-store. The physical servicescape had the same elements but they were measured in B&M shops. Other dimensions were modelled as reflective first-order factors, with each factor comprising three to four items. WSI was measured as a single item. All the measurement scales were drawn from existing scales (see Appendix). The scales were modified to fit to the research context, per the findings of the focus group discussions (see Chapter 5 of this book). In the data analysis phase, we first ran an exploratory factor analysis to identify the factor components. The analysis revealed that the items representing social service CX and emotional service CX loaded on the same factor. Similarly, the items representing cognitive and sensory experiences had the highest coefficients on the singular factor. Hence, they were examined as unified constructs of the emotional experience (including the social element) and the cognitive experience (including the sensory element). Subsequently, the data was analysed using partial least squares confirmatory factor analysis.

In general, construct measures showed high internal reliabilities. The evaluation of the constructs showed acceptable reliability and validity as the factor weights were all either equal to or larger than 0.77. Composite reliabilities were all above 0.88, and Cronbach's alphas were larger than the recommended cut-off value of 0.70. Age, gender, and home region of a respondent were set as control variables. Discriminant validity was achieved by using the Fornell–Larcker criterion and testing the Heterotrait–Monotrait (HTMT) ratio. The square root of the average variance extracted (AVE) of each latent variable exceeded the correlations with all the other latent variables (excluding dimensions within second-order factors), and HTMT ratios were below the cut-off value of 0.90. In addition, the Standardized Root Mean Square Residual (SRMR) value of 0.061 was well below the threshold, which indicated a good model fit (Henseler et al., 2014). To summarize, the evaluation of the reflective constructs met the criteria set in the literature, the model's predictive relevance was high in terms of outcomes, and all $R^2$ values were well above cut-off values. The measurement model is depicted in Table 6.3.

## Structural model

The data confirms that the digital service environment and online customer service were significantly related to the digital servicescape, which was measured as a second-order factor. The data also verifies that the lower level components of the physical service environment and in-store customer service were strongly significantly related to the second-order factor that measured the physical servicescape. With respect to H1a and H1b, positive associations between the digital servicescape and emotional CX ($\beta = 0.116$; $p < 0.001$) and cognitive CX ($\beta = 0.114$; $p < 0.001$) were supported by the data. The data mutually supports H2a and H2b by indicating positive associations between the physical servicescape and emotional CX ($\beta = 0.554$; $p < 0.001$) and cognitive CX ($\beta = 0.410$; $p < 0.001$). However, the servicescape in B&M stores had a stronger effect on both aspects of service CX in comparison to e-stores. With respect to H3a and H3b, the positive effect of perceived cross-channel integration on both cognitive CX ($\beta = 0.295$; $p < 0.001$) and emotional CX ($\beta = 0.263$; $p < 0.001$) is supported by the data.

The data supports H4 and H5 by confirming the positive effect of both emotional CX ($\beta = 0.178$; $p < 0.001$) and cognitive CX ($\beta = 0.366$; $p < 0.001$) on WSI. Subsequently, with respect to H6a and H6b, the positive effects between emotional CX ($\beta = 0.154$; $p < 0.01$) and cognitive CX ($\beta = 0.115$; $p < 0.01$) on SOW in e-stores are supported by the data. The data also supports positive associations

**Table 6.3** Statistical results

Average variance extracted (AVE), composite reliabilities (CR), construct correlations, square root of AVE (on the diagonal), means and standard deviations

| | CR | AVE | 1 | 2 | 3 | 4 | 5 | 6 | 7 | 8 | 9 | 10 | 11 | 12 | 13 |
|---|---|---|---|---|---|---|---|---|---|---|---|---|---|---|---|
| Age in years (1) | n/a | n/a | n/a | | | | | | | | | | | | |
| Living area (2) | n/a | n/a | 0.02 | n/a | | | | | | | | | | | |
| Cognitive CX (3) | .93 | .82 | -.07 | .03 | 0.9 | | | | | | | | | | |
| Emotional CX (4) | .94 | .80 | -.03 | 0.7 | .78 | .89 | | | | | | | | | |
| Digital servicescape (5) | .92 | .65 | .00 | .04 | .56 | .62 | .80 | | | | | | | | |
| Physical servicescape (6) | .95 | .73 | -.02 | .10 | .68 | .80 | .59 | .85 | | | | | | | |
| Gender (7) | n/a | n/a | -.13 | .09 | .09 | .09 | .05 | .12 | n/a | | | | | | |
| Channel integration (8) | .88 | .71 | .01 | .07 | .65 | .72 | .68 | .68 | .07 | .84 | | | | | |
| SOW in e-store (9) | .89 | .72 | .05 | .01 | .32 | .32 | .42 | .23 | -.06 | .38 | .85 | | | | |
| SOW in B&M store (10) | .89 | .74 | -.30 | .07 | .48 | .54 | .32 | .51 | .09 | .43 | .31 | .86 | | | |
| WSI (11) | n/a | n/a | -.06 | .08 | .51 | .46 | .34 | .36 | .01 | .39 | .24 | .32 | n/a | | |
| WOM of e-store (12) | .92 | .80 | -.01 | .01 | .54 | .56 | .65 | .44 | .05 | .58 | .62 | .36 | .33 | .89 | |
| WOM of B&M store (13) | .94 | .85 | -.03 | .03 | .62 | .68 | .48 | .61 | .12 | .57 | .31 | .62 | .36 | .65 | .92 |
| Mean | | | 48.13 | n/a | 4.33 | 4.78 | 4.68 | 5.21 | n/a | 4.82 | 3.78 | 2.74 | 3.18 | 4.01 | 4.51 |
| Standard deviation | | | 14.01 | n/a | 1.39 | 1.28 | 1.22 | 1.26 | n/a | 1.23 | 1.41 | 1.38 | 1.87 | 1.51 | 1.51 |

Notes: n/a= not applicable, construct measured through a single indicator; composite reliability and AVE cannot be computed; latent variables 5 and 6 measured as 2nd order reflective-formative factors

between emotional CX ($\beta$ = 0.424; $p$ < 0.001) and cognitive CX ($\beta$ = 0.111; $p$ < 0.05) and SOW in B&M stores (H7a and H7b). Further, it supports positive associations between WSI and SOW in e-stores ($\beta$ = 0.087; $p$ < 0.05) with respect to H8a. However, H8b was rejected because the data did not indicate a significant association between WSI and SOW in B&M stores. Finally, the data supports H9 by indicating that SOW in e-stores has a positive effect on WOM of B&M stores ($\beta$ = 0.314; $p$ < 0.001). There is also a positive association between SOW in B&M stores and WOM of e-stores ($\beta$ = 0.356; $p$ < 0.001) with respect to H10.

The data did not confirm the hypothesized moderating effect of perceived channel integration on the effects of digital servicescapes on CX, and therefore did not support H11a and H11b. However, with respect to H12a and H12b, significant moderating effects on associations between the physical servicescape and both emotional CX ($\beta$ = 0.030; $p$ < 0.05) and cognitive CX ($\beta$ = 0.054; $p$ < 0.01) were seen. Regarding control variables, the only significant effect was between gender and WOM of e-stores. As seen in earlier studies, the likelihood to share WOM increased if the consumer was female (see Fan & Miao, 2012; Gefen & Ridings, 2005). Notably, because the effects of the rest of the control variables were insignificant and the effect of gender on WOM of B&M stores was not particularly high, the model can be considered good in terms of validity of examined independent and dependent variables. The results are shown in Table 6.4.

## Customers use the elements of servicescape to form their experiences

The results of our study illustrate how the CX path is formed via the joint effect of both digital and physical servicescapes and how CX enhances WSI and loyalty behaviours across e-stores and B&M shops. This cross-channel path is illustrated in Figure 6.2.

The results of our study firstly show how the interplay of digital and physical servicescapes constitutes an emotional and cognitive retail service CX. As expected, based on prior studies (e.g. Rigby, 2011), F2F human contact and the in-store atmosphere of the physical servicescape had a stronger effect on emotional CX than digital servicescapes that consisted of virtual interaction and audio-visual information. However, in contrast to previous literature (e.g. Rose, Hair, & Clark, 2011), the effect of the physical servicescape on cognitive CX was also stronger than that of the digital servicescape, regardless of its superior amount and availability of information. It can be argued that, in the data used in this study, cognitive CX included a sensory aspect alongside the intellectual dimension; thus, in

**Table 6.4** Results of the structure equation model

| IV | DV | Hypotheses | β | R² |
|---|---|---|---|---|
| Digital servicescape | Emotional CX | H1a | .12*** | .71 |
| | Cognitive CX | H1b | .11** | .53 |
| Physical servicescape | Emotional CX | H2a | .55*** | |
| | Cognitive CX | H2b | .41*** | |
| Perceived channel integration | Emotional CX | H3a | .30*** | |
| | Cognitive CX | H3b | .26*** | |
| Emotional CX | WSI | H4 | .18** | .27 |
| | SOW in e-store | H6a | .15** | .12 |
| | SOW in B&M store | H7a | .42*** | .30 |
| Cognitive CX | WSI | H5 | .37*** | |
| | SOW in e-store | H6b | .12** | |
| | SOW in B&M store | H7b | .11* | |
| WSI | SOW in e-store | H8a | .09* | |
| | SOW in B&M store | H8b | Ns | |
| SOW in e-store | WOM of B&M store | H9 | .31*** | .12 |
| SOW in B&M store | WOM of e-store | H10 | .36*** | .11 |
| **Moderating effects (of perceived cross-channel integration)** | | | | |
| Digital servicescape | Emotional CX | H11a | Ns | |
| Digital servicescape | Cognitive CX | H11b | Ns | |
| Physical servicescape | Emotional CX | H12a | .03** | |
| Physical servicescape | Cognitive CX | H12b | .05* | |

*Notes:* ns/not significant at $p > .05$; * $p < .05$; ** $p < .01$; *** $p < .001$

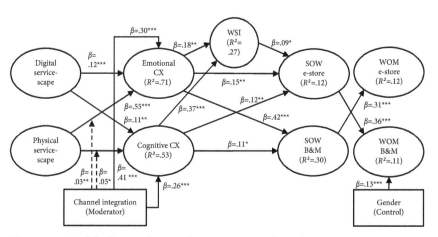

**Figure 6.2** Model of antecedents and consequences of retail service experiences

addition to the information that was provided by each servicescape, consumers utilized sensory cues (e.g. taste and touch) in their cognitive processing. These findings emphasize the role of B&M stores in overall service CX. The results of our study also support prior research by showing that customers' perceptions of channel integration affect the assessment of their overall experience (e.g. Schramm-Klein et al., 2011).

Consistent with prior literature (Leppäniemi, Karjaluoto, & Saarijärvi, 2017), the results of our study secondly show that positive experiences enhance the likelihood of customers to consent to sharing their personal information to retailers. This customers' consent to share data is a prerequisite for extensive customer insight, which is crucial for retailers to develop their business to respond to the Red Queen Race of the disruptive challenges of changing customer needs and technology adoption. Conversely, and in contrast to certain earlier findings (Leppäniemi, Karjaluoto, & Saarijärvi, 2017), there was no significant association between WSI and SOW in B&M stores. However, there was a weak association between WSI and SOW in e-stores. This finding indicates that WSI is a prerequisite for loyalty in the online context but not in the B&M channel.

Thirdly, both cognitive and emotional CX have a direct positive association with loyalty. The effect is strongest between emotional CX and SOW in B&M stores. This finding indicates that emotional processing is most likely to enhance behavioural loyalty towards a physical setting, which is also a key antecedent for emotional CX. However, our results also suggest that this loyalty behaviour migrates to the e-store of the same retailer in the form of positive WOM. Similarly, SOW in e-stores engenders positive WOM of B&M shops of the same retail chain.

Finally, our results illustrate how perceived cross-channel integration enhances the effects of a physical servicescape on emotional and cognitive CX. This finding indicates that the impact of a physical servicescape on overall CX is even stronger if B&M stores are seamlessly integrated with e-stores. Conversely, perceived integration does not enhance the effects of the digital servicescape to overall CX. This can be interpreted such that, regardless of cross-channel loyalty behaviours, for many consumers, an e-store is still an additional channel that enhances their service experiences in a physical servicescape, which is more often the main setting for CXs. To conclude, though the servicescape may initially sound like 'nonsense' or a synonym for store space, customers use the elements of the servicescape to form their experiences and to assess 'how they feel about the retailer'. Therefore, what constitutes a servicescape is as sensible for a customer as a dictionary (cf. Carroll, 1871). CX further links the servicescape to performance management measurements such as WSI, SOW, and WOM.

# Service design and customer relationship management in omni-channel retailing

To conclude the chapter we draw implications for service design and customer relationship management in the omni-channel retail environment. We also suggest future research avenues for academics based on the evaluation of this study.

## Cross-channel integration enables seamless CX

First, from the managerial perspective the findings in this chapter indicate that investments on B&M stores may enhance loyalty as human contacts and sensory elements of the physical servicescape are still key drivers of overall CX. However, B&M retailers may also consider enhancing their service with an e-store, because the impact of the physical servicescape to experience is even stronger if the B&M and e-stores are seamlessly integrated. This highlights the role of service design so that channels are optimized and consistent when it comes to merchandise, accessibility, information, and customer service, as depicted earlier in Chapter 5. For instance, luxury retail chain Neiman Marcus received the 2017 IRT Retailer Innovation Award in Customer Engagement award (Retail Supply Chain Insights, 2016) for its efforts to provide supremely seamless CX. For example, if a customer consistently searches for apparels in a certain size, the retailer's website will remember it, and the next time the customer visits the website it will return search results for that size that are available in the nearest B&M stores of Neiman Marcus.

Even though cognitive, seemingly rational processing is often the main driver of purchase behaviour, our findings acknowledge the importance the emotional processing as well. This emphasizes the importance of human interaction, especially F2F customer service, as emotions are intertwined with social experiences as depicted in our data and evidenced by openings of physical outlets by former pure online retailers such as Bonobos, which were discussed in the introduction section of this chapter.

## Gathering data in a customer-centric way

Second, this chapter illustrates how a positive CX can lead customers to allow the retailer to gather their personal data to receive personalized service in exchange. This finding about the determinants of WSI emphasizes the importance of service design and CX management. The majority of previous literature has over-emphasized the benefits of customer data to the firm while mostly ignoring the customers' perspective (Kunz et al., 2017). In order to enhance WSI, the obtaining and utilizing of customer data can be conducted in a more customer-centric manner so that the customers receive the benefits from the data collected of them. Customer data allows the companies to further develop their servicescape to provide more personalized CXs. In online retailing, consent is not a one-off agreement but it must be sustained. Consent must first be earned by providing satisfactory experience and then maintained by providing perpetually outstanding experiences through better customer insight. For instance, Starbucks does not only provide rewards to their loyal customers but it also utilizes the data collected through their loyalty programme to offer more personalized experiences, such as customized order-ahead options based on purchase history, to enhance CX for further loyalty.

Customers' WSI is a prerequisite for loyalty behaviour in the e-store where the CX can be automatically customized according to customer data and they consent to the retailer to gather data of them during the online shopping. Conversely, WSI is less relevant for customer loyalty towards the B&M channel. This may be due to the fact that customer data in the B&M store is mainly gathered through loyalty card programmes. In line with previous studies (Bellini, Cardinali, & Ziliani, 2011, Leppäniemi, Karjaluoto, & Saarijärvi, 2017), belonging to a loyalty programme in not likely to enhance loyalty as the programmes reward already loyal customers and consumers may also enrol in multiple loyalty programmes to obtain the offers and rewards from all of these programmes.

## Directing customer loyalty behaviours towards profitable channels

Third, this chapter portrays the cross-channel effect of customer loyalty—more specifically, how expenditure in one shopping channel may reflect as recommending another channel of the same retailer. This notion is significant especially from the managerial perspective, because regardless of the revenue growth, digital channels have failed to match the weak profitability or decline of physical sales in many industries such as the music industry (see Chapter 5 of this book). For instance, the major retail chains active in the music category have increasingly emphasized the importance of physical store space in developed markets (Treadgold & Reynolds, 2020). If the retail servicescape is designed seamlessly, the digital channel may be utilized to enhance loyalty towards the more profitable B&M stores, while the e-store initially serves the role of the 'digital catalogue'. Further, our conclusions also emphasize the showroom effect of B&M shops for the retailers that primarily operate online, as depicted earlier in the introduction of this chapter with examples of former pure online retailers such as Warby Parker, who have now established physical outlets to enhance their overall CX though they primarily retail online.

WOM as the final outcome of the model presented in the chapter is the central loyalty metric. As depicted earlier, customers give assessments and communicate about their CXs to a broad network of consumers. Mobile technology has also enabled the spread of online (e-)WOM immediately when CXs occur in the B&M sevicescape. The recommendation systems are an excellent example to illustrate how aggregated customer choices and preferences can be used to generate customer value and encourage reinforcement. This data is captured across a large number of consumers sharing their likes and dislikes and used as a marketing tool to support targeted product recommendations and e-mail campaigns (Kunz et al., 2017). For instance, despite having higher prices when compared to Half.com, Amazon.com performed better and the customer review platform was one of the differentiating factors between these two retailers. According to the chief executive and founder of Amazon, Jeffrey P. Bezos in his letter to the company's shareholders in 1997: 'Word of mouth remains the most powerful customer acquisition tool we have, and we are grateful for the trust our customers have placed in us. Repeat purchases and word of mouth have combined to make Amazon.com the market leader in online bookselling.'

## Future research

This study has some limitations that present opportunities for further research. First, the use of cross-sectional survey data limits the causal interpretations drawn. Cross-sectional studies merely examine associations between the factors and not causation. Future research should thus take up longitudinal studies, conduct experiments, and/or combine together actual behavioural data (i.e. purchasing data) to tease out these potential effects. The major challenges of this type of study are not only tracking customers by the click-stream and loyalty card purchase data and combining these separate data sets, researchers must also record the steps at various touchpoints, such as in-store and window shopping. Thus, there is a measurement gap regarding non-transactional behaviour between the digital and physical channels. Innovative adaptation of multiple metrics, technologies, and incentives for customers to provide data might help draw a more detailed picture of the customer's journey in the future. Second, the chapter studied omni-channel CX in specialty retail in Finland. To further understand CX formation, the effects of contextual factors could be examined, such as differences between industries and cultures.

Finally, Chapters 5 and 6 of this book examined consumers' experiences of retailers that pursue to provide omni-channel CX in some extent. Although many retailers practice retailing through multiple channels, there is still a limited number of successful omni-channel retail service concepts in which the retailer provides a seamless CX across the digital and physical servicescapes. Especially, the evidence is scant regarding how profitably retailers have utilized the digital and physical channels simultaneously, such as by enhancing service CXs with in-store technologies. This may be due to the fact that still a significant minority (11–22 per cent) of consumers use tablets and smartphones at all stages of the buying process (Treadgold & Reynolds, 2020).

# References

Andrade, E. B., Kaltcheva, V., & Weitz, B., 2002. 'Self-disclosure on the web: the impact of privacy policy, reward, and company reputation'. *Advances in Consumer Research*, 29, 350–353.

Autio, M. & Heinonen, V., 2004. 'To consume or not to consume? Young people's environmentalism in the affluent Finnish society'. *YOUNG*, 12(2), 137–153.

Ballantyne, D. & Nilsson, E., 2017. 'All that is solid melts into air: the servicescape in digital service space'. *Journal of Services Marketing*, 31(3), 226–235.

Bellini, S., Cardinali, M. G., & Ziliani, C., 2011. 'Building customer loyalty in retailing: not all levers are created equal'. *The International Review of Retail, Distribution and Consumer Research*, 21(5), 461–481.

Bitner, M., 1992. 'Servicescapes: the impact of physical surroundings on customers and employees'. *Journal of Marketing*, 56(2), 57–71.

Carroll, L. 1871. *Through the Looking-Glass*. New York: Macmillan Publishers Ltd.

Chandon, P., Morwitz, V. G., & Reinartz, W. J., 2005. 'Do intentions really predict behavior? Self-generated validity effects in survey research'. *Journal of Marketing*, 69(2), 1–14.

De Keyser, A., Lemon, K. N., Klaus, P., & Keiningham, T. L., 2015. *A framework for understanding and managing the customer experience*. MSI, 15–121.

De Wulf, K., Odekerken-Schröder, G., & Iacobucci, D., 2001. 'Investments in consumer relationships: a cross-country and cross-industry exploration'. *Journal of Marketing*, 65(4), 33–50.

Dinev, T. & Hart, P., 2006. 'An extended privacy calculus model for e-commerce transactions'. *Information Systems Research*, 17(1), 61–80.

Du, R. Y., Kamakura, W. A., & Mela, C. F., 2007. 'Size and share of customer wallet'. *Journal of Marketing*, 71(2), 94–113.

Econsultancy, 2018. 'Digital Intelligence Briefing: 2018 Digital Trends'. Report by Adobe. Retrieved on 3 February 2020 from https://econsultancy.com/reports/digital-intelligence-briefing-2018-digital-trends-in-financial-services/

Edvardsson, B., 2005. 'Service quality: beyond cognitive assessment'. *Journal of Service Theory and Practice*, 15(2), 127–131.

Fan, Y-W. & Miao, Y-F., 2012. 'Effect of electronic word-of-mouth on consumer purchase intention: the perspective of gender differences'. *International Journal of Electronic Business Management*, 10(3), 175–181.

Frow, P. & Payne, A. J., 2007. 'Towards the "perfect" customer experience'. *Journal of Brand Management*, 15(2), 89–101.

Gefen, D. & Ridings, C., 2005. 'If you spoke as she does, sir, instead of the way you do: a sociolinguistics perspective of gender differences in virtual communities'. *The DATA BASE for Advances in Information Systems*, 36(2), 78–92.

Hennig-Thurau, T., Gwinner, K. P., Walsh, G., & Gremler, D. D., 2004. 'Electronic word-of-mouth via consumer-opinion platforms: what motivates consumers to articulate themselves on the Internet?' *Journal of Interactive Marketing*, 18(1), 38–52.

Henseler, J., Dijkstra, T. K., Sarstedt, M., Ringle, C. M., Diamantopoulos, A., et al., 2014. 'Common beliefs and reality about PLS: comments on Rönkkö and Evermann (2013)'. *Organizational Research Methods*, 17(2), 182–209.

Herhausen, D., Binder, J., Schoegela, M., & Herrmann, A. 2015. Integrating bricks with clicks: Retailer-level and channel-level outcomes of online– offline channel integration. *Journal of Retailing*, 91(2), 309–325.

Jiang, K., Xu, L., & Bao, X., 2015. 'The impact of channel integration on channel reciprocity in the multichannel retail context'. Proceedings on international conference on industrial engineering and engineering management, 1840–1844.

Keiningham, T., Ball, J., Benoit, S., Bruce, H. L., Buoye, A., et al., 2017. 'The interplay of customer experience and commitment'. *Journal of Services Marketing*, 31(2), 148–160.

Kumar, V., Pozza, I., & Ganesh, J., 2013. 'Revisiting the satisfaction–loyalty relationship: empirical generalizations and directions for future research'. *Journal of Retailing*, 89(3), 246–262.

Kumar, V. & Venkatesan, R., 2005. 'Who are the multichannel shoppers and how do they perform? Correlates of multichannel shopping behavior'. *Journal of Interactive Marketing*, 19(2), 44–62.

Kunz, W., Aksoy, L., Bart, Y., Heinonen, K., Kabadayi, S., et al., 2017. 'Customer engagement in a big data world'. *Journal of Services Marketing*, 31(2), 161–171.

Laufer, R. S. & Wolfe, M., 1977. 'Privacy as a concept and a social issue: a multidimensional developmental theory'. *Journal of Social Issues*, 33, 22–42.

Lemon, K. N. & Verhoef, P. C., 2016. 'Understanding customer experience throughout the customer journey'. Journal of Marketing, 80(AMA/MSI Special Issue), 69–96.

Leppäniemi, M., Karjaluoto, H., & Saarijärvi, H., 2017. 'Customer perceived value, satisfaction, and loyalty: the role of willingness to share information'. *The International Review of Retail, Distribution and Consumer Research*, 27(2), 164–188.

Lindell, M. K. & Whitney, D. J., 2001. 'Accounting for common method variance in cross-sectional research designs'. *Journal of Applied Psychology*, 86(1), 114–121.

Malhotra, N. K., Kim, S. S., & Patil, A., 2006. 'Common method variance in IS research: a comparison of alternative approaches and a reanalysis of past research'. *Management Science*, 52(12), 1865–1883.

Mascarenhas, O., Kesavan, R., & Bernacchi, M., 2006. 'Lasting customer loyalty: a total customer experience approach'. *Journal of Consumer Marketing*, 23(7), 397–405.

Metzger, M. J., 2004. 'Privacy, trust, and disclosure: exploring barriers to electronic commerce'. *Journal of Computer-Mediated Communication*, 9(4), JCMC942.

Metzger, M. J., 2006. 'Effects of site, vendor, and consumer characteristics on web site trust and disclosure'. *Communication Research*, 33(3), 155–179.

Neslin, S. A. & Shankar, V., 2009. 'Key issues in multichannel customer management: current knowledge and future directions'. *Journal of Interactive Marketing*, 23, 70–81.

Official Statistics of Finland, 2019a. Retrieved on 3 February 2020 from https://www.stat.fi/til/sutivi/2019/sutivi_2019_2019-11-07_kat_001_fi.html

Official Statistics of Finland, 2019b. Retrieved on 3 February 2020 from https://www.stat.fi/til/sutivi/2019/sutivi_2019_2019-11-07_kat_003_fi.html

Oliver, R. L., 1997. 'Whence consumer loyalty?' *Journal of Marketing*, 36, 33–44.

Palmatier, R. W., Dant, R. P., Grewal, D., & Evans, K. R., 2006. 'Factors influencing the effectiveness of relationship marketing: a meta-analysis'. *Journal of Marketing*, 70(4), 136–153.

Phelps, J., Nowak, G., & Ferrell, E., 2000. 'Privacy concerns and consumer willingness to provide personal information'. *Journal of Public Policy & Marketing*, 19(1), 27–41.

Piotrowicz, W. & Cuthbertson, R., 2014. 'Introduction to the special issue information technology in retail: toward omnichannel retailing'. *International Journal of Electronic Commerce*, 18(4), 5–16.

Reichheld F. F. 2003. The one number you need to know. Harvard Business Review 81(12), 46–55.

Retail Supply Chain Insights, 2016, September 19. 2017 'IRT Retailer Innovation awards'. Retrieved on 3 February 2020 from https://www.retailsupplychaininsights.com/doc/retailer-innovation-awards-0001

Rigby, D., 2011. 'The future of shopping'. *Harvard Business Review*, 89, 64–75.

Rose, S., Hair, N., & Clark, M., 2011. 'Online customer experience: a review of the business-to-consumer online purchase context'. *International Journal of Management Reviews*, 13, 24–39.

Schoenbachler, D. D. & Gordon, G. L., 2002. 'Trust and customer willingness to provide information in database-driven relationship marketing'. *Journal of Interactive Marketing*, 16(3), 2–16.

Schramm-Klein, H., Wagner, G., Steinmann, S., & Morschett, D., 2011. 'Cross-channel integration—is it valued by customers?' *The International Review of Retail, Distribution and Consumer Research*, 21(5), 501–511.

Schwarz, N., 2000. 'Emotion, cognition, and decision making'. *Cognition and Emotion*, 14(4), 433–440.

Shiv, B. & Fedorikhin, A., 1999. 'Heart and mind in conflict: the interplay of affect and cognition in consumer decision making'. *Journal of Consumer Research*, 26(3), 278–292.

Srinivasan, S., Anderson, R., & Ponnavolu, K., 2002. 'Customer loyalty in e-commerce: an exploration of its antecedents and consequences'. *Journal of Retailing*, 78, 41–50.

Szmigin, I. & Bourne, H., 1998. 'Consumer equity in relationship marketing'. *Journal of Consumer Marketing*, 15(6), 544–557.

Treadgold, A. & Reynolds, J., 2020. *Navigating the new retail landscape–a guide for business leaders*. Oxford University Press.

Venkatesh, V., Morris, M. G., Davis, G. B., & Davis, F. D., 2003. 'User acceptance of information technology: toward a unified view'. *MIS Quarterly*, 27(3), 425–478.

Verhagen, T. & van Dolen, W., 2009. 'Online purchase intentions: a multi-channel store image perspective'. *Information & Management*, 46, 77–82.

Verhoef, P. C., Kannan, P. K., & Inman, J. J., 2015. 'From multi-channel retailing to omni-channel retailing'. *Journal of Retailing*, 91(2), 174–181.

Voss, C. A. 2003. Rethinking paradigms of service: Service in a virtual environment. International Journal of Operations & Production Management, 23(1), 88–104.

Wallace, D. W., Giese, J. L., & Johnson, J. L., 2004. 'Customer retailer loyalty in the context of multiple channel strategies'. *Journal of Retailing*, 80(4), 249–263.

Wilska, T-A., 2002. 'Me—a consumer? Consumption, identities and lifestyles in today's Finland'. *Acta Sociologica*, 45, 196–210.

Xu, C., Peak, D., & Prybutok, V., 2015. 'A customer value, satisfaction, and loyalty perspective of mobile application recommendations'. *Decision Support Systems*, 79, 171–183.

Zeithaml, V. A. & Berry, L. L., 1996. 'The behavioral consequences of service quality'. *Journal of Marketing*, 60, 31–46.

# Appendix

Measurement and scales

| Constructs/Items | Alphas | Weights |
|---|---|---|
| Satisfaction toward e-store social interaction (adapted from Verhagen & van Dolen, 2009) | .75 | |
| Customer service is available in the online store of this specific retail chain (e.g. via either chat application, telephone, or e-mail). | | .86 |
| Customer service representatives are friendly in the online store of this specific retail chain. | | .86 |
| I can either share my experiences or read about other customers' experiences in the online store of this specific retail chain (e.g. either using the comment box or social media platform). | | .73 |
| Satisfaction toward the e-store service environment (adapted from Verhagen & van Dolen, 2009) | .89 | |
| The online store of this specific retail chain looks up-to-date (e.g. the website is updated frequently). | | .94 |
| It is appealing to visit the online store of this specific retail chain (e.g. colour schemes, music, audio-visual elements). | | .91 |
| It is easy to find what I am looking for in the online store of this specific retail chain (e.g. search function, navigation). | | .88 |
| Satisfaction toward B&M store social interaction (adapted from Verhagen & van Dolen, 2009) | .93 | |
| Personal customer service is available in the brick-and-mortar stores of this specific retail chain. | | .89 |
| Customer service representatives are friendly in the brick-and-mortar stores of this specific retail chain. | | .92 |
| Customer service representatives have expertise in the brick-and-mortar stores of this specific retail chain. | | .90 |
| I can rely on the customer service personnel of this specific retail chain to give me accurate information (e.g. about product details, guarantee terms). | | .90 |
| Satisfaction toward B&M store service environment (adapted from Verhagen & van Dolen, 2009) | .91 | |
| The brick-and-mortar stores of this specific retail chain are comfortable (e.g. decoration, lighting, music, scents). | | .90 |
| The brick-and-mortar stores of this specific retail chain are well maintained (e.g. up-to-date store decoration). | | .93 |
| The products are displayed in an intriguing way in the brick-and-mortar stores of this specific retail chain (e.g. the products reach the eye, and I can obtain ideas of how to use them). | | .92 |
| Evaluation of cognitive and sensory service experience (adapted from Voss et al., 2003) | .89 | |

*Continued*

| Constructs/Items | Alphas | Weights |
|---|---|---|
| When I visit the online and brick-and-mortar stores of this specific retail chain, I get inspiration and new ideas (e.g. store window displays, product displays, tips from personnel). | | .90 |
| Visiting the online and brick-and-mortar stores of this specific retail chain piques my curiosity and creates a thirst for knowledge (e.g. I want to try new products and services). | | .93 |
| It is nice to test products in both the online and brick-and-mortar stores of this specific retail chain (e.g. offline product demonstrations or using an application in the online store). | | .98 |
| Evaluation of emotional and social service experience (adapted from Voss et al., 2003) | .92 | |
| I become carefree while visiting the online and brick-and-mortar stores of this specific retail chain (e.g. reliance on the quality of merchandise, data privacy, and security matters). | | .90 |
| I feel relaxed while visiting the online and brick-and-mortar stores of this specific retail chain (e.g. proficient customer service, functioning product delivery and returns). | | .89 |
| I am looked after while visiting the online and brick-and-mortar stores of this specific retail chain. | | .87 |
| I feel welcome while visiting the online and brick-and-mortar stores of this specific retail chain. | | .92 |
| SOW in the e-store (adapted from De Wulf, Odekerken-Schröder, & Iacobucci, 2001) | .81 | |
| Estimate the share (%) of your expenditure in a certain product category in the online store of this specific retail chain. | | .87 |
| When you consider your last 10 purchases, how many were made in the online store of this specific retail chain? | | .82 |
| I usually purchase specialty goods from the online store of this specific retail chain. | | .84 |
| SOW in the B&M store (adapted from De Wulf, Odekerken-Schröder, & Iacobucci, 2001) | .83 | |
| Estimate the share (%) of your expenditure in a certain product category in the offline store of this specific retail chain. | | .88 |
| When you consider your last 10 purchases, how many were made in the offline store of this specific retail chain? | | .83 |
| I usually purchase specialty goods from the offline store of this specific retail chain. | | .87 |
| WOM of the e-store (adapted from Reichheld, 2003; Zeithaml et al., 1996) | .87 | |
| I often say positive things about the online store of this specific retail chain to people that I know and/or post them on social media. | | .87 |
| I enjoy telling people that I know and/or posting on social media that I visit the online store of this specific retail chain. | | .89 |
| I would recommend the online store of this specific retail chain to the people that I know and/or post about it on social media. | | .92 |
| WOM of the B&M store (adapted from Reichheld, 2003; Zeithaml et al., 1996) | .91 | |

| Constructs/Items | Alphas | Weights |
|---|---|---|
| I often say positive things about the brick-and-mortar stores of this specific retail chain to the people that I know and/or post them on social media. | | .85 |
| I enjoy telling the people that I know and/or posting on social media that I visit the brick-and-mortar stores of this specific retail chain. | | .93 |
| I would recommend the brick-and-mortar stores of this specific retail chain to the people that I know and/or post about it on social media. | | .94 |
| Evaluation of perceived channel integration (adapted from Schramm-Klein et al., 2011) | .79 | |
| I can pick up my purchases from the online store of this specific retail chain from its brick-and-mortar stores and return in-store purchases via mail. | | .77 |
| The online store and brick-and-mortar stores of this specific retail chain complete each other. | | .86 |
| The online store and brick-and-mortar stores of this specific retail chain are aware of each other (e.g. in terms of selection, special offers, service). | | .88 |
| WSI (adapted from Schoenbachler & Gordon, 2002) | n/a | |
| I am willing to provide this company with personal information in exchange for personalized service both in the online store and at the brick-and-mortar stores of this specific retailer. | | n/a |

*Notes:* Respondents evaluated these 37 statements on a 7-point Likert-type scale (1=strongly disagree to 7=strongly agree).

# 7

# Implementing Strategies to Win the Red Queen Retail Race

*Lauri Paavola*

## Introduction

In today's retail business environment, organizations are confronted not only with unexpected events and crises from which they need to recover but also with continuous adversity that forces them to adapt and transform. Thus, it is crucial for every organization to support the development of capabilities and routines in order to enhance resilience, while at the same time remembering and restoring their ability to run their core business.

As a result, organizations—small and agile ones in particular—have started to transform step by step, from traditional functional siloed organizations into modular ones with loose alliances of autonomous and multi-disciplinary teams (Sahaym, Steesma, & Schilling, 2007). This structural change, which is often aimed at supporting organizational resilience through faster self-organizing (e.g. Stephan & Huysentruyt, 2016), has already started to disrupt a very large number of commercial organizations, and it will also slowly start reaching the less agile ones in our societies—the ones that have traditionally been characterized as stagnant and routinized. Large organizations that operate under a variety of governance structures—including the traditional large retail chains and cooperatives—will also be pressed over the next decades to analyse new information faster, respond more quickly, make better decisions, and coordinate change better—in brief, to perform more resiliently.

However, not all of these large organizations can go through a major transformation in which their entire hierarchies are reshaped. Nor can their vast number of processes or routines be constantly coordinated or redesigned top-down according to a rapidly changing operating environment. Instead, governing bodies must use their existing governance structures to regulate the organizations while simultaneously encouraging rather than discouraging decentralized initiative to solve the surrounding challenges. The ability to respond quickly to societal challenges and innovation opportunities is expected to become a hallmark of effective management in the following decades.

Lauri Paavola, *Implementing Strategies to Win the Red Queen Retail Race*. In: *The Red Queen Retail Race*.
Edited by Richard Cuthbertson, Olli Rusanen, and Lauri Paavola, Oxford University Press.
© Lauri Paavola (2023). DOI: 10.1093/oso/9780192862617.003.0007

In this chapter, we will use a case from the Finnish retail sector to illustrate how a very large cooperative organization, strongly characterized by routinized and stable structures, went through a major turnaround in its resilience with the help of a few central managerial decisions that supported its internal adaptation rather than through an externally led redesign. We conduct a longitudinal research study and illustrate how the turnaround was initiated by the management, which steered routine dynamics through controlling the internal pressures within the organizational structure without redesigning or changing the processes externally. We highlight that managing routines involves effortful enactment and recreation, rather than just straightforward reproduction or replication (Feldman et al., 2016).

## Background

Since there is no existing literature on role of routines in organizational resilience, my following review seeks to combine these two distinct streams of literature: the literature on resilience and literature on routines.

## Organizational resilience: notions and perspectives

Early studies on organizational resilience defined the concept as a resistance or defensive action in the face of adverse situations and external threats, such as financial crises or natural disasters, as well as the recovery from such crises to the normal state or at least an acceptable level of functioning (Horne & Orr, 1998; Robert, 2010). Some scholars have included the notion of anticipating future crises as part of the definition (e.g. Kendra & Wachtendorf, 2003; Somers, 2009). Other definitions go beyond the notion of merely restoring functionality and include an organization's ability to proactively adapt, transform, and develop organizational processes and capabilities after a crisis, or in anticipation of one (Lengnick-Hall, Beck, & Lengnick-Hall, 2011; Somers, 2009).

Recently, research on the concept of resilience has shifted from considerations of an organization's ability to deal with a particular crisis to how an organization continually manages to thrive in the face of adversity (Sutcliffe & Vogus, 2003). According to Sutcliffe and Vogus (2003: 104), the resilience of an organization relies on processes that 'promote competence, restore efficacy, and encourage growth'. Consequently, attempts have been made to gain a deeper micro-level understanding of organizational resilience as an iterative, adaptive process, in which desired outcomes are achieved by means of efficient use of resources (Burnard & Bhamra, 2011; Linnenluecke & Griffiths, 2012).

Due to the interpretation of resilience as an iterative process, it is natural to understand it by means of organizational capabilities and routines. Indeed, several authors have considered the concept of resilience capabilities (Lengnick-Hall & Beck, 2005; Lengnick-Hall, Beck, & Lengnick-Hall, 2011; Ortiz-de-Mandojana & Bansal, 2016); it should be noted that the terminology in the area is rather diverse and heterogeneous, and also notions such as resilience capacity and resilience potential have been employed (Duchek, 2014). According to Lengnick-Hall and Beck (2005) and Lengnick-Hall, Beck, and Lengnick-Hall (2011), an organization's resilience capacity results from its ability to deal with uncertainty and complexity by means of organizational routines.

## Organizational routines: a source of organizational resilience

Failures in enhancing resilience are common, particularly in organizations characterized by stable and routinized processes. It is often claimed that artefacts that are designed to promote new processes often fail to do so (Ohly, Sonnentag, & Plunke, 2006; Pentland & Feldman, 2008). 'It is easy to design artifacts or templates like a chart of accounts, a list of database codes, input forms, checklists, and so on. But these artifacts – no matter how carefully designed – do not necessarily result in changes in the patterns of action' (Pentland & Feldman, 2008: 240). When a process does not produce the intended performances, it is often replaced, which again creates costs and amounts to inefficiencies.

Such problems are prevalent not only in the arena of resilience but are more broadly discussed in the research on routine dynamics (Becker, 2004; Howard-Grenville, 2005; Naduzzo, Rocco, & Warglien, 2000). The significant effort required to transfer or recreate the performance of an organizational routine— to keep the routine alive—has been very recently discussed by D'Adderio (2014), Aldrich and Yang (2014), Danner-Schröder and Geiger (2016), and Cohendet and Simon (2016).

'Live routines are best conceptualized as generative systems that can produce a wide variety of performances depending on the circumstances' (Pentland & Feldman, 2008). The repetitive nature of routines helps organizations coordinate their processes by allowing them to establish an abstract sequence of activities to be performed and by enabling various actors within an organization to observe the progress on the task (Feldman, 2000; Okhuysen & Bechky, 2008). These abstract aspects of routines are referred to as 'ostensive' aspects (Feldman, 2000; Howard-Grenville, 2005), sometimes also as 'dispositions' (e.g. Becker, 2004). The ostensive aspects consist of the shared understandings (embodied as well as cognitive) of the participants, and they can vary across the organization (Feldman, 2000; Feldman et al., 2016; Pentland & Feldman, 2008).

'On the other hand, routines also consist of actual performances by specific people, at specific times, in specific places' (Pentland & Feldman, 2008). We refer to these as the 'performative' aspects (Feldman et al., 2016; Pentland & Feldman,

2008). The ostensive and performative aspects are mutually constitutive; whereas the ostensive aspect enables people to guide, account for, and refer to specific performances of a routine, the performative aspect creates, maintains, and modifies the ostensive aspect of the routine (Feldman & Pentland, 2003). This ostensive-performative mechanism creates the source of the internal adaptation of routines; without these two aspects, the recognizable, repetitive patterns of action that characterize organizational routines cannot be produced or reproduced (Pentland & Feldman, 2008).

## Creating resilience through the management of routines

Whereas the literature on routines is very much focused on routine dynamics and internal adaptation, the literature that considers their management often emphasizes processes that link the change to external sources. Management literature typically offers tools such as redesign, continuous assessment, and replacement to keep the routines alive (Pentland & Feldman, 2008). Such constant transformation is supported by the notion that by understanding its routines an organization can identify its successful operating patterns (Eisenhardt & Martin, 2000; Paavola & Cuthbertson, 2021).

Past research shows that managers can influence employee behaviour (Robertson & Barling, 2013). Investigating action can therefore shed light on the origins of organizational routines and their evolutionary dynamics over time, especially at the individual or micro-foundational level (Bryant, 2014; Felin & Foss, 2009; Winter, 2003). For example, according to Khazanchi and Masterson (2011), trust and social exchange in relationships and behaviours can affect creativity, which, in turn, may play an important role in supporting the adaptation of the performative aspects of routines. There exists a wide range of literature on in-depth research on entrepreneurship related to micro-level factors such as emotions (Antonakis, Ashkanasy, & Dasborough, 2009; Ashkanasy & Daus, 2005; Solinger et al., 2013), organizational culture (Bertels, Howard-Grenville, & Pek, 2016), satisfaction (Baba & Jamal, 1991; Liu, Rovine, & Molenaar, 2012), team climate (Zohar & Hofmann, 2012), and values (Lazaric, 2011), which can contribute significantly to resilience in a micro-foundations context.

## A longitudinal case study: S-Group

In this chapter, we seek to illustrate how skills, personal competencies, and behaviours that managers apply may influence the dynamics behind organizational group-level behaviour. We aim to understand how and why the dynamics in our example case evolved and changed over time, how employees reacted to these changes, and how organizational-level trajectories appeared and disappeared over time.

Our research is a longitudinal process study of the turnaround of S-Group, a large Finnish cooperative retailer consisting of a central organization, SOK, and regional cooperatives around Finland. The turnaround took place in the time period ranging from the early 1970s to the mid-1990s. Due to the longitudinal nature of the research, it is primarily founded on archival data and documents produced over the course of the aforementioned time period. Archival data is particularly suitable for longitudinal process analyses where the past development of an entity over a long time period is observed (Langley, 1999; Langley et al., 2013).

After analysing the public and archival data, we constructed a chronology of the development. To verify our results, we conducted interviews with key middle and top management figures and discussed our findings. All data was triangulated from a minimum of three independent sources. For example, the interview data was verified from the company's annual reports and archival sources.

Since we are interested in the patterns of actions brought about by a routine, statistical methods are not suitable. Instead, as recommended by Pentland, Hœrem, and Hillison (2014), we analysed a large amount of data and interviewed key figures to develop an ostensive understanding of how the analysed routines typically worked. Accordingly, our methodology is a qualitative one.

## Public data

Over the course of the entire research process, we actively studied publicly available material on SOK. This provided us with basic knowledge of the key events, a list of potential interviewees, and a preliminary understanding of the operating environment of the company. This data included all the annual reports from 1970 to 2002, as well as several books written about the company, including, for example, one on the 100-year history of SOK published in 2004.

## Archival data

As stated earlier, our research is primarily founded on archival data. We were granted access to the SOK archives and the vast collection of all past top management minutes, quantitative graphs, and numerical figures describing the state of the company, a plenitude of text documents, memorandums, transcripts of meetings, copies of old contracts, photographs, and a large amount of former CEOs' handwritten notes. The archival data provided us with a temporal insight into the decisions, mindsets, and challenges that arose during the turnaround of SOK. In addition to this data, we also had access to 86 autobiographical accounts from retired middle and top managers of their time at SOK.

## Informants

A total of 28 in-depth interviews with 25 different respondents were organized in order to verify our understanding of the changes that took place at SOK. While interviews are an efficient way to gather empirical data on unique events, the data so obtained may contradict with a longitudinal research approach. To avoid this problem, one should compare the information given by several knowledgeable informants (Eisenhardt & Graebner, 2007). Accordingly, once we had completed the interviews, we compared them, and in cases of contradiction, we sent the transcribed interviews back to the respondents for further clarification. Additionally, in order to achieve maximum accuracy and legitimacy, archival data was repeatedly consulted during the interviews.

The informants included all the living former CEOs from the 1980s onwards as well as the current CEO. We also interviewed the majority of individuals who had been board members and in other leading top management positions during this time period. Hence, most of our respondents had taken part in implementing strategic decisions regarding the analysed turnaround and had observed its development for more than 20 years. The selection of respondents was iterative, since the interviews also provided further information on central decision-makers throughout the interview process. Eventually no further names emerged, and at this point we concluded that a level of saturation had been reached (Glaser & Strauss, 1967). The interviews were semi-structured, with a duration of 60–250 minutes. All interviews were taped, transcribed verbatim, and analysed. The interviews were conducted and transcribed in Finnish, the native language of the respondents.

## Turnaround of SOK

The S-Group, a cooperative society, was founded in 1904 in order to handle the coordination of the cooperative-owned retail store network in Finland. It is comprised of the central organization SOK and regional cooperatives across the country with a large portfolio of businesses also outside of retail. Despite the S-group's diversified business ranging from grocery retail to manufacturing as well as a strong network of cooperatives around the country, it was well known to all stakeholders by the early 1980s that the cooperative was in a poor condition and lacked a clear strategic future direction. The data from our research points out that over the years the company had become very bureaucratic, like a public organization, and it had a relatively large workforce in service of the central organization, despite the central organization being owned by the cooperatives and in practice having only an administrative role, for example, in the centralized purchasing of goods for the cooperatives. At the same time, the company archives and interviewees point out that due to the bureaucracy and public organization-like structure, employees had a low motivation to develop their way of working.

> It was a great, idle machine. A really nice damn machine, everything was in place. It was sort of like a 1986 Ferrari sitting in the garage all cleaned up, polished, shining, ready to be fired up, admired. You can't say this about the stores, they were in poor condition, and in fact the headquarters was not a pleasurable experience either. Before I came here, some newspaper wrote that it is like an office in the Eastern Bloc, with poorly lit hallways, thick doors to every room—and everyone had their own rooms, a lot of rooms.
>
> —Former CEO

In the 1970s, SOK's strategy was developed based on ideologically shaped routines, as the administrative council, the de facto decision-making body, consisted mainly of members from the countryside who saw that SOK should continue its presence in the agricultural sector rather than developing other areas of the business. As a result, it had become a very stagnant and non-sustainable organization.

While the central organization, SOK, had skilled and talented employees in place, they did not have the incentives or motivation to take action or develop the business. Moreover, the cooperatives were only a small player in the grocery sector, and their managers had a low incentive to turn the grocery business around, as they did not view being a manager in the grocery business as a high-profile or respected job in the S-Group.

> When I think about the profile of the company, when I came here I was surprised by how good systems there were. Many of the systems were in really good condition. Really skilled employees. And how pleasant their demeanour—but some kind of edge that they have in the competitive world, was missing from there— they had their shirts tucked straight, they talked in a really civilized manner and for long. But the decision-making, and the implementation that would help get them into motion, was missing.
>
> —Former CEO

Even though the so-called Total Plan of 1970 called for cooperatives to be diverse customer-serving, competitive, and financially efficient working companies, in practice not much changed. While the central organization SOK had a talented, young workforce that was mainly in charge of devising the Total Plan in the 1970s, it was the regional cooperatives that resisted change and prevented the enactment of the proposed plan. The main problem was that the S-Group was very diversified, with the regional cooperatives also owning many of their own manufacturing plants across the country, which meant that there was no unified vision or interest to build capabilities for the future. At the same time, there was a lack of business knowledge in SOK's administrative council, where the farmers and other non-business people had very little knowledge or skills to develop a sustainable business.

By the end of the 1970s, the general mood at SOK was that the current business model and strategic direction could not be continued, as a majority of the cooperatives were making substantial losses. The situation became so severe that SOK's accountants proclaimed at the height of the crisis that only a few of the loss-making quarters could be saved from bankruptcy. For example, in 1977, 112 out of the overall 217 cooperatives were making losses, even though a large number of employees had been laid off during the year and several emergency measures implemented across the organization.

Based on the collected data, the primary reason for the financial difficulties was the so-called 'automatic funding mechanism', that is internal monopoly in which the central organization balanced out the losses of regional cooperatives from the surplus it was making from its purchasing divisions (Figure 7.1). In practice, SOK would channel part of the profits it made to the cooperatives in order to balance out their books, and in the end guarantee the existence of certain cooperatives that could not survive on their own. The automatic funding mechanism thus served as an extra discount for purchases the cooperatives made from the central organization's purchase unit. This led to a routine where the cooperatives expected that each year the central organization would come to their rescue, as it had previously done, if they were not able to turn a profit by the end of the accounting year.

As a result of the financial difficulties of the S-Group, which were well known to the Finnish financial institutions, the cooperatives were paying a significant premium (around 12–14 per cent) for their bank loans. The situation had become so bad that many CEOs of the regional cooperatives had to personally negotiate with financiers to secure loans. Even though the CEOs of the regional cooperatives acknowledged the situation, they did not know what action to take, and in

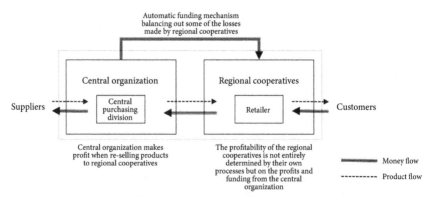

**Figure 7.1** Automatic funding mechanism at SOK

some cases where they did, they did not have the required skills to implement the changes. At the same time, the most severely struggling cooperatives believed that the central organization actually had a lot of hidden assets and that it was not truly struggling. At this rate, the retailers' business model was not sustainable, and reforms were needed in order to wake up the organization and its stakeholders.

As the administrative council did not have the necessary business skills to turn around the company, in 1983 they appointed an external CEO, the first in SOK's history. The new CEO was in charge of turning around the entire S-Group and devising a strategic plan for the future. The new CEO initiated the so-called 'S83' plan, aimed at restructuring the organization. The plan was unanimously accepted by the administrative council and unveiled to the representatives of the regional cooperatives at a large event in the summer of 1983. This strategic plan served as a wake-up call for the entire organization and included three key initiatives:

1. **Restructuring of the cooperatives**. The S83 plan called for the establishment of 36 regional cooperatives to replace the previous structure with 177 cooperatives spread around the country. As a result, some smaller cooperatives had to merge.
2. **Financial autonomy and renewal of the internal accounting system**. The S83 ended, in practice, the 'automatic funding system' and 'internal monopoly' that had been in place, as the creation of larger regional cooperatives meant that SOK would no longer continue to be accountable for the losses of smaller cooperatives that most likely could not survive independently.
3. **Focus on grocery retail**. A central vision was to once again focus on grocery retail as the flagship industry, in order to earn the trust of customers through investments in the store network that had become unappealing and outdated over the years.

When the S83 plan was presented to the cooperatives, it was first met with silence. Many of the representatives expected that the central organization had assets in place that would enable continued funding of the cooperatives, but this was not the case. Members of the cooperatives also stated that the CEO of SOK could not and should not dictate what the cooperatives ought to do to improve their situation. The situation was so tense that some of the cooperative CEOs broke into tears, feeling that their work was not appreciated by SOK.

While in the administrative council the S83 plan received unanimous support and praise, in the field, that is at the cooperatives, the plan faced a lot of opposition, as the cooperative administrative council members did not want to see the position of their own cooperative jeopardized by the reforms. When someone in the audience asked to speak at the unveiling of the S83 plan, the CEO immediately interrupted them by saying that this was a press conference and not a discussion, as described by several of our informants. Naturally the new regional cooperatives into which the smaller cooperatives were forced to merge took the news positively, as these larger cooperatives saw that they would grow as a result and have a future, unlike the smaller cooperatives whose CEOs would most likely be ousted from their jobs. At any rate, eventually the plan went forward, and despite some cooperatives opting out from the mergers, the vast majority of regional cooperatives were formed according to the plan by the end of the 1980s. While 1984 and 1985 were still extremely bad years due to the costs related to the restructuring such as write-offs from property or machinery, from 1986 onwards the financial situation also started to improve slowly.

> It is a weird machine, this S-Group. In practice, the CEO does not have any power over the cooperatives, which are completely independent. In that time [the CEO] ... said that it is quite remarkable that when in a shipping company the company decides what port to go to to load the ship, and where to take the shipment, and then the captain decides how to get there – when all of this is done, in our case the crew then goes to the cargo hold and begins to consider whether we should depart for our destination at all. It was a lot of work, and there were numerous critics who said that [the CEO] can't control us, we do as we do.
>
> —Former board member

Initially, once the restructuring was put into motion, there was resistance and the old way of doing things continued in parts of the S-Group, especially in those cooperatives that were, for the first time in their history, having to substantially reshuffle their structure and way of working. One informant described that after the unveiling of the S83 plan the human resources department of the central organization was constantly on the road for the next few years, traveling across the country to lay off workers in the merging cooperatives. Even though there was some internal resistance, in practice the cooperatives were dependent on the central organization for funding, and as a result the restructuring moved forward, as the cooperatives really had no meaningful alternative.

> Then there was, for example, a problem – feels like it wasn't that great a problem but it was—in the head office, once they had practically agreed that the offices would be shut down completely when possible, they were first reduced and then shut down completely, but in the head office they had a lot of different kinds of consultants and advisors. They had marketing advisors in the food, hardware, textile, cashier, meat, and many other sectors. Then there would come a few key leaders from the cooperatives, it wasn't an acclamation per se but it was crucial that they just maintain the jobs that were crucial. You pay. The cooperative pays. You pay their salaries, SOK has nothing to do with them and doesn't need them. The most skilled employees found jobs, but there were people whom no

one wanted. Of course that created unemployment. But right there was this big divide between who is still needed, and those that are needed are hired by the cooperative and SOK will not pay at all, as they don't need them.

—Former cooperative CEO and board member.

One of the first and most important steps taken during the establishment of the new cooperatives was cutting back on staff, as the organization had grown a lot in the past decades and had thus become inefficient. Earlier the employees did not have a need to develop their capabilities, especially the ones without a business degree; yet the inefficient employees were retained, as roles were to be refilled only once employees retired or otherwise left the S-Group. Overall, the former structure of the cooperative was such that the group consisted of the central organization, the central organization's regional offices making purchases, regional cooperatives, and regional cooperative stores, which meant that there was a lot of overlap in functions, especially as SOK continued to pay for many of the positions, furthermore reducing the cooperatives' incentives for reducing inefficiencies. Thus, the structure was not sustainable, especially insofar as the S-Group's retail chains were not competitive in terms of price level. One of the interviewees stated that it was sad watching the key metric, the grocery retail market share, fall until the late 1980s, though then it slowly started to rise again, after the major transformations had been put into action. Absurdly, our data shows that despite the low interest in developing the grocery retail business in the 1970s and early 1980s, the grocery retail market share was the key metric reported across the organization. Overall, we found that in the mid-1980s, as a result of the establishment of the regional cooperative structure and the elimination of several inefficiencies such as the excessive organization size, everyone now had a clear role to play in the S-Group.

While previously the agricultural focus of the S-Group meant that many employees had an agricultural background, the employment policies of the cooperatives slowly changed, as the main focus now was doing business and growing with a clear strategic direction. As a result, more fresh business school graduates flooded to work for the retailer, and the overall leadership and management of the company became more professional. While the retailers had always had a trainee programme for fresh business school graduates, now these recent graduates also filled many of the top management positions in the central organization and the cooperatives. At the same time, the administrative council changed to consist only of members, that is CEOs, of the regional cooperatives. These changes to the composition of the administrative council were implemented through the late 1980s and early 1990s. This meant that the interests of the regional cooperatives would now be represented in the de facto decision-making body of the S-Group, and at the same time the administrative council would be fully professional, with many members also having an academic degree for example from a business school. For example, the chairman of the administrative council from 1991 and throughout the 1990s came from an academic background with a PhD in economics.

> In many different ways, the new concept of being a retailer was developed. Today it's called 'manager days'. For many years it was called 'retailer days', which was accepted around the cooperatives. For the store or business managers they always had their events in Helsinki, at Finlandia Hall, at such a venue that when they come there, they know that they are important invited guests. They always had speeches from the different divisions: grocery retail, hardware, marketing, and they talked about the future. Then they also had sessions in the cabinets, for example for the restaurant managers they had their own event—about what we have to do in the next couple of years and how do we grow the business. They had over 1,000 participants and we had never had this sort of events before. I argue that this created a kind of social cohesion and group spirit, as the supermarket managers would dress in a certain way with their own clothes for the parties, and all kinds of things like that. They still have these but that was a way to build group spirit and cooperation in the cooperative. I also know that in the administration it had a really big effect.
>
> —Former cooperative CEO, former board member

While hiring and management were important, a major part of the waking-up came through boosting the overall morale of the stakeholders, most importantly the employees. Up until this time, it was clear that employees of the S-Group did not have the same entrepreneurial spirit that existed in its competitor, the K Group, whose stores were run with a franchise-like business model, with entrepreneur retailers. As the employees of the S-Group were not entrepreneurs, they did not do a lot of extra outside their formal job description, while on the other hand the K Group stores were geared to offer customers superior service. As a result, the S-Group launched the 'retailer days' for its chain and unit managers across the country. The retailer days were held once a year for the hundreds of store managers of the retail business, who would come together and attend several sessions held by SOK's managers with their colleagues and learn more about current strategic issues. This helped especially to demonstrate that the cooperative was one big family rather than just a consortium of the regional cooperatives.

> [The education centre Jollas] has long traditions. With it we have wanted to ensure the practical know-how of the store managers, in order to help them fight off their competition. At first it was vocational education, but a little bit higher. But suddenly, or quite fast it turned out to be almost equivalent to a university – [it provided the participants with pretty much all the necessary skills and knowledge to work in the field of retailing]. There was a lot of general managerial education, strategy work, and also at some level, practical applications. The education took

two years. It started from scratch, you would work in the warehouse during the summer, then you had to be in the store at some point doing marketing. Then in the areal office of the central organization for half a year. It gave you a good view of the work in retail. It was an exceptionally good education. It is a retail field training, nowadays. I saw that [the education programme] should be renewed so that good education is the starting point, and then from there, as competitive managers as possible to the field to manage the stores or chains.

—Former CEO

Based on the collected data, in the 1980s the S-Group shifted the focus of its internal training and education programmes towards university students in order to gain skilled employees straight from business school. While previously the training programme consisted more of a vocational education for those interested in the retail business, since the early 1980s it started to consist of more strategic management-related education geared at developing future managers for several different functions at the S-Group. For example, one interviewee stated that even when the company was going through its worst crisis years in the early 1980s, it was considered wise to actively train new employees, as qualified managers would be needed once the business was successful again. The training and education programme also served as a moral boost, as employees saw that they had a clear path up the S-Group's hierarchy, towards top management positions. Over the years, the S-Group also cooperated with several foreign universities and executive education programmes in order to help further educate existing managers as well as stay on top of recent managerial trends.

In these administrative days in these big events they always rewarded one cooperative as the best – [the award] was formally given to the chairman of the administrative council and the CEO of the coop.

(Former cooperative CEO and board member)

While previously the cooperatives had more autonomy, as a result of the change in the organizational structure, more effort was put into standardizing managerial practices. For example, in the 1980s a managerial handbook was compiled for the CEOs and administrative council members of the regional cooperatives. The standardization of managerial practices created more transparency, as now all cooperatives were evaluated with the same criteria. At the same time, since the late 1980s and early 1990s each regional cooperative was ranked from the best to worst, with the ranking communicated to each cooperative. All of these activities made employees feel more connected to the cooperative and also increased internal competition, as now everyone was actively trying to increase the profitability of the group as well as their own cooperative. Now the pressure to develop and succeed came from the 30+ cooperatives and was not only dictated by SOK.

If we look at it positively, we had a strong administrative council, I mean a really strong administrative council... we had a leadership team that was very skilful. That created a really strong discussion culture, and also in some ways a small amount of tension, of course you can see that negatively, as there was a lot of discussion and different opinions. So decisions were thought out carefully, and then we would go forward on the path we decided together.

—Former CEO, former chairman of the administrative council

In terms of managerial practices, our data indicates that an important part of the retailers' success arose from a strong administrative council that helped the board in managing the group and in developing strategy. While in the 1970s and 1980s the administrative council consisted largely of non-business people, the new structure meant that there was a strong business sense among the top management team that allowed the administrative council to support the leadership team in the daily management of the S-Group, as they had complementary skills and a joint vision for the future. This meant that decisions were discussed together and the future was mapped out carefully in order to ensure the future success of the group, representing a marked difference to the routines with which decisions were previously made.

## Developing routines through their internal dynamics

We have seen how the direction of SOK and the S-Group has changed after the new management entered the organization. It may be noted, however, that the changes have not primarily resulted from the implementation of new routines or work practices but rather from the ability of the new management to steer the existing routines in a more efficient direction. As noted in our data, our interviewees found the systems and routines of SOK to be in very good condition already before the turnaround. Reportedly these routines, which, for example, Feldman (2000), Howard-Grenville (2005), Becker (2004), and Eisenhardt and Martin (2000) have considered to be the backbone of organizational behaviour, largely remained the same throughout the analysed turnaround—they were primarily not replaced. However, as we discussed in our literature review, carefully designed artefacts and routines do not guarantee the intended organizational behaviour or development. We saw this to be the case before the implementation of the S83 plan.

We recall that the ostensive aspect of an organizational routine refers to the routine as an abstract pattern, whereas the performative aspect refers to the actual execution of the routine in specific instances (Becker, 2004; Feldman, 2000; Howard-Grenville, 2005; Naduzzo, Rocco, & Warglien, 2000). Whereas the templates behind the routines that we have considered have largely remained the same, we have witnessed a major change in the internal dynamics of the routines.

This change was reportedly crucial in the turnaround that the entire organization went through. Throughout the years, the relatively independent decision-making of the individual cooperatives had stagnated the centralized development of the S-Group. The employees of SOK were good, punctual workers, but only after the changes in management were they given the incentive to develop their work practices. A new culture emerged within the central organization as well as in the regional cooperatives around the country. 'The employees started to care about the way they did their thing.' This enabled the ostensive and performative aspects of the routines to act in a mutually constitutive manner—the routines were produced and reproduced internally.

As an example of a key organizational routine that evolved in a new direction, we consider the human resources management routine of the individual cooperatives. While the template of such a routine included components such as hiring, employee evaluation, and training already prior to the implementation of the S83 plan, in practice these were not executed effectively, if at all. For example, inefficient employees were usually retained until they retired. However, after the impetus given by the S83 plan, this routine began to develop stage by stage, following the feedback provided by the observed results. At first, as the individual cooperatives were forced to start developing their efficiency, they laid off many redundant employees. Next, the cooperatives began to hire new employees more carefully according to specific needs, with business skills being valued over the previously typical agricultural background of many employees. Finally, the education of employees shifted from a vocational training to strategic management. We conclude that the human resources management routine, while remaining essentially the same routine, began organizing internally and developed significantly through its own routine dynamics; this observation is similar to that in the work of Feldman (2000).

## Managing routines to enhance organizational resilience

In contradiction with the current theory (e.g. according to Pentland & Feldman, 2008) of managing routines, hardly any of the routines or processes we observed were replaced or redesigned but rather just awakened or steered towards a new, more resilient direction. Almost nothing completely new was created, but rather routines fell into place and developed internally due to various pressures and reactions to them. This important aspect is largely neglected in the current management literature focusing on organizational routines. For example, the education centre Jollas was founded already in 1961, but only with the pressures created by the deteriorating economic situation and diminishing market share of the S-Group, and the S83 plan that was implemented as a result, did the education provided in the centre evolve towards a clearer goal of training highly competitive managers who could deal with tightening competition and other adversity.

We have considered organizational resilience as 'a firm's ability to effectively absorb, develop situation-specific responses to, and ultimately engage in transformative activities to capitalize on disruptive surprises that potentially threaten organization survival' (Lengnick-Hall, Beck, & Lengnick-Hall, 2011). In accordance with Lengnick-Hall and Beck (2005) and Lengnick-Hall, Beck, and Lengnick-Hall (2011), the routines of SOK, in our case specifically changes in their internal dynamics, improved the organization's ability to deal with and react to uncertainty and complexity. Moreover, we recall that Sutcliffe and Vogus (2003) have considered resilience as an organization's *continual* ability to thrive in the face of adversity; the routine dynamics observed in our case clearly provided the organization with an ability to react and adapt continually and thus stay up-to-date, eliminating the need for great turnarounds in the future. Consequently, we finally argue that a continuous renewal of routine dynamics may enable an organization to anticipate, with the help of antecedents, the nature of future crises and disruptions and to adapt to changes; thus we find the different types of resilience discussed previously to be closely connected with the study of routine dynamics.

In Table 7.1 we illustrate how the management of SOK was able to shape the *internal* pressures within the S-Group to support the dynamics of routines. In our case, the change was primarily driven by social and economic pressures. In the following, we will focus on these. As discussed in the data section, by far the biggest reason behind the change in the routine dynamics was the termination of the so-called 'automatic funding mechanism' or 'internal monopoly', in which SOK balanced out the losses of regional cooperatives from the surplus it was making from its purchasing divisions. This increased the economic pressure on individual cooperatives and, as a result, increased their incentives to start thinking about efficiency. This led to a top-down chain reaction of cutting funds, as losses were no longer balanced out at any organizational level. In practice, the cooperatives became the profit centres of the S-Group and SOK assumed a supporting role for the cooperatives, although the full implementation of this change was slow.

The new management also initiated an internal ranking system where the individual cooperatives were compared with one another. The managements of the successful cooperatives were granted bonuses and rewards, whereas the rest were pressured to increase their efficiency. This made employees feel more connected with the cooperative and increased both the economic and the social pressure within the cooperative. Motivated by this new competitive culture, everyone began to form opinions and take an interest in how to develop their work as well as the whole organization. Naturally, disagreements and tensions also arose, but decisions were thought out carefully and executed with the backing of both the administrative council and the board.

Finally, this culture that was built around the economic and social pressures was spread in various social and educational events where individual cooperatives were in contact with one another. These events, the 'retailer days' in particular, supported the formation of one united organization.

**Table 7.1**  Illustrating how different pressures were created in SOK to support routine dynamics

| Quote on action | Interpretation | Pressure(s) |
|---|---|---|
| 'I argue that this [education/social events] created a kind of social cohesion and group spirit because it went so that the supermarket managers would dress in a certain way with their own clothes for the parties and all kinds of things like that. They still have these but that was a way to build group spirit and cooperation in the cooperative. I also know that in the administration it had a really big effect.' | New education and social events had influence on work motivation. The whole cooperative became more united. | Social pressure |
| 'While previously the cooperatives had more autonomy, as a result of the change in organizational structure, more effort was put into standardizing managerial practices.' 'The standardization of managerial practices created more transparency as now all coops were measured with the same criteria. – [it] increased internal competition as now everyone was fighting to increase the total benefit of the group as well as their own cooperative.' | It increased transparency created internal pressure and competition. | Social and economic pressure |
| 'At the same time since the late 1980s and early 1990s each regional cooperative was ranked from best to worst, with the ranking communicated to each cooperative.' 'This increased motivation – not only because of the money…but everyone wanted to show their skills.' | The applied ranking of individual cooperatives increased competition and work motivation. | Social and economic pressure |
| 'The biggest reasons for the financial difficulties was the so-called "automatic funding mechanism" or internal monopoly in which the central organization balanced out the losses of regional cooperative from the surplus it was making from its purchasing divisions.' 'The S83 in practice ended the "automatic funding system" and "internal monopoly" that had been in place, as the creation of larger regional cooperatives meant that SOK would no longer continue to be accountable for the losses of smaller cooperatives that most likely could not survive independently without financial support.' | Ending the automatic funding system increased economic pressure on individual cooperatives. Individual cooperatives were forced to start developing internally. | Economic pressure |

**Table 7.1** *Continued*

| Quote on action | Interpretation | Pressure(s) |
|---|---|---|
| 'In the head office they had a lot of different kinds of consultants and advisors. They had marketing advisors in the food, hardware, textile, cashier, meat sectors and many more. Then there would come a few key leaders from the cooperatives; it wasn't an acclamation but it was crucial that they just maintain the jobs that were crucial. You pay. The cooperative pays. You pay their salaries; the central organization has nothing to do with them and doesn't need them. The most skilled employees found jobs, but there were people who no one wanted. Of course that created unemployment. But just there was this big divide between who is needed anymore, and those that are needed are hired by the cooperative and the central organization will not pay at all, as they don't need them.' | Eliminating the inefficiencies and establishing a regional cooperative structure provided everyone with a specific role within the organization. This provided employees with a feeling of importance among others. | Social pressure |
| 'As a result of the establishment of the regional cooperative structure and the elimination of several inefficiencies such as the excessive organization size, everyone now had a clear role to play in the cooperative.' | | |
| 'The main interest of the administrative council, the de facto governing body, was to maintain the strong position in the agricultural sector rather than develop other areas of SOK's already diversified operations.' | Strong management increased the pressure on individual employees. This created a positive discussion culture as everyone had an opinion on how to develop his/her work practices. | Social pressure |
| 'But there came, if we look at it positively that we had a strong administrative council, I mean a really strong administrative and then a leadership team that was very skilful. That created a really strong discussion culture, and also in some ways a small amount of tension, of course you can see that negatively, as there was a lot of discussion and different opinions.' | | |

## The possibility to bring about change

In our illustration, we have witnessed a major turnaround of SOK, a highly stable and routinized organization. We found that a company that is simply able to integrate the required pressures into the ostensive aspects of its routines is able to develop in a more resilient direction. Based on our research, the development of routines seems to be characterized by flexible ostensive aspects and a real autonomy and the possibility to bring about change. This possibility to bring about change in routines is essential in adapting to the current changes brought about by digitization in the Red Queen Retail Race. Our case indicates that there are many things that entrepreneurs can do to achieve the ambitious goal of developing their organizations' routines into more resilient ones while ensuring that employees are keeping pace.

# References

Aldrich, H. E. & Yang, T., 2014. 'How do entrepreneurs know what to do? Learning and organizing in new ventures'. *Journal of Evolutionary Economics*, 24(1), 59–82.

Antonakis, J., Ashkanasy, N. M., & Dasborough, M. T., 2009. 'Does leadership need emotional intelligence?' *The Leadership Quarterly*, 20(2), 247–261.

Ashkanasy, N. M. & Daus, C. S., 2005. 'Rumors of the death of emotional intelligence in organizational behavior are vastly exaggerated'. *Journal of Organizational Behavior*, 26, 441–452.

Baba, V. V. & Jamal, M., 1991. 'Routinization of job context and job content as related to employees' quality of working life: a study of Canadian nurses'. *Journal of Organizational Behavior*, 12, 379–386.

Becker, M. C., 2004. 'Organizational routines: a review of the literature'. *Industrial and Corporate Change*, 13, 643–677.

Bertels, S., Howard-Grenville, J., & Pek, S., 2016. 'Cultural molding, shielding, and shoring at Oilco: the role of culture in the integration of routines'. *Organization Science*, 27, 573–593.

Bryant, P. T., 2014. 'Imprinting by design: the microfoundations of entrepreneurial adaptation'. *Entrepreneurship Theory and Practice*, 38(5), 1081–1102.

Burnard, K. & Bhamra, R., 2011. 'Organizational resilience: development of a conceptual framework for organizational responses'. *International Journal of Production Research*, 49(18), 5581–5599.

Cohendet, P. S. & Simon, L. O., 2016. 'Always playable: recombining routines for creative efficiency at Ubisoft Montreal's video game studio'. *Organization Science*, 27, 614–632.

D'Adderio, L., 2014. 'Replication dilemma'. *Organization Science*, 25, 1325–1350.

Danner-Schröder, A. & Geiger, D., 2016. 'Unravelling the motor of patterning work: toward an understanding of the microlevel dynamics of standardization and flexibility'. *Organization Science*, 27, 633–658.

Duchek, S., 2014. 'Growth in the face of crisis: the role of organizational resilience capabilities'. *Academy of Management Meeting Proceedings*, 2014(1), 861–866.

Eisenhardt, K. M. & Graebner, M. E., 2007. 'Theory building from cases: opportunities and challenges'. *Academy of Management Journal*, 50, 25–32.

Eisenhardt, K. M. & Martin, J. A., 2000. 'Dynamic capabilities: what are they?' *Strategic Management Journal*, 21, 1105–1121.

Feldman, M. S., 2000. 'Organizational routines as a source of continuous change'. *Organization Science*, 11, 611–629.

Feldman, M. S. & Pentland, B. T., 2003. 'Reconceptualizing organizational routines as a source of flexibility and change'. *Administrative Science Quarterly*, 48, 94–118.

Feldman, M. S., Pentland, B. T., D'Adderio, L., & Lazaric, N., 2016. 'Beyond routines as things: introduction to the special issue on routine dynamics'. *Organization Science*, 27, 505–513.

Felin, T. & Foss, N., 2009. 'Strategic organization: a field in search for micro-foundations'. *Strategic Organization*, 3(4), 441–455.

Glaser, B. G. & Strauss, A. L., 1967. *The discovery of grounded theory: strategies for qualitative research*. Aldine Publishing Company.

Horne, J. F. & Orr, J. E., 1998. 'Assessing behaviors that create resilient organizations'. *Employment Relations Today*, 24(4), 29–39.

Howard-Grenville, J., 2005. 'The persistence of flexible organizational routines: the role of agency and organizational context'. *Organization Science*, 16, 618–636.

Kendra, J. M. & Wachtendorf, T., 2003. 'Elements of resilience after the World Trade Center disaster: reconstituting New York city's emergency operations center'. *Disasters*, 27(1), 37–53.

Khazanchi, S. & Masterson, S. S., 2011. 'Who and what is fair matters: a multi-foci social exchange model of creativity'. *Journal of Organizational Behavior*, 32, 86–106.

Langley, A., 1999. 'Strategies for theorizing from process data'. *The Academy of Management Review*, 24, 691–710.

Langley, A., Smallman, C., Tsoukas, H., & Van de Ven, A., 2013. 'Process studies of change in organization and management: unveiling temporality, activity, and flow'. *Academy of Management Journal*, 56, 1–13.

Lazaric, N., 2011. 'Organizational routines and cognition: an introduction to empirical and analytical contributions'. *Journal of Institutional Economics*, 7(2), 147–156.

Lengnick-Hall, C. A. & Beck, T. E., 2005. 'Adaptive fit versus robust transformation: how organizations respond to environmental change'. *Journal of Management*, 31(5), 738–757.

Lengnick-Hall, C. A., Beck, T. E., & Lengnick-Hall, M. L., 2011. 'Developing a capacity for organizational resilience through strategic human resource management'. *Human Resource Management Review*, 21(3), 243–255.

Linnenluecke, M. K. & Griffiths, A., 2012. 'Assessing organizational resilience to climate and weather extremes: complexities and methodological pathways'. *Climatic Change*, 113(3/4), 933–947.

Liu, S., Rovine, M. J., & Molenaar, P. C. M., 2012. 'Selecting a linear mixed model for longitudinal data: repeated measures analysis of variance, covariance pattern model, and growth curve approaches'. *Psychological Methods*, 17, 15–30.

Naduzzo, A., Rocco, E., & Warglien, M., 2000. 'Talking about routines in the field'. In G. Dosi, R. Nelson, & S. Winter (eds), *The nature and dynamics of organizational capabilities*: 27–50. Oxford University Press.

Ohly, S., Sonnentag, S., & Plunke, F., 2006. 'Routinization, work characteristics and their relationships with creative and proactive behaviors'. *Journal of Organizational Behavior*, 27, 257–279.

Okhuysen, G. A. & Bechky, B. A., 2008. 'Coordination in organizations: an integrative perspective'. *The Academy of Management Annals*, 3, 463–574.

Ortiz de Mandojana, N. & Bansal, P., 2016. 'The long term benefits of organizational resilience through sustainable business practices'. *Strategic Management Journal*, 37(8), 1615–1631.

Paavola, L. & Cuthbertson, R. 2022. Redefining capabilities as drivers of adaptation, incremental change, and transformation: Recognizing the importance of strategic and operational intent on performance. Journal of Management & Organization, 28(3), 522–539.

Pentland, B. T. & Feldman, M. S., 2008. 'Designing routines: on the folly of designing artifacts, while hoping for patterns of action'. *Information and Organization*, 18, 235–250.

Pentland, B. T., Hœrem, T., & Hillison, D., 2014. 'Comparing organizational routines as recurrent patterns of action'. *Organization Studies*, 31, 917–940.

Robert, B., 2010. *Organizational resilience: concepts and evaluation method*. Presse de l'École Polytechnique de Montréal.

Robertson, J. L., & Barling, J., 2013. 'Greening organizations through leaders' influence on employees' pro-environmental behaviors'. *Journal of Organizational Behavior*, 34, 176–194.

Sahaym, A., Steesma, H. K., & Schilling, M. A., 2007. 'The influence of information technology on the use of loosely coupled organizational forms: an industry level analysis'. *Organization Science*, 18(5), 865–880.

Solinger, O. N., van Olffen, W., Roe, R. A., & Hofmans, J., 2013. 'On becoming (un)committed: a taxonomy and test of newcomer onboarding scenarios'. *Organization Science*, 24, 1640–1661.

Somers, S., 2009. 'Measuring resilience potential: an adaptive strategy for organizational crisis planning'. *Journal of Contingencies and Crisis Management*, 17(1), 12–23.

Stephan, U. & Huysentruyt, M., 2016. 'Resisting temptation—the case of Triodos Bank'. *Stanford Social Innovation Review*, Fall, 20–25.

Sutcliffe, K. M. & Vogus, T. J., 2003. 'Organizing for resilience'. In S. Cameron, J. E. Dutton, & R. E. Quinn (eds), *Positive organizational scholarship: foundations of a new discipline*: 94–110. Berrett-Koehler Publishers.

Winter, S. G., 2003. 'Understanding dynamic capabilities'. *Strategic Management Journal*, 24, 991–995.

Zohar, D. M. & Hofmann, D. A., 2012. 'Organizational culture and climate'. In S. W. J. Kozlowski (ed.), *The Oxford handbook of organizational psychology*: 643–666. Oxford University Press.

# 8

# Managing Organizational Routines to Win the Retail Race

*Lauri Paavola and Richard Cuthbertson*

## Introduction

The advent of big data and novel analytic technologies provides an opportunity for new organizational work practices that are designed to promote faster and more efficient change. An example of this can be observed in the retail sector, which has seen a shift from analyses based on product-centric data to analyses based on more complex customer-centric data (Hänninen & Paavola, 2020; Paavola & Cuthbertson, 2021). In this chapter, we examine the use of customer data in the field of UK grocery retailing, which has been perceived as one of the frontrunners in the area. The field has undergone major changes within the past few decades, with various loyalty card programmes operating as tools for data collection and organizational change. From the viewpoint of marketing, loyalty programmes are designed to encourage and reward buying behaviour that is beneficial to the retail organizations, and often also to their product suppliers. However, more significantly in terms of promoting change in organizational processes, loyalty programmes also provide retail organizations with data on their customers and their shopping behaviour. This data can be increasingly exploited in strategic and operational decision-making concerning, for example, pricing, merchandising, and store development, making the insights worth 'a thousand pounds a word'. However, an implementation of data analytics enabling technologies is only the first step in this transformation. Understanding the various factors that influence the successful use of the data is required to seize benefits from it.

The customer data-led transformation of the field of grocery retailing in the United Kingdom began in 1995 when Tesco, a large grocery retailer, launched its Clubcard. The substantial benefits gained by Tesco from this loyalty programme have redefined the competitive dynamics within the field, forcing competitors to start their own loyalty programmes. Despite the intended transformational influence of these programmes, our conclusions highlight that their outcomes vary depending upon various situational variables. Understanding these variables is crucial for the success and efficiency of the change, and we will observe how the management of specific routines has resulted in varied performance outcomes

Lauri Paavola and Richard Cuthbertson, *Managing Organizational Routines to Win the Retail Race*. In: *The Red Queen Retail Race*. Edited by Richard Cuthbertson, Olli Rusanen, and Lauri Paavola, Oxford University Press. © Lauri Paavola and Richard Cuthbertson (2023). DOI: 10.1093/oso/9780192862617.003.0008 and varying paths of development within the field. Generally, we are interested in understanding how specific organizations initiate change and how a change diffuses within the field.

We begin this chapter by discussing organizational work through a theoretical lens of organizational routines. After providing the theoretical background for our approach, we apply it to understand the change that the field of UK grocery retailing has undergone. We provide a brief analysis that focuses primarily on Tesco, a large grocery retailer, which has been driving the data-led transformation within the United Kingdom. Finally, we conclude the chapter by providing some more practical learnings.

## The ubiquity and complexity of routines

Routines can be found everywhere. To a certain extent, everything that surrounds us has repetitive and cyclical characteristics that provide predictability and the ability to build knowledge. Thus, routines nowadays occupy an increasingly central position in organization theory. 'As genetic material, they are used to explain the inertial quality of organizational structure in evolutionary theories' (Pentland & Rueter, 1994: 484). As memory, routines have become a cornerstone in theories of organizational learning and adaptation. They occupy the crucial nexus between structure and action, between the organization as an object and organizing as a process (Pentland & Rueter, 1992).

During the past decade, organizational routines have been actively studied. The concept has turned out to be more ubiquitous than previously imagined, and organizational routines can be identified in retail, healthcare, logistics, research, and so on. Broadly speaking, organizational routines determine the everyday operations of an organization (Cohen et al., 1996; Feldman et al., 2016; Paavola & Cuthbertson, 2018). Having well-functioning routines in place, even relatively minor ones, can greatly improve the performance of an organization, and hence it is crucial for the management of an organization to understand its routines (Eisenhardt & Martin, 2000). For example, in the design process of a new automobile, as the component parts become finalized, an important step consists of simply verifying that each part fits in the space provided. Not carrying out this step properly can lead to product failure and necessitate a recall of the car model from the market. Overall, research on organizational routines is motivated by their central importance as well as the complexity of the concept and of the interactions among routines.

Previously, the term 'routine' had been commonly used to refer to the standard, repetitive nature of certain actions, but recently the role of routines in change has started to become more apparent. It has become accepted that routines are not clearly defined entities, as previously thought, but rather 'repetitive streams of situated action' (Feldman et al., 2016). Situated actions are enacted in specific times and places, at least partially in an ad hoc manner. Consider driving a motor vehicle. The sequences of actions performed, such as accelerating and changing lanes, are clearly routine-like in nature, yet the specifics always depend on the particular route, the surrounding traffic, and so on. Performing situated actions and transferring them to different situations require effort, and performing the same action (or an action with the same outcome) can be more difficult than performing something different.

Pentland and Rueter (1994) referred to the effort of producing the same pattern of action as 'effortful accomplishment'. As noted by Feldman and Pentland (2003), here one must draw a line between a few distinct concepts, such as *variation* and *change*. Sometimes significant flexibility, and even variation, in a routine is required to produce the same or similar outcome. Generally, achieving stability requires suitable adaptation; for example, driving a specific route at a particular time is of course informed by the knowledge and skills one has learned in driving school, but conversely, a specific experience can influence one's overall understanding of safe driving.

On the other hand, routines are of course not always stable but may change. In fact, variation may emerge on any occasion where a routine is enacted (Bucher & Langley, 2016; Dittrich, Guérard, & Seidl, 2016). Routines are not simply mindlessly executed but are rather carried out by knowledgeable and reflective actors. Moreover, because the actions produced by a routine are situated, actors are not even always aware of producing changes in routines.

In Chapter 7 we found that bringing about and sustaining the functioning of a routine, and in other cases preserving the outcome of a certain routine, requires their suitable management. In this chapter, our main focus is on the study of *higher order routines* in change, that is routines that are designed to manage and coordinate existing more operative routines (Adler, Goldoftas, & Levine, 1999; Paavola & Cuthbertson, 2022), amounting to exogenous change in the latter. More specifically, we focus on understanding the role of customer data analytics routines in wider organizational transformation.

## A multi-case study on the collection and use of customer data

Given the organization- and context-dependent nature of the questions regarding the relationship between transformational routines, customer behaviour, and organizational change, a multi-case study is a suitable approach for research (Eisenhardt, 1989; Yin, 1994). Hence, this research is based on an in-depth, inductive multi-case study on the collection and use of customer data in the field of UK grocery retailing. Since we consider all the major players in the field, the study can also be seen as a field-level study. Moreover, we apply an inductive case research strategy, which by definition utilizes an empirical case or cases to build theory in an inductive fashion (Bacharach, 1989; Eisenhardt & Graebner, 2007).

In addition, by taking a long-term historical perspective, we gain insight into the evolutionary nature of the field and the organizations within it. The purpose of such longitudinal process analysis is, by definition, to observe the unfolding of events and processes over time (Langley et al., 2013). There are several advantages to combining a longitudinal study with a number of individual case studies (Leonard-Barton, 1990).

The research part of a qualitative study usually relies on a combination of participant observation, interviews, and historical research (Glaser & Strauss, 1967). Accordingly, in our study public data, company archives, and interview data were collected on the evolution of the various organizations' activities related to both the use of customer data and organizational development.

Publicly available data included a complete set of historical annual reports, financial analyst reports, prior studies on the development of UK grocery retailing, and business press articles on organizations operating in the field of UK grocery retailing. Company archives supplemented the publicly available data. Historical strategic plans, organization charts, internal memos, and technical papers helped document the evolution of the organizations in question. Archival data is particularly suitable for longitudinal process analyses where the development of an entity is observed over a long period of time (Langley, 1999; Langley et al., 2013).

Finally, we organized discussions with a sample of current and ex-employees of the organizations under analysis. The interviews were focused on certain key figures who have played a major role in developing the use of customer data in one or even several of the organizations in question.

## Case study: development of customer data in UK grocery retailing

In the early 1990s, Tesco was running trials of several marketing programmes. One of these trials in a few stores, codenamed 'Omega', was a new card-based customer loyalty programme. Customers could sign up for their Clubcard, and by making purchases at Tesco they would accumulate points that were converted into vouchers that could be used to purchase items at Tesco. This was intended to increase customer loyalty.

Sainsbury's was also conducting trials with a loyalty programme of its own, but neither Sainsbury's nor Tesco's programme was considered transformational. In general, Tesco's promotional initiatives were expected to be useful only in a certain locality or for a limited period of time, and the scope of the Clubcard trial was according to the interviewees 'modest even compared to other marketing pilot programmes'.

Tesco's marketing staff had actively assessed retail loyalty schemes in the United States but had concluded that such schemes were unlikely to provide sufficient return on the investment. In 1993, Grant Harrison was selected to head the development of the Clubcard. Research that Harrison had conducted on loyalty marketing had revealed that a crucial additional benefit that could be obtained from Clubcard was the accumulation of customer data. Customers would give their names, addresses, and information on the size and ages of their family, and in this way, Tesco was able to identify the customer in each transaction performed at one of its stores (similar to the online identification of customers today, e.g., at Amazon). The focus on customer data was apparently underestimated by Sainsbury's, which launched a customer loyalty card in 1995.

During the first two months of the trial in 1993, Clubcard turned out to be a success in terms of the proportion of sales attributable to Clubcard owners in the stores participating in the trial, rising to 60–80 per cent. Moreover, the 1 per cent reward for their spend turned out to be a sufficient incentive for customers to sign up for Clubcard. However, there remained a problem. In order to gain information on individual customers and to respond to their preferences, massive amounts of transactional data needed to be processed. With the limited computing power available at the time, this was proving to be too time-consuming and expensive. To obtain the data analysis expertise they required, Tesco turned to a small consumer data analysis company named Dunnhumby. Dunnhumby showed that instead of analysing all of the transactional data that had been gathered, they could analyse around 10 per cent of it and reach conclusions that were 90–95 per cent accurate.

Various interesting facts were discovered by Dunnhumby from the Clubcard trials that were extended to 14 stores in 1994. For example, previously it had not been known that a small proportion of customers produced a very large part of Tesco's profit. Information was obtained on how far customers were willing to travel to shop, as well as which departments within the stores failed to attract particular customers who shopped heavily in other areas.

As several of our interviewees explained, when Dunnhumby presented its results to the Tesco board in 1994, Ian MacLaurin famously remarked: 'What scares me about this is that you know more about my customers after three months than I know after thirty years.' With its culture of innovation and bold decision-making, the Tesco board decided at the end of 1994 to launch the Clubcard nationally 12 weeks later.

It should be emphasized that many of Tesco's competitors were simultaneously trialling or launching their own loyalty cards, but Tesco had certain advantages over each of them. Being the first nationally launched loyalty card, Clubcard received huge media attention. By contrast, for example, Sainsbury's 'Saver Card', which was piloted in 1995, never received widespread attention and indeed was only initially introduced in a little more than half of its stores. When Sainsbury's lost customers to Tesco, apparently due to Clubcard, it did not know which customers it was losing, whereas later on Tesco could identify customers that apparently returned to Sainsbury's by monitoring those customers that stopped using Clubcard.

Crucially, the Tesco management understood the value of customer data. Sainsbury's viewed a loyalty card mostly as an in-store promotional device and had no real focus to utilize the data. According to one of the interviewees, 'They [Sainsbury's] never really had the same leadership drive to be using customer data from their executive.' With its 'Reward Card', launched in 1996, Sainsbury's chose to reward customers at the checkout. By contrast, Tesco rewarded its customers who had a Clubcard by sending them vouchers and coupons four times a year. Apart from the fact that Tesco's method reportedly received a more positive response from customers, by providing a larger (quarterly) and more tangible (paper coupon) reward, it is notable that Sainsbury's method provided customers with no incentive to provide their address information. Over time, as computing power developed and so Tesco was able to analyse more and more transactional data, it was able to mail coupons and offers that were tailored to different customer groups such as vegetarians and diabetics, and finally tailored, in effect, to individual customers based on individual historic and predicted purchasing patterns.

In 1995, even though Sainsbury's was the market leader, the most significant competition to Tesco's Clubcard came from Safeway (now Morrison's). With its ABC card, Safeway did place emphasis on gathering accurate data of individual customers, avoiding the oversight made by Sainsbury's. An analysis of this data revealed to Safeway that the segment of its clientele that would bring in most of its profits was families with young children. Safeway focused its marketing accordingly and simultaneously ended up distancing other customer segments. Safeway's approach was in stark contrast with Tesco's desire to be an inclusive brand that appeals to the mass of potential customers. For example, initially Tesco awarded Clubcard points only to customers that spent a minimum of 10 pounds in order to reduce the costs of the Clubcard programme and encourage higher basket spend. However, when this limit was found to be too high for many seniors in particular, Tesco began to offer them Clubcard points for any purchase that exceeded 5 pounds, despite the increased costs of operation.

In sum, Safeway failed to engage the widest possible range of customers with its ABC card, despite having superior technology compared to Tesco. Due to a change of leadership and the move to a Hi-Lo promotional strategy that differentiated on product rather than customers, Safeway ended up withdrawing the ABC programme in 2000, citing the high costs of running it. Dunnhumby, the data analysis company working for Tesco, managed the costs much better by focusing their analysis on small samples of the data and using it to draw conclusions with implications for all customers and operations.

Hence, Tesco took a highly pragmatic approach to data analysis, always focusing on questions that could realistically be answered at the time with the technological resources available. At the time Clubcard was launched, it was fashionable to store huge amounts of operational data in databases with the intent of eventually analysing it thoroughly. However, the cost of storing and analysing such quantities of data was very high, and in retailing, data can become out of date very quickly. Instead, Dunnhumby made the pragmatic decision of taking in only part of the available data and delivering its analysis once a week.

According to the interviewees, Tesco developed a simple but effective method of collecting data, analysing it, and acting upon it, in a short period of time. Other organizations could collect large quantities of data and analyse it to find interesting results, but Tesco focused on creating routines that allowed the findings from the data to be operationalized in a short period of time.

While the quarterly mailings could eventually be, in essence, tailored to individual customers, other uses of customer data took place at a broader level. An important way in which Tesco used this data was the process of segmenting its customers. The idea was to classify customers into different groups, say, environmentally conscious buyers, those looking for the best nutritional quality at the lowest price, bulk shoppers, and so on, by analysing key product sales. At first, 80 high-volume products that each had a particular attribute were selected, and the number of items customers bought of each of these products produced data points in an 80-dimensional space. As a result, a total of 27 different clusters were identified in this space and interpreted as customer segments.

In 1998, this segmentation proved highly useful for Tesco in the price wars against competitors, especially Asda, which has had a consistent reputation of being cheaper than Tesco. A traditional method for such price wars is to simply compare prices with the competitor and then to lower prices on the biggest-selling items. However, this costs a lot of money, some of which is effectively wasted, especially as few customers choose where to shop exclusively based on price. Instead, based on customer segmentation, Tesco was able to identify price-conscious shoppers and the particular products bought almost exclusively by them. According to the management of Dunnhumby at the time, '6 per cent of products typically account for 40 per cent of the sales to price sensitive customers'. By focusing price cuts on these few products, Tesco was able to make a large impact at a comparatively low net cost.

Customer segmentation was also successful more generally: when coupons mailed to customers were targeted according to the segment they belonged to, redemption rates doubled. However, this early segmentation had its weaknesses; for example, some of the 27 segments were simply too small to address effectively. Entirely new segments were defined by placing every product on a certain point in a total of 20 different scales, such as 'low fat' against 'high fat' and 'ready to eat' against 'needs preparation'. When customers were classified according to the quantities they purchased on these scales, 14 segments were identified. The results were again highly interesting: for example, it was found that one group of loyal customers regularly shopped at 12 of 16 Tesco store departments, implying that encouraging these customers to shop even sporadically in the other four departments would produce large profits.

A process that is also related to customer segmentation is the so-called Customer Plan Process. This is an annual process where customer data is used to identify what is important to customers, what their opinions are of Tesco, and so on. As a result, a small number of Customer Plan Projects are conceived each year and put into effect. As one interviewee explained,

> The nature of these is that it's done at a high level because in order to change, let's say, to make Tesco better for quality customers, who are called Finer Food Customers within our segmentation, then that's going to have implications on what products you sell but also how you merchandise them, how you source and distribute them, how you think about them not just in isolation but also in combination.

Crucial in the whole transformation concerning the use of customer data was a switch in the mindset—the focus at Tesco was shifted from analysing sales of products to analysing (and understanding) customers. As the knowledge of how and what to sell is the backbone of retailing, this change in thinking necessarily revolutionized almost all operational processes within Tesco. Furthermore, the transformation in operations was not limited to Tesco itself, as the next important step in the utilization of customer data was providing it to the supply chain partners. In the United Kingdom, and perhaps globally, this was pioneered by Tesco in 2002. Sainsbury's took a similar step much later, in 2012, and according to one of our interviewees, 'pretty much all of their suppliers now have access to their customer behavioural data'.

As stated in the interviews, 'The suppliers are always going to be the greatest experts on their particular product area. Unilever and P&G will always know more about detergent than Tesco'. On the one hand, a retailer might wish to use this specialized knowledge. On the other hand, customer data collected by a retailer is useful for its suppliers, who are indeed willing to pay for it. However, in both cases, finding a 'common language' is crucial. The goal is that suppliers and retailers are both 'talking about the same segmentation, talking about the same customers. They're both seeing the same metrics in terms of sales performance'. For example, a particular promotion can increase the sales of Coca Cola but decrease the sales of Pepsi by almost an equal quantity. This results in no overall sales benefit to the retailer—though the supplier is likely to be paying the retailer for the privilege of targeting specific customers. According to the interviewees, retailers such as Sainsbury's are 'increasingly pushing suppliers ... to design promotions and to fund promotions that actually increase the total category purse rather than just product sales'.

On top of the successful innovations that Tesco achieved in collaboration with the data analysis company Dunnhumby, selling data to supply chain partners provided an opportunity to obtain revenue from the customer data collected. Partly due to these reasons, in 2001 Tesco purchased 53 per cent of Dunnhumby and in 2006 increased its share to 84 per cent. Finally in 2010, Tesco acquired Dunnhumby entirely, and at this point the founders of Dunnhumby left the business. Soon after, in 2011, the management team of Tesco also went through significant changes as the CEO, Terry Leahy, resigned. Consequently, Dunnhumby's influence on Tesco has not been as significant as with the previous management teams, who had worked together with the same leadership team for 14 years. As a result of this and the fact that data was now being routinely sold to interested parties, the collection, analysis, and selling of customer data became a more mechanical operation. Hence, Dunnhumby appeared to have less of a strategic impact on Tesco, and became more transactional. Moreover, providing customer data to the supply chain required increasing the number of personnel in Dunnhumby significantly. In the last few years, Tesco has conducted negotiations about selling Dunnhumby. According to the interviews, in acquiring Dunnhumby, Tesco ended up losing a significant amount of innovativeness, and the selling of data to the supply chain has also not been as profitable as expected. One of the interviewees even went so far as to call the acquisition 'one of the worst acquisitions of all time'.

According to the interviewees, 'Up until the last few years, Tesco was unassailable anyway and was leading the pack in everything that was done.' This included 'formats, just running the business. All the others were on the back foot playing catch up all the time.' For example, Sainsbury's reward card had not proved profitable. Simultaneously, the loyalty card programmes of several other companies in the United Kingdom, including outside the field of grocery retailing, had proved costly to operate and complicated for customers to use. As a result, the Nectar card programme was developed in 2001–2002 by a privately owned and managed firm, Loyalty Management UK (LMUK), led by Keith Mills, who had previously founded Air Miles, the airline-based loyalty programme. The concept was that several retailers would share a loyalty card programme, dividing the costs among them and allowing customers to use the same card and the same points in all of the participating outlets.

The four founding partners of the Nectar programme were Sainsbury's, the department store Debenhams, the oil and gas company BP, and the bank Barclays. The Nectar card was launched in 2002 and proved successful in terms of customer participation: by September 2003, some 13 million UK households had activated a Nectar account. For Sainsbury's, the Nectar card was quite explicitly intended to be a competitor for Tesco's Clubcard: 'From Sainsbury's point of view, this was really copying competitors.' However, use of the customer data was largely limited to contact data and demographic data, involving a customer's name, address, gender, and the number of people in the household. '[Sainsbury's] did have some attempts to use purchasing data that would surface through the loyalty card, but it wasn't a massive focus for them.'

According to the interviews, the collection and use of transactional behavioural data became a focus for Sainsbury's only around 2007. At this time a representative of Sainsbury's reportedly said: 'We think this is giving Tesco a real competitive advantage. We now really want to use deep customer data.' A role was also played by the suppliers, who had earlier been allowed access to Tesco's customer data for a fee and were eager to collaborate and to create some competition in this area. Sainsbury's was the key player in the Nectar programme, and the programme would have fallen apart had Sainsbury's left it. Thus, when Sainsbury's renewed its contract with LMG (owner of LMUK), it was able to gain access to LMG's new data analytics service. In 2007, the Canadian company Groupe Aeroplan acquired the Nectar programme and later became known as Aimia.

The cooperation between Sainsbury's and Aimia became very close. Following Sainsbury's demands, in 2007 Aimia began to invest heavily to create its customer analytics platform. According to Mike Coupe, Group Commercial Director at Sainsbury's (and now CEO), 'We see the Aimia team as an extension of our own business. Their data insights continue to be invaluable in the evolution of our business.' According to a report by Aimia from 2013, in the year 2007 a pioneering group of four consultants worked alongside Sainsbury's to extract insight from Nectar data; by 2013 that team had grown to 44 analysts and consultants, half of whom were embedded in Sainsbury's offices. Furthermore, in 2012, Sainsbury's and Aimia together created the marketing solutions company Insight 2 Communication (i2c). Consequently, Aimia was becoming more than a behind-the-scenes loyalty management provider—it was becoming a trusted strategic partner.

Other competitors in the field of UK grocery retailing followed suit. In 2008, Iceland introduced the 'Bonus Card', Waitrose introduced a loyalty card in 2011, and Morrison's introduced a loyalty card in 2013. As advances in technology have become available and cheaper to all competitors, the initial advantage that Clubcard gave Tesco has diminished as the sector has transformed around routines based on customer rather than product data.

Nevertheless, many of these retailers have had qualms about introducing a loyalty card programme. In 2013, Morrison's appointed Crawford Davidson as its customer marketing director, after he had previously worked for Tesco on the Clubcard programme. As an interviewee stated, 'I think it probably wouldn't have gone without that senior director level endorsement and drive, because it's a big, scary decision. It does impact operating margins and so on, so it's easier to take the default position of, "Let's maintain the status quo."' However, extensive use of customer data has now become almost ubiquitous in the field. According to the interviewees, 'Even now, Asda, who doesn't have a loyalty card … what I'm hearing is they're doing a lot of work trying to get customer data via other means. I think the importance of customer data is, even to people without a loyalty card, at the forefront of everyone's thinking.' The advent of e-commerce has enabled retailers to gain further customer insight without the need of a loyalty card programme.

Due to increases in computing power, in 2003 Tesco was able to use 100 per cent of the customer data gathered—as one of the interviewees explained: 'There was probably a glorious period from 2003 until 2013 when everything was being done off of 100 per cent Clubcard and also sales data.' Nowadays, with the huge amounts of non-sales data gathered from other areas, such as social media, this is impossible. One may speak of a new kind of transition in the field of grocery retailing, where the significance of customer data generated in Facebook, Google, Amazon, and so on is widely recognized, but the best ways to utilize this data have yet to be discovered. 'I think probably the grocery industry is, in this particular space, being driven for the first time more by what they're seeing outside of their industry.' With the advent of 'big data', including customer data, obtained from Internet sales, the various grocery retailers are once again competing on a more even basis in driving innovations based on customer data.

## Customer data routines as drivers of field evolution

In the case on Tesco discussed here, we have presented how the field of grocery retailing in the United Kingdom and various organizational routines such as the use of customer data have evolved during the past two decades. Many of the routines that we have observed, such as environmental assessment and the collection of product sales data, have remained fairly stable throughout the development, with only small adaptations. Traditionally, organizational routines have indeed been viewed as a source of organizational inertia and stability (Pentland & Feldman, 2005).

Other developments have resulted in changes in organizational routines. For example, the development of technology, especially increases in computing power, has significantly facilitated data analysis in UK grocery retailing. However, the introduction of Tesco's Clubcard in 1995 was not really based on the invention of any new technology but rather on innovative thinking on the part of Tesco's board, as well as on the part of Dunnhumby that needed to find ways to effectively analyse data with the computing power that was then available. While observing one's competitors has seen little change and the role of technological development has been mostly a facilitating one, ideas about collecting customer data have changed radically.

Past research suggests that organizational routines can be used to explain variance and deviation in organizational outcomes. As seen in our case example, during the time when other UK grocery retailers were not yet actively collecting or analysing customer data, Tesco stood out from its competitors in the way it viewed the surrounding world. For example, while Sainsbury's did collect sales data as well as contact data and demographical data from its customers, the focus of this data collection was on improving product sales, as opposed to Tesco's drive to understand and communicate with individual customers.

Altogether, the collection and analysis of customer data and its utilization in decision-making can be seen as a higher order routine that was first introduced in the mid-1990s and has now become ubiquitous in the field. In accordance with the view that routines are a source of organizational change and adaptation (Howard-Grenville, 2005), customer data has been the decisive factor that has resulted in the transformation of the field of retailing during the past two decades.

## Digitalization can be far more than just an adjustment to existing routines

Our understandings on field transformation have traditionally focused on explaining how structures within the industries affect organizational work processes. Particular attention has been given to the conforming behaviour of organizations' routines and practices—for example on how new technologies shape the way in which we do our daily work. Such daily routines have been traditionally viewed as stable and repeated behavioural patterns, but in digitalization, their role in bringing about transformation and innovations has also become a phenomenon of interest.

The advent of digitalization and big data provides an opportunity for completely new or different work routines that are designed to promote transformation. One such example can be found in the retail sector where the move from routines based on periodic product-centric data to routines based on more complex, real-time, customer-centric data provides a potential for change. In our research, we have examined the use of customer data in the industry of UK grocery retailing, which has been perceived as a leader within this transformational space. This industry has undergone a major transformation within the past few decades, with various loyalty programmes operating as a vehicle for change. From a marketing perspective, loyalty programmes are structured to reward both specific and general buying behaviours—encouraging changes in customer behaviour that are beneficial to the retail organizations and/or their product suppliers, and presumably to the customer. However, of more significance in promoting change within the firm, loyalty programmes also provide retail companies with data on their customers and their shopping behaviours, which can influence strategic and operational decision-making and may result in changes to organizational processes, such as those involving pricing, promotions, merchandising, and store development.

Our research has taught us that digitalization is far more than just a change in the way we do our daily work. In addition to changes in our work routines, our research illustrates how the entire transformational potential of an organization may result from the implementation of new technologies. However, the change does not come about only by implementing the most sophisticated digital processes and purchasing the newest technologies. Instead, it means institutionalizing a new culture and mindset, where employees are ready and willing to transform their existing work practices.

At the firm level, digitalization is usually associated with stronger financial growth and a higher level of efficiency. As in our case of UK grocery retailing, we argue that companies where the digital mindset is institutionalized from the highest strategic level are able to create new innovations most efficiently. It is not about having the most brilliant researchers working on digitalization, but instead, it is more about the institutionalized belief in the new way of doing things. Successful digital firms are characterized by a flexible, less hierarchical culture where employees enjoy a real autonomy and the possibility to bring about change through their own work routines.

There is no point running these expensive processes without gaining the maximum advantage out of them. The biggest challenge for managers is to figure out how to capture the benefits of digitalization, while minimizing the costs. This places additional responsibility on managers, in terms of anticipating changes in skills, adapting new training policies, and most importantly, institutionalizing the right mindset within the firm. While the goal is ambitious, there are many things managers can do to evolve their conventional organization into a digital one while ensuring that employees are keeping pace.

# References

Adler, P. S., Goldoftas, B., & Levine, D. I., 1999. 'Flexibility versus efficiency? A case study of model changeovers in the Toyota production system'. *Organization Science*, 10, 43–68.

Bacharach S. B. 1989. Organizational Theories: Some Criteria for Evaluation. The Academy of Management Review, 14(4): 496–515.

Bucher, S. & Langley, A., 2016. 'The interplay of reflective and experimental spaces in interrupting and reorienting routine dynamics'. *Organization Science*, 27(3), 594–613.

Cohen, M. D., Burkhart, R., Dosi, G., Egidi, M., Marengo, L., et al., 1996. 'Routines and other recurring action patterns of organizations: contemporary research issues'. *Industrial and Corporate Change*, 5, 653–698.

Dittrich, K., Guérard, S., & Seidl, D., 2016. 'Talking about routines: the role of reflective talk in routine change'. *Organization Science*, 27(3), 678–697.

Eisenhardt, K. M., 1989. 'Building theories from case study research'. *Academy of Management Review*, 14, 532–550.

Eisenhardt, K. M. & Graebner, M. E., 2007. 'Theory building from cases: opportunities and challenges'. *Academy of Management Journal*, 50, 25–32.

Eisenhardt, K. M. & Martin, J., 2000. 'Dynamic capabilities: what are they?' *Strategic Management Journal*, 21, 1105–1121.

Feldman, M. S. & Pentland, B. T., 2003. 'Reconceptualizing organizational routines as a source of flexibility and change'. *Administrative Science Quarterly*, 48, 94–118.

Feldman, M. S., Pentland, B. T., D'Adderio, L., & Lazaric, N., 2016. 'Beyond routines as things: introduction to the special issue on routine dynamics'. *Organization Science*, 27, 505–513.

Glaser, B. G. & Strauss, A. L., 1967. *The discovery of grounded theory: strategies for qualitative research*. Aldine Publishing Company.

Howard-Grenville, J., 2005. 'The persistence of flexible organizational routines: the role of agency and organizational context'. *Organization Science*, 16, 618–636.

Hänninen, M. and Paavola, L. 2020. 'Digital Platforms and Industry Change', in Society as an Interaction Space: A Systemic Approach, H. Lehtimäki, P. Uusikylä, and A. Smedlund (Eds.), Springer Singapore: Singapore.

Langley A. 1999. 'Strategies for Theorizing from Process Data'. Academy of Management Review, 24(4): 691–710.

Langley A. Smallman C, Tsoukas H & Van de Ven A. 2013. 'Process Studies of Change in Organization and Management: Unveiling Temporality, Activity, and Flow'. Academy of Management Journal. 56(1): 1–13.

Leonard-Barton, D., 1990. 'A dual methodology for case studies: synergistic use of a longitudinal single site with replicated multiple sites'. *Organization Science*, 1, 248–266.

Paavola, L. J. & Cuthbertson, R. W. 2018. 'Routines as drivers of adaptation, incremental change and transformation'. *Academy of Management Proceedings* 2018(1): 15686.

Paavola, L. & Cuthbertson, R. 2021. 'Algorithms Creating Paradoxes of Power: Explore, Exploit, Embed, Embalm', *Information Systems Management*, 38(4): 358–371.

Paavola, L. & Cuthbertson, R. 2022. 'Redefining capabilities as drivers of adaptation, incremental change, and transformation: Recognizing the importance of strategic and operational intent on performance'. *Journal of Management & Organization*, 28(3): 522–539.

Pentland, B. T. & Feldman, M. S., 2005. 'Organizational routines as a unit of analysis'. *Industrial and Corporate Change*, 14, 793–815.

Pentland, B. T. & Rueter, H. H., 1994. 'Organizational routines as grammars of action'. *Administrative Science Quarterly*, 39, 484–510.

Yin, R. K., 1994. *Case study research—design and methods* (2nd ed.). SAGE.

# 9

# The Timing of Innovation

*Lauri Pulkka and Richard Cuthbertson*

## Introduction

Not all innovations are successful. While innovation is vital to keeping ahead (or at least level) in the Red Queen Retail Race, it must be the right innovation at the right time. Thus, the capability to innovate has tremendous importance. The continued success and survival of firms depend on it. Innovation gives an edge on competition, and failure to change has been the undoing of many companies. Innovation is also linked to economic growth, and governments around the world enact policies in support of innovation. Moreover, external pressures, whether long-term changes, such as the ongoing digital revolution, or short-term shocks, such as the recent coronavirus pandemic, highlight the importance of innovation capability even further. Depending on the organization, such external pressures can present a cornucopia of opportunities or a kiss of death.

This innovate-or-die rhetoric can be overwhelming. It arguably creates a sense of urgency and enforces a mentality that more innovation is better. Moreover, it overshadows another highly interesting phenomenon: sometimes demonstrably capable companies choose not to innovate. They choose not to innovate and, importantly, seem to be performing well.

Innovation is defined as a non-trivial idea, practice, or object that is perceived as new by an organization (Rogers, 2003). The management of innovation is a complex process, which consists of searching for, selecting, implementing, and capturing value from innovations (Tidd & Bessant, 2013). The Covid-19 pandemic has forced many retailers to innovate due to public policies limiting the use of physical stores and encouraging online retailing. In this chapter, we examine the factors that determine when organizations innovate, not only at times of crisis, such as during a pandemic, but also in more normal circumstances.

History is littered with examples of companies entering the market too late (e.g. Nokia missing the smart phone train or Morrisons' belated entry into online grocery retailing in the United Kingdom) or too soon (e.g. Xerox introducing the graphical user interface a decade early or Webvan starting an online grocery business in the United States in 1996). How do organizations with the right capabilities know *when* to innovate? What does timing of innovation even mean?

Lauri Pulkka and Richard Cuthbertson, *The Timing of Innovation*. In: *The Red Queen Retail Race*. Edited by Richard Cuthbertson, Olli Rusanen, and Lauri Paavola, Oxford University Press. © Lauri Pulkka and Richard Cuthbertson (2023). DOI: 10.1093/oso/9780192862617.003.0009

We begin this chapter with a short overview of the innovation literature, with a focus on why the timing of innovation is relevant. This is followed by a review of innovation capability. We propose a construct of innovation capability consisting of capacity, ability, and value. Capability is important but alone insufficient in explaining the timing of innovation. Therefore, we also examine the external forces that act as impetus to innovation. We then proceed to show how the implementation of innovation depends on both capability and impetus. Finally, we develop a new model of the timing of innovation that is a function of capabilities, impetus, and implementation.

The retail sector is undergoing an unprecedented transformation. The broadest strokes of the future retail landscape are evident: increasingly digital, global, and diverse (for a detailed description, see Treadgold & Reynolds, 2020). The pace of change and details of its manifestation vary, however, depending on the context. For example, why is online grocery retail a thing in the United Kingdom but not in Finland?

The concept of innovation and the issue of timing are central to understanding the dynamics of what is happening in the retail sector. Innovation involves not only an idea but the implementation of such an idea. The timing of that implementation may be the difference between success and failure. Hence, in any marketplace, there are leaders and laggards (Rogers, 2003). As highlighted in the previous chapters, innovation feeds on and contributes to changes in technology, consumer behaviour, business models, organization structure and strategy, and public policy.

## From why and how to when

The question 'why innovate?' has already been convincingly answered: if you do not, you eventually cease to exist. Failed businesses across sectors can attest to that. This dynamic is the essence of the Schumpeterian notion of creative destruction, whereby waves of technological and socio-economic change sweep unprepared organizations into obsoletion (Schumpeter, 1942).

Innovation capability is considered one of the most important determinants of firm performance (Hult et al., 2004; Mone, McKinley, & Barker, 1998). Being able to implement new products, processes, and services is a source of competitive advantage. In the long term, it enables organizations to adapt to competition and other changes in their environment (Elmquist & Le Masson, 2009; Olsson et al., 2010).

In high-tech industries, innovation has been routinely prioritized. Now, in the wake of digitalization, organizations in traditionally low-tech industries like retail and construction, which have enjoyed a period of relative stability, are increasingly compelled to think about change. Digitalization is half promise, half threat.

It opens up opportunities for efficiency and productivity gains and new products and services. The threat for an organization is that its competitors are more skilled in exploiting those opportunities.

Digitalization is a catalyst to innovation; the ongoing disruption highlights the importance of renewal across industries. Importantly, how organizations innovate is also changing. After the introduction of open innovation (Chesbrough, 2003), it is increasingly acknowledged that organizations do not innovate in isolation (Dahlander & Gann, 2010). The main principle of open innovation is that organizations should utilize internal as well as external ideas and paths to markets (Chesbrough, 2003, 2008). In other words, open innovation encourages cross-pollination of ideas and innovations across organizational boundaries.

This is in stark contrast to the traditional, closed model of innovation management. Its features include detailed planning, relying on in-house development, operating under secrecy, and strictly enforcing intellectual property rights (Chesbrough, 2003). A common practical application is the stage-gate system, in which the innovation process is divided into sequential stages with quality control checkpoints, or gates, between them (Cooper, 1990; O'Connor, 2002). A typical sequence consists of (1) preliminary assessment of potential R&D ideas, (2) detailed investigation, (3) development, (4) testing and validation, and (5) full production and market launch (Ettlie & Elsenbach, 2007).

The paradigm shift from closed to open innovation is more profound than a shift from in-house to collaborative development. The best practice in closed innovation processes has long since evolved from the single-organization, technology-push model of the 1950s into a dynamic, non-linear process that incorporates collaboration and external factors (Rothwell, 1994). What the shift from closed to open innovation really changes is the goal.

Traditionally, the goal of innovation activities has been to gain a temporary monopoly position in a market by offering or doing something unmatched (Schumpeter, 1942). Whether the innovator is an organization or a network does not matter. This mode of operation encourages organizations to keep their ideas to themselves and force competitors to play catch-up. Open innovation, on the other hand, starts from the premise that neither ideas nor innovations are scarce resources. The innovator benefits mainly not from being the first and only to the market—a so-called first-mover advantage—but from getting others to adapt the innovation (Chesbrough, 2003).

The main implication is that innovation has become more about implementation and less about development. There are more opportunities for innovation available than before. Globalization makes it more pronounced; organizations have access to a global pool of ideas and solutions. For many organizations, access to global markets has also removed constraints like the limited production capacity of local partners or reliance on the national financial sector that may have previously prevented them from considering some options altogether.

The move from development to implementation in innovation is mirrored in the shift from a goods-dominant to a service-dominant (S-D) logic in business. The concept of the S-D logic originates from marketing literature (Grönroos, 1982, 2006; Vargo & Lusch, 2004). It represents a fundamental change in how value is considered. The prevalent goods-dominant logic holds that value can be embedded into the goods and services an organization produces and sells to customers, that is, that value is created by organizations for customers.

The S-D logic is built on a different set of premises. Rather than seeing value as something that is created for the customer, 'the customer is always a co-creator of value' (Vargo & Lusch, 2008, p. 7). The organization cannot create value independently; it can only offer value propositions. Value itself is derived through use and determined by the beneficiary, which means that the value of a particular service is unique to the customer. Moreover, according to the S-D logic, service is defined as the application of knowledge and skills (operant resources) for the benefit of another party (Vargo & Lusch, 2004). Goods such as physical products (operand resources) are merely a way to distribute services. Therefore, the same product, for example, can be part of very different value propositions in different organizations.

What follows is that the value of any instance of innovation is not determined by its qualities per se but by how it is integrated with the operant resources of the organization and used by the customers and other beneficiaries (Michel, Brown, & Gallan, 2008). This approach highlights implementation rather than development of innovation: even if the innovation is not new to the world, it can be implemented in a way that results in a unique value proposition. The integration of the innovation and the organization's resources into a coherent value proposition can be described using the Service Innovation Triangle (SIT) framework (Furseth & Cuthbertson, 2016).

The organization is at the centre of the SIT framework. It is divided into three layers. The outcome layer is at the top and has only one element: value. This represents the value the organization is proposing to customers and other beneficiaries with the innovation. Because it depends on the organization's resources, it rests at the top, supported by the two other layers. The ability layer represents how the organization goes about activating its resources and creating the value with others: customer experiences delivered by the service system, united by a business model. At the base of the triangle is the capacity layer, which represents the stock of operant and operand resources of the organization: tangible, financial, and intangible assets, as well as people and technology. The SIT framework is apt for our purposes because it highlights that the implementation of innovation concerns both the internal elements of the organization and external forces.

To summarize, innovation capability is as important as ever for both short-term competitive advantage and long-term survival. The foundational reasons for why organizations should innovate have remained stable. In how organizations innovate, the largest change is arguably the paradigm shift from closed to open innovation. While both modes of innovation continue to co-exist, the utilization of external ideas and pathways to market has become more prominent. It has resulted in a shift of focus from the development to the implementation of innovation. In the retail sector, there are more opportunities for implementing innovations than ever, but organizations have limited resources and need to choose where to commit them. This and the uncertainty created by the ongoing digital revolution beg the question of when to innovate. 'As quickly as possible' is an often-heard, intuitively appealing but observably false answer, and we are committed to providing a better one. In the next section, we introduce the components of our model of the timing of innovation.

## Components of the model: capability, impetus, and implementation

Based on our analysis, there are three important questions impacting the timing of innovations. Does the organization have the capability to innovate? Does the organization have the impetus to innovate? And how could an organization implement an innovation? Each of these components are now discussed.

### Innovation capability

One of the challenges related to studying innovation capability is that it cannot be directly observed. That is, innovation capability is not a distinct entity within a firm but a higher level construct that consists of multiple elements and their interactions that support innovation. Innovation activities concern the entire organization, and innovation capability has knowledge, organizational, and human dimensions (Martínez-Román, Gamero, & Tamayo, 2011). Typical elements include innovation-oriented culture, supportive and participatory leadership, work climate, ideation management, organizational structure and systems, and individual activity (Saunila, Pekkola, & Ukko, 2014).

The manifestation and combination of the above elements is firm specific. What works for one organization may fail at another. Due to the complexity of the innovation capability construct and the variation among organizations, it is impossible to come up with a universal recipe for success. Furthermore, it has been argued that different types of innovation call for different sets of capabilities (Tuominen & Hyvönen, 2004).

There is reason to suspect that existing conceptualizations of innovation capability do not readily fit our purposes. Innovation capability is typically discussed in terms of enabling product innovation. Retailers are often involved in the non-technical service and process innovation that takes place alongside everyday business. Traditional metrics of innovative output fail to account for much of what happens in retail. Similarly, existing constructs of innovation capability do not necessarily reflect the proper capability for innovation in the retail sector.

Sometimes the innovation capability of an organization is equated with its innovative performance, emphasizing quantity, continuity, and speed. For example, one widely used measure consists of the company's readiness to experiment with new ideas, creativity in its operations, ability to take risks, keenness on being the first to market, and increase in new innovations in the last five years (Calantone, Cavusgil, & Zhao, 2002; Lin, 2007).

While having no doubt that some firms in retail, just like in any other industry, want to continuously maximize their innovative output and be at the forefront of change, we argue that many other organizations are more conservative and careful in selecting which innovative opportunities to pursue. Not all organizations are 'innovation engines' (see Lawson & Samson, 2001). Some firms thrive on stability.

Moreover, we cannot start with a premise that an organization's innovation capability is good when it is geared towards uncovering and exploiting innovative opportunities as quickly as possible, for the simple reason that we are examining the issue of the timing of innovation. We have already argued that more innovation is not necessarily better. Many innovative opportunities are known and available for organizations. Therefore, what we need is a construct of innovation capability that (1) can be used on a case-to-case basis to discern whether a particular instance of innovation can be implemented and (2) is also compatible with the non-technical service and process innovation.

For this purpose, we suggest a construct of innovation capability that is based on the nine elements of an organization in the SIT framework: innovation capacity (tangible assets, technology, financial assets, people, and intangible assets), ability (service system, business model, and customer experiences), and outcome (value), where:

Capability = organization's operant + operand resources

and

Impetus = demand and expectations for the value proposition.

Using the SIT as a basis for the construct of innovation capability fits our purposes, because the SIT is designed for analysing the implementation of service innovation and has been used extensively in the context of retailing. Moreover, it is compatible with the so-called holistic view of innovation capability, according to which innovation activities concern the entire organization. For example, based on an extensive literature review, Martínez-Román, Gamero, and Tamayo (2011) divide innovation capabilities into knowledge, organizational, and human dimensions, all of which have managerial implications. The capacity and ability layers of the SIT cover the three above-mentioned dimensions, and the ability layer in particular is concerned with their management.

## Impetus to innovate

Innovation capability is crucial because it determines whether an organization has the capacity and ability to implement a particular instance of innovation. However, it does not determine whether the organization will implement the innovation. This is where the concept of impetus comes in. Impetus is defined as the force or energy that sets things in motion. In the context of innovation, impetus can be seen as a combination of forces that set the demand and expectations for the innovation.

Sources of impetus are external to the organization. In line with the previous discussion on innovation capability, our conceptualization of impetus also builds partly on the SIT. The main elements of the construct are highlighted in Figure 9.1. The elements can be divided into layers based on how much control the organization is able to exert on them. Owners, suppliers, and customers are participants of the organization's value network. The organization typically directly interacts with them. Surrounding the organization and its immediate value network is the market/society layer. It includes actors and forces such as competitors, regulation, and social trends. The gradient symbolizes both its breadth and limited observability from the organization's perspective.

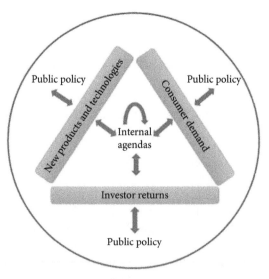

**Figure 9.1** Sources of impetus to innovate

The actors in the value network can influence impetus to innovate in many ways. Institutional investor owners typically seek long-term gains from their investments, meaning that they appreciate innovativeness and may influence firms to increase innovation (Kochhar & David, 1996). Because large investors work with many organizations and sectors, they are in a good position to pollinate ideas across firm boundaries. It is of course possible for owners to inhibit innovation by actively opposing it, decreasing impetus. Due to the interdependencies between organizations, suppliers play an integral role in an organization's innovation activities (e.g. Christensen, 2013; Miller et al., 1995). Similarly to owners, they can increase or decrease impetus with their own actions.

Customers are one of the main sources of impetus. If we accept the premise of the S-D logic that customers are always co-creators of value, then organizations should be very sensitive to what kind of value propositions their customers are after. Customer demand can drive growth of impetus from owners and suppliers, too. On the other hand, Christensen (2013), for example, warns against serving only current customers, because disruptive innovation may serve the needs of a completely new customer segment. Current customers may therefore constrain impetus.

Competition stimulates innovation (Schumpeter, 1942; Souder & Chakrabarti, 1978). It applies generally but also to particular instances of innovation. If a competitor implements an innovation, it can increase the focal organization's pressure to implement its version of it. For example, when none of the grocery retailers in a given market offer an online delivery service, the pressure to implement that service is limited. However, when any of the retailers makes it available, customers start to expect it, which increases the impetus for other retailers to implement their own delivery services.

Innovation policy is used increasingly to support innovation in general, but regulation can also create impetus for particular innovations. This is the case especially in the context of environmentalism (Beerepoot & Beerepoot, 2007; Jordan et al., 2003). Building regulations is an obvious example, whereby tightening energy requirements has forced building designers and construction companies to implement some form of heat recovery ventilation into the buildings.

Impetus is related to the concept of change-based momentum, which is used in the strategy literature to describe the energy and enthusiasm associated with pursuing a new trajectory (Jansen, 2004). It is a dynamic element, whose level fluctuates in response to events, perceptions, and interactions. Pulkka and Junnila (2015) have applied the concept of change-based momentum to the innovation process. Gaining momentum decreases the amount of the firm's own resources that the organization needs to implement an innovation. Losing momentum increases the need for the firm's own resources and hinders implementation. Impetus can be considered as the potential of different actors to contribute to the momentum of the implementation process.

## Implementation of innovation

Capability describes if an organization can innovate, and impetus describes how much an organization has to innovate in order to create enough momentum to change the market. How an organization innovates is a question of implementation. It refers to all the steps the organization takes in order for the innovation to be adopted (Tidd & Bessant, 2013). Implementation is shaped by capability and impetus. We illustrate this through the gravitational slingshot analogy of innovation, originally developed by Pulkka and Junnila (2015).

The gravitational slingshot or gravity-assist manoeuvre is a proven method of interplanetary travel, which utilizes the gravity and motion of planets to change the speed and path of a spacecraft. Here, space travel is used as a metaphor for the innovation process. The analogy is illustrated in Figure 9.2. The planets represent organizations and other actors (e.g. suppliers, customers, owners, competitors, regulators) that can affect the innovation process. Their orbital direction is signified by the arrowheads.

The arrow spiralling outwards represents the implementation of the innovation. It originates at the innovating organization, and its path bends upon interaction with different organizations and actors—much like a spacecraft's path does in planetary flybys. In addition to redirecting the path of the implementation process, these interactions also serve the purpose of gaining or losing momentum. A spacecraft accelerates when it flies with the orbital motion of the planet and

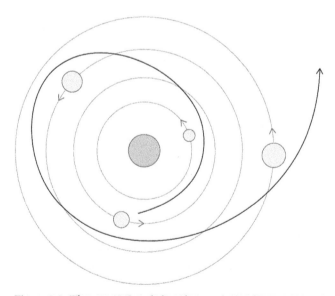

**Figure 9.2**  The gravitational slingshot analogy of innovation (adapted from Pulkka and Junnila, 2015)

decelerates when it flies against it. Analogously, the implementation gains momentum in interactions with supportive actors and loses momentum in interactions with non-supportive actors.

Implementation is shaped by capability and impetus. In the space travel metaphor, capability is the propellant. It is needed for take-off and for manipulating the trajectory. Impetus corresponds to the orbital direction, position, and gravity of the planets, that is the potential for using the gravity-assist manoeuvre. The gravitational slingshot method is often the fastest and—because it greatly reduces the amount of propellant required—the most feasible way of space travel. Similarly, a combination of capability and impetus is required for the implementation of innovation.

The planetary system is largely innovation and market-specific. That is, the impetus to innovate is for the most part shared by different organizations pursuing the same innovation in the same market. It is important to note, however, that while the impetus may be the same, how different organizations perceive it, as well as how they are positioned to utilize it, varies.

Figure 9.2 depicts a successful outcome whereby the innovation is adopted. This is indicated by the line flying out, or the spacecraft gaining necessary velocity to escape the system. Other outcomes are of course possible. A lack of capability may lead to the innovation not getting off the ground in the first place. A combination of low capability and high impetus (little capacity to steer and many planets with high gravity) or high capability and low impetus (lots of fuel but few opportunities for flybys) may leave the innovation stuck in orbit within the system.

We have so far covered the three main components of the model of the timing of innovation: capability, impetus, and implementation. What is missing is time. In the following section, we illustrate through a model how timing is a function of the development of capability and impetus over time. Moreover, we argue that timing is very relevant to the implementation of innovation and show through practical examples how the model explains different outcomes.

## The model of the timing of innovation

Neither capability nor impetus alone explains when it is the right time to implement a particular innovation or what good timing means. Therefore, we propose a new model of the timing of innovation, which is a function of capability, impetus, and implementation. The timing of innovation model is illustrated in Figure 9.3 and described in more detail below.

Capability and impetus are plotted on a graph that has their relative levels on the Y-axis and time on the X-axis. The dashed line denotes innovation capability and the solid line the impetus to innovate. More specifically, the lines represent

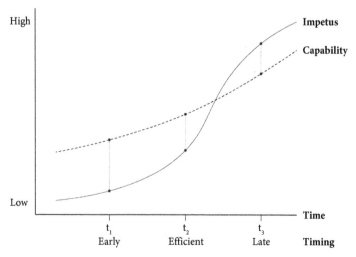

**Figure 9.3** The timing of innovation

the development of capability and impetus over time regarding a specific instance of innovation. Whether timing is early, efficient, or late is indicated by the relative levels of the two variables.

The model has been developed primarily for new services, but it is also applicable to product, process, and organizational innovation. It does not have to be new to the world. For example, there is little revolutionary about the global e-commerce giant Amazon opening a physical bookstore or the Finnish multi-sector cooperative S-Group introducing self-checkout machines, but the examples are new to the organization and therefore qualify as innovations.

It is not possible to discern from the model whether implementing the innovation is desirable or will be beneficial to the organization. The focus is strictly on timing and its implications for the implementation process. Moreover, in the following discussion, it is assumed that the organization is capable of implementing at least some version of the innovation, no matter how flawed (e.g. limited rollout, poor functionality, or regulatory non-compliance). Otherwise, there would be no capability line to draw, and the question of timing would be irrelevant.

When capability exceeds impetus, the organization is ahead of external demand for the innovation. The organization is able to initiate implementation, but with more push and less pull for the innovation. Low impetus can indicate that the timing is early. This is the case at $t_1$ in Figure 9.3. Impetus at that point is not only lower but also developing slower than capability. Implementing the innovation with little impetus can be arduous, costly, and potentially unsuccessful. In terms of the space travel metaphor, more propellant is not a replacement for the gravitational slingshot method.

Impetus at $t_2$ remains lower, but it is growing at a faster pace and will eventually surpass capability. The timing becomes more efficient as the lines converge until they intersect. In Figure 9.3, the point at which the lines intersect indicates the most efficient timing. Higher impetus translates into higher potential for gaining momentum for the implementation. Matching capability means that the organization is able to exploit that potential. Efficiency applies to space travel, too: the planets are aligned just right and the spacecraft has enough propellant for take-off and necessary manoeuvring.

When impetus is higher than capability, the timing is late. The organization is not able to exploit the potential momentum to the fullest, leading to suboptimal implementation of the innovation. Remember, the timing of innovation is determined by the relative rather than absolute levels of capability and impetus. Therefore, although capability has increased from $t_2$ to $t_3$ in Figure 9.3 impetus has increased even more and exceeded capability, resulting in the timing at $t_3$ being late.

The implications of timing for implementation are illustrated in Figure 9.4. When the timing is efficient, the organization can focus on the execution of the implementation. Innovation is always a risky endeavour, but the balance between capability and impetus facilitates the process. When the timing is late, the risk of failure is greater. To mitigate that risk, the organization should focus on developing its capability while it is implementing the innovation. When the timing is early, the risk is again higher, and the organization should focus on developing impetus. Especially the last item, development of impetus, is often overlooked in the capability-emphasizing and management-oriented innovation literature. It is also the part that really stretches the analogy, as manipulating the planetary system is much easier in the organizational than physical universe.

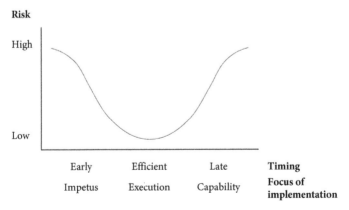

**Figure 9.4**  Risk of failure and focus of implementation with different timings

The abstract model seems logically consistent, but a true test of its relevance is how well it is able to explain different outcomes. In the following sections, we apply the model to some practical examples of innovation. We then examine how capability and impetus develop and how the model can be utilized by organizations in practice.

## Implications of timing on innovation outcomes

Before going into more detail, a few general remarks are in order. First, it is important to remember that capability and impetus are constructs that consist of multiple elements. Individual elements can develop at different paces and directions. Second, the elements do not exist in isolation; they influence one another. Third, the organization has limited control over the development of capability and impetus. Fourth, the act of implementing the innovation affects capability and impetus.

Experimenting with an innovation before its large-scale implementation is common in retail. Practical experimentation is sometimes preceded or accompanied by R&D around the topic. Experiments increase capability in many ways. They can familiarize the organization with new technology, people involved acquire new knowledge and skills, and experimenting enables quick feedback on new customer experiences. Experimentation is often a process of trial and error, which increases capability in incremental steps rather than discontinuous leaps.

A major limitation of experiments is that they typically concern a small share of personnel and locations. For example, Citycon, an owner and operator of multiple shopping centres in Northern Europe, recently developed a smartphone app, which initially had functionality for just one of its centres. The benefits of the experiment on the capability of Citycon regarding digital services are not spread evenly. Without an effort to disseminate the learnings of the people involved in the experiment to the rest of the organization, the overall impact can be modest.

Increasing capability is not the only purpose of experimentation. It is also a means to influence impetus on many levels. Experiments can generate excitement within the organization and garner top-level commitment for innovations. Moreover, they increase demand and interest among customers and suppliers, by exposing them to new possibilities. Experiments can also have even broader, sometimes unexpected consequences. Pässilä, Pulkka, and Junnila (2015) detail how a successful pilot project changed regulation concerning low-energy housing in Finland because the organization simply invited politicians and public officials to come look at it.

If experimentation is a possible reason behind incremental capability development, organizational acquisitions or mergers represent a discontinuous leap. Amazon's acquisition of Wholefoods in 2017 is a prime example. In the $13.7 billion deal, Amazon gained a vast stock of tangible and intangible assets: a network of brick-and-mortar stores, private-brand product, and data on affluent customers (Petro, 2017). On a related side note, Amazon made its move after years of experimentation with physical stores.

The actions of an organization can also decrease capability and impetus for an innovation. Discontinuing R&D on an area not only stops the generation of new information but also undermines the organization's ability to assimilate and exploit related existing information (Cohen & Levinthal, 1989), which leads to a gradual decrease in capability. A discontinuous drop in capability can result from, for example, a disinvestment. Since 2008, the energy company BP invested an estimated $750 million into the development of cellulosic biofuels before pulling the plug in 2015, effectively removing that capability from its organization (Lane, 2015).

When it comes to impetus, one important reason for its decrease is the success of business as usual. Why prioritize and commit resources to change when the organization is doing great as is? This is related to the 'innovator's dilemma', whereby an organization is blinded by existing demand, gets locked in into an incumbent technology, and fails to innovate until it is too late (Christensen, 2013). But the issue is not only internal to the organization. The desirability of the status quo can arguably suppress impetus from virtually any source: for example initiative of the owners, innovativeness of suppliers and the sector, customer demand for new services, or even structural policy change.

The previous examples were intended to illustrate that there is great variety in possible reasons for the development of capability and impetus. To what extent are they in the hands of the organization? The elements of capability are mainly internal, and therefore they are more easily influenced by the organization. The elements of impetus are mainly external. However, none of them should be considered completely outside the organization's sphere of influence.

The organization is continuously interacting with its customers, suppliers, and owners. It was already mentioned how experimentation, for example, can create impetus within these groups. Regulation and competition are separate from the organization but, again, not necessarily outside the sphere of influence. In Europe alone, lobbying is a billion-euro industry. And, many organizations share membership with their competitors in the same professional and industry networks.

The variation in the examples may make the development of capability and impetus seem random. However, there are some general rules or trends to it. The diffusion of innovation, meaning its adoption by users, follows an S-curve; the adoption starts from a small group of frontrunners, followed by the majority, and ending with a small group of laggards (Rogers, 2003). This implies that impetus in the form of customer demand tends to increase after the innovation has been implemented by an organization.

There are similar 'laws' governing the development of technology. For example, after radical breakthroughs, technological development typically continues along a trajectory in incremental steps (Dosi, 1982). There is agreement on what constitutes an improvement. In this process, the technology becomes more accessible and gets adapted by more actors. Therefore, over time, capability in the form of technological capacity tends to increase simply because the technology becomes more mature.

Finally, the act of implementation affects capability. It is widely acknowledged that organizations with greater innovation capability have, on average, greater innovation activity. However, the relationship is argued to be reciprocal, meaning that implementing the innovation strengthens the development of the organization's capability (Withers, Drnevich, & Marino, 2011). Therefore, innovative organizations may have an easier time implementing innovations overall, although it does not guarantee impetus and good timing.

## Considerations on using the model

With the previous discussion in mind, the model of the timing of innovation should look less like Figure 9.4 and more like Figure 9.5 with the elements doing their own things. However, we want to say:

1. Thinking of capability and impetus as uniform lines is helpful, because it forces the organization to think about what the boundary conditions are, that is the vital elements of capability and impetus.
2. To what extent do the lines represent reality or perceptions? For some elements, there are metrics more readily available than for others. For example financial assets or regulations are more or less factual.

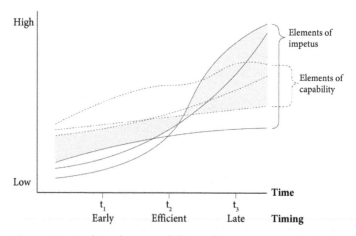

**Figure 9.5** Breaking down capability and impetus into individual elements

3. The model can be used in an organization by surveying personnel, suppliers, and potential customers to see how they perceive capability/impetus.

## Commitment and timing

The model of the timing of innovation is intended as both a research and decision-making support model, that is, as a helpful conceptual tool for researchers and practitioners who are trying to make sense about the time dimension of innovation.

Interestingly the lessons for practitioners appear to be more about commitment and implementation rather than timing. There are examples of success and failure in all timeframes, suggesting that trajectory is more important than timing. For example, Webvan created great momentum for change but there was little impetus coming from the market.

The concept of innovation binds together the chapters of this book. The disruption of the retail sector is largely driven by innovation. Changes in organization structure are closely related to the development of innovation capabilities. Changes in strategy can generate impetus to innovate. Changes in customer experiences and the emergence of new business models result from and feed into innovation. In this chapter, we presented the model of the timing of innovation on a conceptual level. Other parts of the book contain more details and practical examples of the individual components that make up innovation capability and impetus to innovate. Taken together, those chapters and the model of the timing of innovation offer a fresh perspective on the ongoing Red Queen Retail Race. Retailers are not only competing against other retailers (competition) but also against themselves (capability) and changes in the external environment (impetus).

## References

Beerepoot, M. & Beerepoot, N., 2007. 'Government regulation as an impetus for innovation: evidence from energy performance regulation in the Dutch residential building sector'. *Energy Policy*, 35(10), 4812–4825.

Calantone, R. J., Cavusgil, S. T., & Zhao, Y., 2002. 'Learning orientation, firm innovation capability, and firm performance'. *Industrial Marketing Management*, 31(6), 515–524.

Chesbrough, H. W., 2003. *Open innovation: the new imperative for creating and profiting from technology*. Harvard Business School Press.

Chesbrough, H. W., 2008. 'Open innovation: a new paradigm for understanding industrial innovation'. In H. W Chesbrough, W. Vanhaverbeke, & J. West (eds), *Open innovation: researching a new paradigm*: 1–12. Oxford University Press.

Christensen, C. M., 2013. *The innovator's dilemma: when new technologies cause great firms to fail*. Harvard Business Review Press.

Cohen, W. M. & Levinthal, D. A., 1989. 'Innovation and learning: the two faces of R&D'. *The Economic Journal*, 99(397), 569–596.

Cooper, R. G., 1990. 'Stage-gate systems: a new tool for managing new products'. *Business Horizons*, 33(3), 44–53.

Dahlander, L. & Gann, D. M., 2010. 'How open is innovation?' *Research Policy*, 39(6), 699–709.

Dosi, G., 1982. 'Technical paradigms and technological trajectories: a suggested interpretation of the determinants of technical change'. *Research Policy*, 2(3), 147–162.

Elmquist, M. & Le Masson, P., 2009. 'The value of a "failed" R&D project: an emerging evaluation framework for building innovative capabilities'. *R&D Management*, 39(2), 136–152

Ettlie, J. E. & Elsenbach, J. M., 2007. 'Modified stage-gate regimes in new product development'. *Journal of Product Innovation Management*, 24(1), 20–33.

Furseth, P. I. & Cuthbertson, R. W., 2016. *Innovation in an advanced consumer society.* Oxford University Press.

Grönroos, C., 1982. 'An applied service marketing theory'. *European Journal of Marketing*, 16(7), 30–41.

Grönroos, C., 2006. 'Adopting a service logic for marketing'. *Marketing Theory*, 6(3), 317–333.

Hult, G. T. M., Hurley, R. F., & Knight, G. A., 2004. 'Innovativeness: its antecedents and impact on business performance'. *Industrial Marketing Management*, 33(5), 429–438.

Jansen, K.J., 2004. 'From persistence to pursuit: a longitudinal examination of momentum during the early stages of strategic change'. *Organization Science* 15(3), 276–294.

Jordan, A., Wurzel, R. K., Zito, R., & Brückner, L., 2003. 'Policy innovation or "muddling through"? "New" environmental policy instruments in the United Kingdom'. *Environmental Politics*, 12(1), 179–200.

Kochhar, R. & David, P., 1996. 'Institutional investors and firm innovation: a test of competing hypotheses'. *Strategic Management Journal*, 17(1), 73–84.

Lane, J., 2015. 'BP's exit from cellulosic ethanol: the assets, the auction, the process, the timing, the skinny'. *Biofuels Digest*, 18 January, available online: http://www.biofuelsdigest.com/bdigest/2015/01/18/bps-exit-from-cellulosic-ethanol-the-assets-the-auction-the-process-the-timing-the-skinny/

Lawson, B. & Samson, D., 2001. 'Developing innovation capability in organizations: a dynamic capabilities approach'. *International Journal of Innovation Management*, 5(03), 377–400.

Lin, H. F., 2007. 'Knowledge sharing and firm innovation capability: an empirical study'. *International Journal of Manpower*, 28(3/4), 315–332.

Martínez-Román, J. A., Gamero, J., & Tamayo, J. A., 2011. 'Analysis of innovation in SMEs using an innovative capability-based non-linear model: a study in the province of Seville (Spain)'. *Technovation*, 31(9), 459–475.

Michel, S., Brown, S. W., & Gallan, A. S., 2008. 'An expanded and strategic view of discontinuous innovation: deploying a service-dominant logic'. *Journal of the Academy of Marketing Science*, 36(1), 54–66.

Miller, R., Hobday, M., Leroux-Demers, T., & Olleros, X., 1995. 'Innovation in complex systems industries: the case of flight simulation'. *Industrial and Corporate Change*, 4(2), 363–400.

Mone, M. A., McKinley, W., & Barker, V. L., 1998. 'Organizational decline and innovation: a contingency framework'. *Academic Management Review*, 23(1), 115–132.

O'Connor, P., 2002. 'Implementing a stage-gate process: a multi-company perspective'. *Journal of Product Innovation Management*, 11(3), 183–200.

Olsson, P., Bodin. Ö, & Folke. C., 2010. 'Building transformative capacity for ecosystem stewardship in social–ecological systems'. In D. Armitage and R. Plummer, editors. Adaptive capacity and environmental governance: 263–285. Springer-Verlag.

Petro, G., 2017. 'Amazon's acquisition of whole foods is about two things: data and product'. *Forbes*, 2 Aug, available online: https://www.forbes.com/sites/gregpetro/2017/08/02/amazons-acquisition-of-whole-foods-is-about-two-things-data-and-product/#fccc18fa8084.

Pässilä, P., Pulkka, L., & Junnila, S., 2015. 'How to succeed in low-energy housing—path creation analysis of low-energy innovation projects'. *Sustainability*, 7(7), 8801–8822.

Pulkka L. & Junnila, S., 2015. 'Gravitational slingshot analogy of discontinuous sustainability innovation in the construction industry'. *Construction Innovation: Information, Process, Management*, 15, 409–427

Rogers, E. M., 2003. *Diffusion of innovations* (5th ed.). Free Press.

Rothwell, R., 1994. 'Towards the fifth-generation innovation process'. *International Marketing Review*, 11(1), 7–31.

Saunila, M., Pekkola, S., & Ukko, J., 2014. 'The relationship between innovation capability and performance: the moderating effect of measurement'. *International Journal of Productivity and Performance Management*, 63(2), 234–249.

Schumpeter, J. A., 1942. *Capitalism, socialism and democracy*. Harper & Brothers.

Souder, W. E. & Chakrabarti, A. K., 1978. 'The R&D/marketing interface: results from an empirical study of innovation projects'. *IEEE Transactions on Engineering Management*, (4), 88–93.

Tidd, J. & Bessant, J., 2013. *Managing innovation: integrating technological, market and organizational change* (5th ed.). Wiley.

Treadgold, A. & Reynolds, J., 2020. *Navigating the new retail landscape: a guide for business leaders*. Oxford University Press.

Tuominen, M. & Hyvönen, S., 2004. 'Organizational innovation capability: a driver for competitive superiority in marketing channels'. *The International Review of Retail, Distribution and Consumer Research*, 14(3), 277–293.

Vargo, S. L. & Lusch, R. F., 2004. 'Evolving to a new dominant logic for marketing'. *Journal of Marketing*, 68(1), 1–17.

Vargo, S. L. & Lusch, R. F., 2008. 'Service-dominant logic: continuing the evolution'. *Journal of the Academy of Marketing Science*, 36(1), 1–10.

Withers, M. C., Drnevich, P. L., & Marino, L., 2011. 'Doing more with less: the disordinal implications of firm age for leveraging capabilities for innovation activity'. *Journal of Small Business Management*, 49(4), 515–536.

# 10

# The Future of Retailing

*Richard Cuthbertson and Lauri Paavola*

"They were running hand in hand, and the Queen went so fast that it was all she could do to keep up with her: and still the Queen kept crying 'Faster! Faster!' but Alice felt she could not go faster, though she had not breath left to say so. The most curious part of the thing was, that the trees and the other things round them never changed their places at all: however fast they went, they never seemed to pass anything."

Lewis Carroll (1871)

## Introduction

Throughout this book, we have seen how retail firms, like many businesses, are undergoing dramatic changes. As described in Chapter 1, the very nature of the retail sector is changing. The boundaries between distribution and communication channels are blurring (Chapter 2) and re-forming in new networks or ecosystems of manufacturers, retailers, consumers, and investors, with regulators struggling to keep up (Chapter 3). While retail public policy has always been split across many different government departments, such as environment, planning, taxation, competition, and employment, as well as being split between national and local decision-making, one constant has remained, geography. Decisions were always based on location: too many stores in that area, too little competition in that town, recycling requirements of that country, taxation rates of that city centre, and so on. However, the digital revolution has undermined such location-based decision-making, as discussed in Chapter 4. This gives rise to a dynamic within the retail sector that makes it necessary for firms to develop their resources faster in order ultimately to remain competitive at all. The Covid-19 pandemic has accelerated the pace of this innovation in many areas. This innovation pandemic is necessary to stay in the Red Queen Retail Race. The concept of the Red Queen Retail Race is a metaphor inspired by Alice's encounters with the Red Queen in the classical novel *Through the Looking-Glass, and What Alice Found There* by Lewis Carroll (1871). When observing the Red Queen Race, Alice wondered why,

Richard Cuthbertson and Lauri Paavola, *The Future of Retailing*. In: *The Red Queen Retail Race*. Edited by Richard Cuthbertson, Olli Rusanen, and Lauri Paavola, Oxford University Press. © Richard Cuthbertson and Lauri Paavola (2023). DOI: 10.1093/oso/9780192862617.003.0010 unlike in her country, most contestants appeared to remain still despite running intensively. 'That is a slow sort of country!' the Queen commented, and continued: 'Now, here, you see, it takes all the running you can do, to keep in the same place. If you want to get somewhere else, you must run at least twice as fast as that.' As competition breaks down across geographies and sectors, retailers must now continue to run twice as fast as today just to stay in the race.

## Competition in a global marketplace for consumer services

We began this book with Chapters 1 and 2 outlining the retail context today. In Chapter 2 we discussed how global marketplaces have transformed during the past two decades. We saw how major retail chains have traditionally competed through investments on volume-driving resources that have leveraged supply innovation, wide product assortment, and large physical space that has delivered competitive advantage through economies of scale. Lately, however, the value of these volume-driving resources has declined, creating a major challenge for retail resource management. Retailers are thus forced to find new sources of growth and to identify emerging value drivers, particularly through developing better consumer experiences. The requirements for resources have changed, and continue to change, to keep up not only with new trends in product development but also with how those products are delivered to the customer.

Chapter 2 presented a model that explored the gap between large retailers' current competencies and these emerging value drivers. The twentieth century witnessed the rise of large retail firms reaching out across the globe. These firms leveraged innovations on the supply side and through standardization and economies of scale empowered their customers with broader assortments coupled with low prices. During the last decade, many of these traditional businesses have been struggling due to the declining unit value of volume-driving resources.

The model presented summarized four tangible key competencies and four emerging intangible value drivers. Retailers' core competencies are built around supply technologies, product orientation, physical environment, and standardization-driven economies of scale. Emerging drivers of resource value are increasingly intangible: demand-driven innovations through big data, service orientation, digital solutions, and personalized relationships. The goal of this chapter was to open up our discussion on the dematerialization of resource value drivers due to the megatrends of digitalization and servitization. Accordingly, the capability needs of retailers have undergone a huge change during the past decade.

To take the discussion further, in Chapter 3, we focused on the emergence of platforms that have provided retailers with a tool for responding to this changing landscape. More specifically, we discussed the theoretical, managerial, and public policy implications of the platform economy on the retail sector. Three public policy issues were highlighted. First, multi-sided markets and marketplaces base their business model on the aggregation of demand- and supply-side data, which raises questions around privacy, particularly if this data is collected in countries with lax data protection rules. Second, as retail has become increasingly global, many multi-sided markets and marketplaces have been able to create competitive advantages that may be considered unfair compared to traditional store-based retailers. For example, companies such as Amazon can base their central operations in any market, rather than being limited to local responsibilities regarding income tax, employment, investments and so on, due to their very different core resource base of data rather than physical stores. Third, as multi-sided markets and marketplaces primarily intermediate transactions between end customers and third-party suppliers, questions around the responsibilities of platforms become increasingly prominent from a public policy perspective. Compared to more traditional retailers, platforms may have only limited responsibility for their end customers and suppliers and tend to emphasize their role as intermediaries when faced with such questions. Chapters 2 and 3 highlighted the increasing need for public policy, as well as retail strategies, to keep up with the changing landscape of the Red Queen Retail Race, where key resources and capabilities are changing.

## Planning physical space in a digital world

A second theme in this book is the evolving digital customer behaviour and omni-channel consumption, which we discussed in Chapters 4, 5, and 6. While the focus of retailing has increasingly shifted towards the customer (Chapter 2), particularly through technologies providing better online services (Chapter 3), it has also forced physical spaces to transform. In Chapter 4, we focused on shopping centres, entities that play an important role in the retail infrastructure, seeking to understand how these traditionally very physical marketplaces perceive the future with increasing digitalization and online offers.

The perceptions of threat associated with the Red Queen Retail Race comes mainly from the technological nature of the disruption. New technologies are seen to benefit e-commerce players more than shopping centres. Digital technologies can be used in shopping centres in many ways. For example, they can enable new services alongside the collection and analysis of customer data. However, digital technologies do not appear to offer shopping centres a competitive edge over their e-commerce rivals because digital platforms, such as Amazon, Google, and Facebook, are typically the developers of such technologies. Moreover, e-commerce platforms such as Amazon (discussed in Chapter 3) were conceived and raised in the digital world. Shopping centres were not. It became apparent in the focus group discussions that many organizations in the shopping centre business do not have the right people to take advantage of digitalization. This applies not only to owners and operators but also to real estate developers and regulators.

The policy implications of Chapter 4 are twofold. First, the participants in our study felt that the playing field is tilted in favour of e-commerce players, partly due to regulation that has failed to keep up with the constant change associated with the Red Queen Retail Race. Online retailing was perceived to be a decisive element in how any of the future scenarios play out. The Covid-19 pandemic has increased this awareness. Global platform retailers may be able to circumvent local rules and regulations that shopping centres with their physical presence find harder to avoid. As noted in the chapter, policymakers should ensure that similar rules apply to all types of retailers. If not, it is easy to foresee that e-commerce platforms will continue their aggressive growth, and the relationship between e-commerce and shopping centres will continue to be adversarial. Ultimately, this may not be in the consumers' best interest, and may not be in the local interest either.

## Consumer demands on public policy

Earlier, we have seen how new technologies have disrupted retail markets but also provide retailers with new growth opportunities. From the retailer's perspective, this growth can be achieved through creating new products and services or by providing existing products and services in a better way. For example, completely new products and services may be developed, more effective substitutes for existing products and services may be found, or existing tasks and processes may be improved through the application of new technologies. Consumers are at the heart of many of these systems. New, smarter, and interconnected technologies are influenced by the increasing role of the consumer in their adoption and use. Consumers increasingly expect retailers to provide shopping processes that are continuously available, deeply transparent, and provide for more personalization and customization. The Red Queen Retail Race often focuses on a firm's capability to transform and, in retailing customers, form an important part of the medium for change.

To address the impact of customers, Chapters 5 and 6 discussed the impact such digitalization has on brick-and-mortar (B&M) stores. In Chapter 5, the digitalization of retailing was seen to augment the physical servicescape through digital features and touchpoints. This was explained through modelling the behaviour of customers within the service environment, Customers construct retail service experiences by utilizing different channels for different tasks, missions, and occasions, as well as by using them simultaneously at times. Thus, instead of taking place exclusively in one channel, service experiences are formed by a network of experiences across both the digital and physical servicescapes. Experiences in different channels tend to be interconnected; if a service is perceived as satisfying in a specific physical store, then customers expect it to be consistent in that brand's digital store and vice versa. However, the experience manifests in different ways in both the physical and digital servicescapes. Overall, Chapter 5 elucidates how social interaction and the retail environment in both online and B&M stores can affect the cognitive as well as the emotional aspects of a service experience.

Although retailing is still dominated by B&M stores, the rapid growth of online shopping, especially during the Covid-19 pandemic, is transforming the rules of retailing. Thus, practitioners and scholars are trying to better understand the interaction between online and offline channels. Chapter 6 sought to examine this interplay from the perspective of the cognitive and emotional aspects of service experiences, including how they build loyalty in this omni-channel retail environment. The results show that, among customers using multiple channels, physical stores still play a crucial role in forming the perception of the overall service experience. Additionally, the findings illustrate how positive experiences enhance a customer's willingness to share their personal data with firms. In addition to this, Chapter 6 examined the relationship between share of wallet and positive word of mouth in both the online and offline environments. Overall, findings in Chapters 5 and 6 indicated that investments in physical stores may enhance loyalty as physical human contact and sensory elements of the physical servicescape are still key drivers of the overall customer experience. However, traditional B&M retailers may also consider enhancing their service through an online e-store, because this enhances the impact of the physical servicescape, making it even stronger if the physical and digital stores are seamlessly integrated. This emphasizes the importance of service design, such that channels are optimized and aligned when it comes to merchandise, accessibility, information, and customer service. Even though cognitive, and seemingly rational, processing is an important driver of purchase behaviour, the findings also acknowledge the importance of emotional processing. This emphasizes the importance of human interaction, especially face-to-face customer service, as emotions are intertwined with social experiences.

Furthermore, the research portrayed the cross-channel effect on customer loyalty, more specifically, how expenditure in one shopping channel may be reflected in recommending another channel of the same retailer. This notion is significant, especially from the managerial perspective, because regardless of the revenue growth, digital channels can often suffer from weak profitability. If the retail servicescape is designed seamlessly, the digital channel may be utilized to enhance loyalty towards more profitable physical stores, while the online store serves as the 'digital catalogue'. Hence, such conclusions emphasize the showroom effect of physical shops for retailers even for those that primarily operate online.

## Changing work in retail companies

The third theme of this book is the organization structure and the ability to adapt to a changing environment, which is discussed in Chapters 7, 8, and 9. We began with Chapters 7 and 8 focusing on the changing nature of work within retail firms that seek to transform. As we saw in Chapters 2, 3, 4, 5, and 6, the advent of big data and novel analytic technologies has provided an opportunity for new organizational work practices that are designed to promote faster and more efficient change. The Red Queen Retail Race transforms the routines of daily work.

Chapter 7 focused on the way a change in routines can be managed. While the academic literature on routines is focused on routine dynamics and internal adaptation, the literature that considers their management often emphasizes tools such as redesign, continuous assessment, and replacement to keep the routines alive.

Not all organizations can survive a major transformation in which their entire hierarchies are reshaped. Nor can their vast number of processes or routines be constantly coordinated or redesigned top-down within a rapidly changing operating environment. Governing bodies and managers must be able to use their existing governance structures to regulate organizations while simultaneously encouraging decentralized initiatives to solve the emerging challenges.

In Chapter 8, we focused on the use of customer data in the field of UK grocery retailing, which has been perceived as one of the frontrunners in this field worldwide. This field has undergone major changes, with loyalty card programmes and online retailing operating as tools for data collection and subsequent organizational change. From the viewpoint of marketing, loyalty programmes are designed to encourage and reward buying behaviour that is beneficial to retail organizations, and often also to their product suppliers. However, more significantly in terms of promoting change in organizational processes, loyalty programmes also provide retail organizations with a better understanding of their customers and their shopping behaviour. This data can be employed in strategic and operational decision-making in many areas, such as pricing, merchandising, and store development. However, implementing data enabling technologies is only the first step in this transformation. Understanding the various factors that influence the successful use of the resulting data is required in order to fully realize the benefits available.

The customer data-led transformation of the field of retailing through loyalty programmes and online data has redefined the competitive dynamics within the Red Queen Retail Race, forcing competitors to respond through their own loyalty programmes and online offers. Despite the intended transformational influence of these programmes, the conclusions in Chapter 8 highlight that their outcomes vary according to multiple situational variables. Understanding these variables is crucial for the success and efficiency of the changes implemented. We observe how the management of specific routines has resulted in varied performance outcomes and varied paths of development within the field. Not even the best routines or technologies provide competitive advantages unless suitable mindsets are in place.

## The drive to transform

We have seen how technologies have enabled new forms of services (Chapters 2 and 3), we have seen how physical spaces have transformed (Chapter 4), and we have seen how all of this is changing customer behaviour (Chapters 5 and 6). In Chapter 9, we focused on the management of innovations that support all these changes. As suggested by the Red Queen Retail Race, retailers must constantly innovate in order to adapt and evolve in a constantly changing environment.

In line with the conclusions from Chapters 5 and 6, the conclusions from Chapter 9 suggest that the newly emerging service economy has not rendered established ways of doing business obsolete. Consumers still demand novel products and low prices. However, as recent empirical evidence suggests, this is the minimum level, or the best practice. The value-added is shifting towards digitalized services in a relationship-driven ecosystem. Firms need to further develop capabilities that utilize these aspects of a 'consumer society'. According to the model presented in Chapter 9, we are currently facing a situation where the capabilities of many firms are still locked into a physical world, while future value is increasingly moving towards a more digital world. Firms can either take advantage of this shift or fall victim to it.

In the twentieth century, major retailers utilized modern supply innovations to develop broad product assortments with substantial economies of scale. Now, supply innovation, product orientation, physical spaces, standardization, and volume-based strategies are still important, but their performance has declined. These strategies have become easier to imitate and so become minimum best practices in the retail sector, not sources of sustained competitive advantage. So, retailers have begun to identify new sources of growth. The emerging value drivers that characterize contemporary retailers' investment patterns are increasingly based on an innovation pandemic on the demand side, incorporating service elements, utilizing intangible resources, and focused on a more personal form of relationship management.

## The innovation pandemic

The field of retailing has undergone dramatic change over the last few years, especially in surmounting restrictions due to the Covid-19 pandemic. Firms continue to develop their services through deploying new technologies and creating a better understanding of customers and related activities through data. The Red

Queen Retail Race is moving us further and further away from the situation where competitive advantage was created through economies of scale based on bulk buying, huge sales capacities, and increasing physical retail space. The situation is changing and continues to change. Small start-ups can take on established giants by providing richer customer experiences, a more convenient service, or a better business model. Value-driven relationships are replacing the more traditional, physical resources as sources of competitive advantage. Success is based more on the ability to innovate and change rather than the inherent capacity to grow, leading to new questions for public policy decision-makers and researchers. It is increasingly common that retailers face challenges with legislation and public policies that were designed for a different version of retailing.

With future competition defined by the ability to innovate and change rather than the inherent capacity to grow, firms and their management need to focus much more on themselves rather than on running a race against competitors. It is their own ability to change, to develop their service system and new customer experiences, and to adapt their business model that will lead to success. In the Red Queen Retail Race, where boundaries between sectors are disappearing, competition may come from anywhere.

Thus, the focus of strategic management has been shifting from capturing resources to capturing relationships—hence the success of the platform ecosystem approach. While this book has been all about change and we have witnessed a variety of transformations taking place, the Red Queen Retail Race has only just started. The impact of digitization began the Red Queen Retail Race at the start of this century but the Covid-19 pandemic forced the pace of change, bringing about an innovation pandemic in order to respond to the rapidly changing retail landscape. Those firms that thrive will need to continue to innovate as the rules of this new race are still unclear. While policymakers will take time to consider what frameworks and tools from the past century are still relevant today, firms must invest now in order to stay in the Red Queen Retail Race.

## Reference

Carroll, L., 1871. *Through the looking-glass, and what Alice found there.* Macmillan.

# Index

*For the benefit of digital users, indexed terms that span two pages (e.g., 52–53) may, on occasion, appear on only one of those pages.*